MW00331260

GORGEOUS WAR

GORGEOUS

WAR

★

THE BRANDING WAR
BETWEEN
THE THIRD REICH
AND THE UNITED STATES

TIM BLACKMORE

WILFRID LAURIER
UNIVERSITY PRESS

This book has been published with the help of a grant from the Canadian Federation for the Humanities and Social Sciences, through the Awards to Scholarly Publications Program, using funds provided by the Social Sciences and Humanities Research Council of Canada. Wilfrid Laurier University Press acknowledges the support of the Canada Council for the Arts for our publishing program. We acknowledge the financial support of the Government of Canada. This work was supported by the Research Support Fund.

Library and Archives Canada Cataloguing in Publication

Title: Gorgeous war : the branding war between the Third Reich and the United States / Tim Blackmore.
Names: Blackmore, Tim, [date] author.
Description: Includes bibliographical references and index.
Identifiers: Canadiana (print) 20190114193 | Canadiana (ebook) 20190114266 | ISBN 9781771124201 (hardcover) | ISBN 9781771124225 (EPUB) | ISBN 9781771124218 (PDF)
Subjects: LCSH: Germany—Armed Forces—Insignia—History—20th century. | LCSH: United States—Armed Forces—Insignia—History—20th century. | LCSH: Branding (Marketing)—Political aspects—Germany—History—20th century. | LCSH: Branding (Marketing)—Political aspects—United States—History—20th century. | LCSH: Nazi propaganda. | LCSH: World War, 1939-1945—United States—Propaganda.
Classification: LCC UC535.G3 B63 2019 | DDC 355.1/34209430904—dc23

Cover and text design by Michel Vrana. Cover texture from iStockphoto.com.

© 2019 Wilfrid Laurier University Press
Waterloo, Ontario, Canada
www.wlupress.wlu.ca

This book is printed on FSC® certified paper.
It contains recycled materials, and other controlled sources,
is processed chlorine free, and is manufactured using biogas energy.

Printed in Canada

Every reasonable effort has been made to acquire permission for copyright material used in this text, and to acknowledge all such indebtedness accurately. Any errors and omissions called to the publisher's attention will be corrected in future printings.

No part of this publication may be reproduced, stored in a retrieval system, or transmitted, in any form or by any means, without the prior written consent of the publisher or a licence from the Canadian Copyright Licensing Agency (Access Copyright). For an Access Copyright licence, visit http://www.accesscopyright.ca or call toll free to 1-800-893-5777.

For you, the best, the stalwart, the sane:
Ruby, Gilda, Mary Anne, Richard, Joe & Gay

It was a town by Brueghel. All the small towns around here were by Brueghel. When I told Beckman that, he said, no, van Eyck. It never occurred to either of us that they were not built by some artist, that they were not the work of pure imagination. Even the people moved about the streets with Utrillo-like stiffness, and the castle was by Rembrandt, the king, Major Falconer, a Rouault, and all the whores were by Modigliani.

The war was by us.

—William Eastlake, *Castle Keep*

CONTENTS

A MAN OF HIS SEASON

IN THE COURSE OF RESEARCHING AND WRITING THIS book, my father, Russell Blackmore, died. As I thought and wrote, I pondered the inordinately complex life he'd lived. When he was a teen he learned to drive on a Model T Ford, but at the end of his life stored his book about the brain, cognition, and computers on "the cloud." He was born between wars and times. A child of science and rationalism, he also loved music of the romantics as widely spaced as Beethoven and Dvořák. He revelled in the moderns—Stravinsky, Berlioz, Sibelius—and equally in the writings of George Orwell, Sinclair Lewis, T. S. Eliot ("But how his arms and legs are thin," he'd quote dryly, eyebrow up). Although he enjoyed science fiction and enthusiastically read Frank Herbert's 1965 *Dune* (fascinated as much by the technology of spice harvests as Fremen culture, which he much admired), he was for many decades a Bertrand Russell positivist. His dedication to stability and stubbornness made Robert Bolt's play about the minority of one, Thomas More, "A Man for All Seasons," his favourite. Toward the end of his life he used statistics and biology to work on Fermi's paradox, dreaming of aliens in a universe he believed existed by design, just not that of a god or gods. Intellectually he understood the power of words and images, but always claimed that advertising never affected him, although he could and did quote ad jingles from prior decades. His truth was in number and scientific method. As a mathematician and chemist he cut into the world with new tools—X-rays, then computers. He laughed when remembering early mechanical computers like Whirlwind, ruefully thinking about how much 1950s lab time was lost searching for blown vacuum tubes at MIT. Corporate demand for forecasting and large-system management ultimately pushed the physical chemist out of the lab, moved him from measuring atomic matter to weighing information. By the 1960s he was deep into operations research, the science of rationalization that had governed so much of the Second World War at places like Bomber Command. When digital computers began to process data fast enough to make large-scale simulation viable, he shifted into management information systems, became a professor, began teaching, joined the union and shed the corporate world he had come to loathe. He spent his last public years labouring in the virtual, creating multiple unreal models of what might be. He was a thoroughly modern man, produced by and comfortable with modernity and its cultural response, modernism. Like so much inherent in modernism, his aesthetics were contradictory—he loved fall colours, the "Archduke Trio," and well-made machines; these were not separate in his world of mind. His life was full of revolutions in science, understanding, and unexpected hybrid colours. I miss him every day.

ACKNOWLEDGEMENTS

IT'S A HARD THING TO WRITE KNOWING THAT SOME READ-
ers, so crucial to the process of producing both a book and one's
life, will never read the text. I miss my father, who always supported
me and my work, as much as he thought it was, basically, crazy. He
wouldn't have read this book when I gave him a copy, but he would
have put it on his desk, said a pleased "Good" to me, and then gone
back to work. In a very different way Edward (Ned) Hagerman,
military historian, cultural scholar, and my lifelong teacher and
mentor, also supported me without question. It was Ned who
taught me to think, to have courage, who worked to deepen my
understanding of the world and my own work. Ned would have
read the book and we would have had our usual six-hour-long
discussion about it and everything else related to it. After his
sudden death a year ago there was a stark silence where there had

been a mind full of understanding. Ned took me in like family and helped at every stage of migration from adult undergraduate at night school to university professor. I think of him, miss him, hear his delightful chuckle, and know that the time I spent with him on the earth was some of the best I'll ever have. More thanks than I have, as well, for Richard Swinson and Quentin Rae Grant, who taught me and were patient—man were they patient.

My academic cheering team is jammed with people I'm lucky to know. Willem (Bill) Vanderburg, director of the Centre for Technology and Social Development at the University of Toronto and Jacques Ellul's last protégé, opened his heart and home to me and has been a wonderful guide through what he calls the "labyrinth of technology." Siobhan McMenemy has been an invaluable thinker, advisor, colleague, reader, and editor for well over a decade. I am enormously lucky and grateful to have her insight, wit, humour, help, and friendship. Joe and Gay Haldeman, showing the typical unstinting generosity with which they approach the world, took me in decades ago and have ever since been scholarly colleagues, wonderful friends, family. Bob ("Chickenhawk") Mason and Patience Mason, both authors and war watchers, have helped me through. Sheila Embleton, linguistics professor, colleague, friend, and long-time mentor continues to be resolutely there when I need something. Paul Headrick is, as always, that utterly stable rock in the river of chaos. Gilda Blackmore typed and typed and *typed*, day and night for weeks, getting documents ready for me—whatever flavour ice cream, I'm happily buying pretty much forever. Many thanks to Ted Kaye for his vexillological help and generosity. I am very grateful to Rifat Al-Chadirji for his permission to reproduce his flag designs. Thanks also to Ahmed Al-Mallak, who made communication and understanding between the two of us possible: it was a late and important education that made me reflect on how little it can take to make bridges where there were none before. My sincere thanks to Chris Wheeler, who worked some excellent digital magic on an old piece of film and made the book more "gorgeous." Similarly, I am hugely grateful to my teaching buddy Mark Rayner for his desperately needed graphic help. Thanks to my anonymous readers, who worked to improve this book—I appreciate the advice. If there are still problems, they're on me. A special note of thanks to designer Michel Vrana, who put the smartest, sharpest, most "gorgeous" cover on this book. My list of graphical embargoes (no swastikas, no Statues of Liberty draped in variegated flags, and so on for hundreds of words) made me feel hopeless about ever seeing a cover that could seize the book's gestalt. Michel Vrana has beautifully captured the two deeply contrasting brands and their different notions of modernity without resorting to any clichés. I'm delighted and grateful.

The people who made a space for me at Western—Carole Farber, Catherine Ross, and Gloria Leckie—have been the best co-workers one could have, always ready to listen to some tale of grief. David Spencer, another recent loss to us, was another enormously welcoming force in my life. I miss him and am glad I had time to work with him. My sincere thanks, too, to Susan Knabe and Kathie Hess for being there with good counsel. My own students, many now colleagues, have educated me about war and trauma, engaging in work that was surprising, exciting, and made me proud to see: Dr. Elle Ting, Daryl Hunt, Dr. Jeff Preston, Rebecca Elias, Chang (Melody) Song, Rhea Harris (Johnson), Dr. Patti Luedecke, Dr. Kyunghee Kim. My thanks particularly to the inaugural class of MIT 2161 (now 3440), War for War, a remarkable communal experience, and the many astounding groups who have taken MIT 3215, Killer Culture: working with all of you always impresses me with how incisive and wonderful people can be. I have full confidence in Millennials; it's people of my generation who have their hands on the levers of power who stop my heart in terror. Everything else comes from, and to, the family: Jesse, Gilda, and Russell.

GORGEOUS WARNING

WAR IS THE APEX CONSUMER. IT GATHERS EVERYTHING to itself. First to go are bodies, but soon after it recruits human systems of organization, as well as useful tools like science, math, and technology, and other ways of knowing. Nothing escapes its reach and grasp: not philosophy or music, not ballet, opera, or poetry. Of all the things caught and made fat by war, the graphic arts—design, fine art, illustration, posters, banners, badges, textile patterns—are some of the earliest to be seized. In the late nineteenth and early twentieth centuries, graphic forms, once mostly static, were extended by new media like film and animation, and both were immediately bent to war's purpose.

This book is about the convergence of the graphic arts, two Western cultures—Germany and the United States—and modernism. It is about the ways in which both countries engaged in a war of images against each other, the surrounding world, and their own people. The book is an interpretation of what happened when, before and during the widest war the planet has yet seen, two very different political systems tried their best to co-opt and deploy contemporary cultural forms for their own purposes. At the heart of the book is the point that, for all that human beings complain about war, we also make it attractive enough that we compulsively return to, fetishize, and fantasize about it. Industrial war of the kind seen from the late nineteenth century to the present day is, by most accounts, a horrific affair. Yet we have also dedicated ourselves to making it intriguing and compelling, to creating war which, even in its dreadfulness, is gorgeous. "Gorgeous" comes flanked by other words like "dazzling," "striking," "magnificent"— words we use to capture the undeniably impressive. Describing night combat in Vietnam, Tim O'Brien struggles for clarity: "It's not pretty, exactly. It's astonishing. It fills the eye. It commands you. You hate it, yes, but your eyes do not ... [it has] the aesthetic purity of absolute moral indifference—a powerful, implacable beauty."[1] O'Brien is careful to note the complex entanglement of beauty and amorality. Something that astonishes and dazzles, that fosters awe in us, may be beautiful and also lethally uncaring. Near the end of Michael Herr's *Dispatches* (1977), photographer Tim Page is offered a publishing contract for a book that will "once and for all 'take the glamour out of war.'" A dumbfounded Page lists the astonishing things he's seen during his time in Vietnam, finally reduced to incoherence, "working his hands up and down to emphasize the sheer insanity of it. 'I mean, you *know*, it just *can't be done!* ... Ohhh, what a laugh! Take the bloody *glamour* out of bloody *war!*'"[2] This book doesn't seek to take the lustre off war, but instead to focus on it, to determine why and how we make war gorgeous.

Bringing a nation into a war is hard work, particularly if there has been no overt attack on the homeland. Such an assault, particularly if it's a surprise, can mobilize the population reasonably quickly. But to take a peacetime society and convert it into one bent on making, sustaining, and winning a war requires the state's full resources and energy. The causes for wars may also be difficult to determine. Those not alert to the politics of the Great Powers in mid 1914 with their interrelated agreements—the triple entente—might have been baffled as to how the assassinations of an otherwise unimportant archduke and his wife could detonate a political explosion that would engulf the world in fours years of industrial warfare. The killing of Ferdinand and Sophie required all nations involved to produce some kind of explanation, no matter how cursory, about why a war against people they had likely never met or interacted with was about to be necessary.

Governments, the media, and historians speak about "going to war," but arguably it is more of a process of coming to it. The whole state apparatus must labour to bring a people to war and then work even harder to keep them there. Apparently endless slaughters like the First or Second World Wars require that societies, democratic or not, enlist all manner of lies and coercion to sell the war. Not only will governments have to make the case for war, but every other quasi-governmental authority—religion, junior and senior education, branches of media, medicine, science and engineering, sports and entertainment organizations, social groups and clubs, the whole of the law enforcement structure, including police, courts, and prisons—must support the argument. Most of all, the war must be backed by business and must employ business methods. Information will have to be managed so that sufficient outrage at the enemy can be manufactured, enough that people are prepared to go away and fight strangers they don't know in places of which they've never heard. Those who stay at home will have to sacrifice materials necessary for the war. The state is the new prime consumer of energy, raw and manufactured material, foodstuffs, and labour. Civilians will just have to wait: lack of steel will prevent new cars from being made, and anyway, there won't be sufficient gas for their tanks. Oils, fats, sugars, and solvents will be drained out of the public pantry for use in the manufacture of chemicals, explosives, and weapons. Everywhere people will be asked, coerced, or simply forced to surrender their bodies and goods in exchange for the political ideas the government advances. Those ideas have to be communicated forcefully, convincingly.

It's become common to call such communication "propaganda," that is, the deliberate curation and turning of information against another group or groups in order to harm them. Propaganda, the conversion of any possible piece of information or its representation in *any* form (still or moving images, sounds, radio transmissions, songs, printed text, textiles like clothing, caps, armbands, flags, jewellery) into an argument for an official political point of view, employs all possible media without observing any rules of conduct. During the event, daily, even hourly, reminders will be evident all around one, reassuring us that war-making is a glorious business, particularly as it becomes increasingly difficult, ugly, and intolerable. The worse it gets, the more necessary, the more heroic. Across the media one will be perpetually reminded that each beautiful object is integral to the joint national struggle that makes the present survivable, the fearful endurable. Each object is a reminder that, as terrible as war is, it is also, sadly, indispensable. Propaganda will sell this story because it follows only the rule of success. It lies by omission and commission, twists events and narratives, tells partial truths and presents particular narratives that may shift over the course of time. Such shifts don't require admissions that previous propaganda was wrong, only that it has been revised to fit the new normal. From the propagandist's point of view, the only bad propaganda is that which fails.

This book begins at the point that propaganda picks up images, specifically military images in the United States and Nazi Germany, and uses them to create cohesion and loyalty between people during wartime. Many things that don't appear to be propaganda will be called into service by propagandists. On their own, pieces of information may appear to be innocent, free of political purpose. An image or military marker, like a heraldic crest or shield, or what is known in the United States military as a Distinctive Unit Insignia (the patch that appears on a uniform's left shoulder), initially seems to be merely a way of organizing masses of people involved with the military. But heraldry, like all things made by human beings, has a multitude of meanings, most social and political. Heraldry isn't just an identification system, a way of differentiating one group from another, or "us" from "them," but also a way of making people proud to be identified as the member of a group. As time passes, a military unit builds up a history of action—battles fought, lost, won—to become an organization with its own life. The unit comes to be associated with the patch it bears, to have a reputation for battlefield heroism, diligence, even war crimes and atrocities. Famous military patches (in the United States, the 101st Airborne's Screaming Eagle, the 1st Cavalry's black-on-yellow horsehead patch) can inspire devotion, even reverence, from civilians and soldiers alike. Many civilians will specifically wish to join a particular unit based on a family member's service in that same group or because of the unit's famous history. By the same token, units that earn bad reputations are disbanded, such as the United States Army's 23rd Infantry Division (better known as the Americal Division), which was taken apart following the atrocities committed by its soldiers against hundreds of unarmed civilians in My Lai in 1968. The unit patch comes to operate in the same way as a corporate brand: it can inspire dedication, loyalty, and fervent commitment to a worldview, but can also become toxic enough that it must be erased, remade, rebranded.

My argument about images, propaganda, heraldry and corporate identity is generally focused on the years 1919–1939 and the Second World War in the United States and Nazi Germany. The interwar period is marked by the maturation of a vast, complex social, political, philosophical, and artistic movement called modernism that had gotten underway, depending on the country one considers, as early as the beginning of the nineteenth century and by the beginning of the twentieth century is in full flood. Because design is directly informed by social ideas and pressures, fads, habits, and residual traditions, the creation of new military identities is intimately entwined with modernism as much as with the shocking effects of the two world wars. Modernism, which I take up in much greater detail at the book's start, was determined to replace old ideas with new ones, to shift the way people approached the world and the condition of their lives in it. There were new ideas about labour, class, gender and race, art, the mind, and science, but also new ways of making meaning of the global slaughter that had been the First World War.

Both America and Germany, in preparing for and fighting the Second World War, had intricate relationships with modernism. The Allies and the West have remained invested in the idea that modernism, and artistic freedom in general, is a sign of basic societal goodness. Paralleling that claim is the assertion that a liberal democracy was and is the only place where modernism can exist, let alone flourish. These claims turn out to be more of what Studs Terkel identifies as the "Good War's" myths. The American and Nazi militaries both embraced and rejected modernism as it suited them. The Nazis' superb use of modernist design demonstrated that modernism was no guarantee against fascism. Examining American heraldic design shows that the United States military had a scattershot attitude to its official graphic program. Instead, it was often large corporations that learned the lessons about the kind of graphic clout the Nazis produced, lessons they were already applying to the growing world of logos and their associated brands.

Much is made by historians of the Nazis' obsession with the occult, with Wagnerian and Norse mythology, all of them drawn into a romantic world of ancient traditions, nature, and tragic deaths. As much as these forces had a powerful impact on the Reich's beliefs and public expressions, they were met with arguably equal or greater force by the demand for newness. There were new forms of efficiency, of industrial organization and design, of media, art, and film-making. Included in that hunger for a new way of making the world was a renascent military, at the heart of which rotated the swastika and a related empire of striking graphics. How did the Nazis, so attached to the past and to "blood and soil" ("*Blut und Boden*") rituals, come to embrace the swastika and a whole world of modernist design? This was the question I first came to answer in the writing of this book.

Given the staggering success not only of the Reich's design but also its propaganda, I subsequently pondered how the United States, which had mobilized (and demobilized) so rapidly for the First World War, responded to the Nazi propaganda threat. Once the United States entered the war, first against Japan and then Germany, in 1941, was there, I wondered, an equal demand from Americans for graphic freshness? These questions drove my research and pushed me to further consider how much what I knew of modernism was accurate and how much was a set of agreements about Western democracies. In North America modernism is presented as an explosion of expression, art, science, and social science, irrevocably tied to democratic freedom. Recently modernism has been viewed with more suspicion, understood as a lever used to repress all kinds of differences in gender, race, and class, something that supported kindlier forms of colonialism.

I came to look again, to inquire about the ways that the Nazis engaged with modernism, to reconsider how modernism lived up to its tenets before and during the Second World War. I wanted to understand, as much as such a thing can be possible, how modernism had functioned for Nazis and Americans, how they responded to each other, and who, ultimately, was the winner in that contest.

I concluded that, as with our present (and really any period of intense human activity), the interwar era presents a problem known to us as "wicked complexity." Wicked complexity is a condition that describes what happens when we try to predict any sufficiently intricate behaviour, such as how a new technology will be taken up and used by people in a mass society. We can model future human actions as much as we please, but beyond a very limited point, we're probably guessing more than anything else. The result is that we're soon off the rails and plunged into the unknowable. Understanding who our grand- or great-grandparents were is incalculably difficult. For many of us, it's impossible. Why, then, bother with any of this stuff from the past, these attic findings?

As a contemporary citizen, I am unwilling to quit and walk away. In order to understand, to teach, and to write about the present aggravating, often terrifying and disheartening cultural moment, I have found it a necessity to connect it to the past. Understanding a world now governed by corporations with transnational boundaries that seem to have made global markets their obedient donkeys, I have tried to take one small piece of the present and roll it sufficiently far back in time that it was clear enough for me to picture. This book is a set of slightly shifting images filled with information not just about military heraldry and propaganda, but about brands as wielded first by military organizations and the states that co-created them and then by global multinationals that have encased challenge within difficulty, as

Churchill once characterized a political puzzle: "a riddle wrapped in a mystery inside an enigma." Coming to terms with complexity is one of the central issues in this book. The necessity of unravelling some of the past and tracing lines into the present is another. Understanding our complicity in the way the world continues to be structured yet another.

This cultural moment, a slight second that holds us and the world in which we exist, sits on top of a deep crust of accumulated events, objects, and bodies. Many things we use without reflection originated in or were shocked into being by the Second World War. If the reader finds some discussions of recent texts or events apparently out of place (an extended discussion of *American Sniper*, contemporary clothing, or advertising), they are present as a reminder of just how much we live in a shared cultural environment of space and time. We are always shuttling back and forth between where we were and where we are now, but we may not always be alert to the motion.

This book exists because it has been preceded by foundational texts in visual culture, media, propaganda, military heraldry, modernism and modernist art in each country, fascist modernist art. Those seeking a deeper view of the above fields might begin at any of the following entry points: for visual culture, Marita Sturken and Lisa Cartwright's *Practices of Looking* (2009), and slightly antique though it may be, Roland Barthes's *Mythologies* (1957, 2014 new translation); Michael Ryan and Douglas Kellner's *Camera Politica* (1988) and Paul Virilio's *War and Cinema* (2000), for media; Jacques Ellul's still-on-target *Propaganda* (1973) for a structural discussion of the same; and for visual propaganda, Sam Keen's indispensable *Faces of the Enemy* (1991), Steven Heller's *Iron Fists* (2008), Walton Rawls's *Wake Up, America!* (1988), and Anthony Rhodes's *Propaganda: The Art of Persuasion, World War II* (1994); for heraldry, Guido Rosignoli's *Illustrated Encyclopedia of Military Insignia of the 20th Century* (1986); Terry Smith's

Making the Modern (1994), for a discussion of American modernism; Jeremy Aynsley's *Graphic Design in Germany 1890–1945* (2000), and Modris Ekstein's *Rites of Spring* for discussions of Weimar and Nazi modernism; Roger Griffin's book *Modernism and Fascism* (2007) for an overall picture of the interrelation of the two forces, followed by Frederic Spotts's *Hitler and the Power of Aesthetics* (2004). The study's broader context is formed by Paul Fussell's revelatory discussions of the worlds inside the world wars: *The Great War and Modern Memory* (1975) and *Wartime* (1989); Philip Beidler's irreplaceable *American Literature and the Experience of Vietnam* (1982); Klaus Theweleit's two-volume *Male Fantasies* (trans. 1987, 1989); Cynthia Enloe's ongoing treatment of war and gender across a number of excellent books, from *Does Khaki Become You?* (1988) and *Maneuvers* (2000) to *Globalization & Militarism* (2016), among others. There is a growing catalogue of anthropology at war, to which Enloe's *Nimo's War, Emma's War* (2010) is a welcoming introduction. The issue is enormously fraught, however, enough that I set it aside here.

While the process of trying to reconstruct how modernism was used by the Nazis and Americans during the Second World War was difficult and required many different kinds of information, not all things are that complex. Some really are what they seem to be. As I worked on this book the United States elected a president who accepts support from known Ku Klux Klan leaders like David Duke, who in 2017 embraced neo-Nazis demonstrating in Charlottesville, Virginia, saying that they were "very fine people," and who has encouraged hate crimes at the nation's southern border, as well as bestowed a presidential pardon on Sheriff Joe Arpaio of Arizona's Maricopa County, an officer convicted by his own state courts of illegally persecuting a particular group of Americans. Trump's rise to power has been paralleled by leaders who present themselves as throwback strong men: Vladimir Putin, Viktor Orban, Bashar al-Assad, Recep

Erdogan, and the few women leading alt-right anti-immigration, often anti-Semitic as well as anti-Muslim parties like Frauke Petry's *Alternative für Deutschland* (Petry is known affectionately by her supporters as "*der Führerin*" and "Adolfina") and Marine Le Pen's *Front National*, or parties pledged to generalized racial intolerance like Britain's United Kingdom Independence Party (UKIP). While some of the personalities have shifted over time, the parties themselves have only grown stronger and gained seats in their respective governments, even in countries that have reputations for being the world's most tolerant, advanced democracies (the Netherlands' Party for Freedom [PVV] or Sweden's Sweden Democrats).

As of this writing, nativist and racist parties have only gained ground popularly and politically. Growing worldwide expression of hatred for the Other, scapegoating, and the politics of fear following the worldwide market crash of 2007, coupled with the surge in migration from wars in Syria and other North African countries, have direct parallels to the rise of nativist populism in Canada, the United States, and most of Europe during the 1920s and 1930s. Worse are the attacks on forms of democratic government and a free press in the United States, Turkey, Poland (the Justice and Law Party [PiS]), and Hungary, behaviour that marked fascist or authoritarian regimes that took control just prior to the Second World War. The brute rage that comes from fears of dispossession, imagined attacks on a way of life, these are once more our daily meal, even though we declared, after seeing their end results in the Nazi death camps and Stalin's gulags, that we would never eat this again. In our new century hatred has been rebranded, to use a comfortable business word, as freedom of expression where the alt-right presents itself as an ironic voice tweeting from the wilderness about liberal identity politics. Leave it to a modernist like Bertolt Brecht to be prescient about the ongoing popularity of fascist leaders, which he predicted in his 1941 play *The Resistible Rise of Artuo Ui*, concluding "Do not rejoice in his defeat, you men. For though the world has stood up and stopped the bastard, the bitch that bore him is in heat again."

The reader will find that this book generally alternates between the visual and propaganda worlds of America and Germany, with a few chapters here and there dedicated to specific topics common to both countries. The text begins with a deliberate refresher about the way modernity—which I typify as the force of the machine, a metaphor for the West's full-throttle industrialization in the twentieth century—evoked the artistic response of modernism. That short visit is followed by a comparative look at modernism, first in the United States and then Nazi Germany. With a basic discussion of modernism in place, I then move on to consider how the United States military's rather haphazard use, and more accurately abuse, of a heraldic system inherited from the United Kingdom came into being. At the same cultural moment the Nazis were also inventing not only their politics, but also the beginnings of the sign system they would use to obtain and hold power. These chapters are followed by two more that step out of the chronological narrative for the moment to examine the way brands and heraldry are entwined both in the United States and Germany. As with the discussion of modernism, we need to have a common footing concerning brands so that the comparison can continue smoothly. The parallels I make in the subsequent chapters about United States military patches and the deployment of the swastika by the Nazis are not always one to one, partly because the Nazi program is, if nothing else, an obvious one. In the penultimate discussion I consider the two different propaganda efforts used by both nations. The United States military's failure in meeting the Nazi brand program left the job hanging. The resolution came from a surprising quarter, which takes up the final chapter.

CHAPTER 1

SAME OLD NEW

Interwar American Modernism

BEFORE ANYTHING, SAY NOW WHO ARE THE MOST CUL-
turally significant musicians, film-makers, writers, poets, cartoonists, dramatists, architects of the moment. Also say why they're
significant. You can't like all of them—that would just be your
particular top ten. You're choosing on behalf of the whole culture
here. Put the book down and write a list of ten names in each
category, and as you go through them, figure out which ones we'll
remember in ten years, twenty, one hundred. Now figure out what
unites them. I'll wait.

There is no quick, complete picture of chaotic sets of ideas like
modernism. I find it easier to begin with things that are obvious to
us now. The grid of technology and industry is deeply embedded
in the present century's substrate, even more than it was at the
beginning of the nineteenth century. Industrial revolutions have

been the multiple hearts of our contemporary world. Water and wind power steadily retreated before coal-fired steam engines, where the coal itself could be coked and reduced to a substance much denser in energy than wood or lignite. Although we have yet to put coal aside, the story of twentieth-century power generation was marked by refining and compression of energy-rich materials like oil and nuclear ores. As the century proceeded, advances in science drove technology and engineering, producing better versions of older materials—stronger forms of steel, new products like celluloid, eventually plastics. Electricity made long-distance communication devices like the telegraph and telephone possible, shifted the world over from wax and gas burning to electric light, which on its own radically altered not only when people could work, but for how long. Electric light made it possible for manufacturing to move to two or three shifts a day, banishing farm time organized around daylight. Scientific, medical, and engineering advances brought about, over the space of a lifetime in North America, Britain, and the industrialized nations of Europe, changes in what people used to communicate, how they dressed, what they read and how they wrote, how they got to work, the kind of work they did once they were there, when their days began and ended, how long they lived. The second industrial revolution brought about what we identify as modernization and modernity.

Modernity has come mean that the tools of the mind prized by the Enlightenment—reason, observation, the scientific method applied to physics, chemistry and biology, math, logic, economics, systemic organization and statecraft—would be converted into methods and devices that not only shape the world, but seek to dominate it. Modernity privileges efficiency, which in the late nineteenth and early twentieth century meant that humans labouring at repetitive farming tasks would be replaced by machines. The people who once worked the land would find themselves driven by rural unemployment and poverty into centralized environments where many could be housed and fed at once. Those captive populations would be pressed by their new urban settings, whose lack of green space prevented the growth of the family subsistence garden, into semi- or unskilled labour in new factories that were organized around rigid factory methods designed by efficiency experts like Frederick Taylor and Henry Ford to generate a geometric rise in production numbers (in 1904 the Ford Highland Park plant's annual output was 1,745 cars: by 1914 it was 82,388).

Modernity can be represented as the force of a collective machine presence that propels society, whether that machine is composed of the first moving assembly line as developed during 1914 at the Ford factory or the present moment's digital handheld devices that have created a transparent world of workers on call 24/7. But the machine goes deeper than that. Understanding the planet as a giant ball of resources that humans feel they deserve to extract endlessly is as much part of the machine as the earth-moving or fracking equipment necessary to accomplish the task. Methods and ideas are integral to the machine. As understood by Marx and Engels, modernity powered by capital alienated workers from their labour, progressively eliminating skilled craft and meaningful work with which people could identify. It also reduced family to a commodity such that the worker's "children [are] transformed into simple articles of commerce and instruments of labor."[1] From capital's point of view the worker had won freedom by earning wages, didn't have to assume the burden of organization or operation, and could shift readily from job to job seeking the best going rate for labour. It didn't matter whether you were a Communist or capitalist to understand that work had changed drastically. In 1900 Americans had to adapt to modernity by moving into urban anthills and taking factory jobs where they repeated a few identical motions as rapidly as they could; by 1999 they had to accept that modernity meant factory work was over and that millions of jobs, as well as a way of life, had been replaced by fast computerized information exchanges that dissolved human bonds, making capital "transgressive, boundary-breaking, all-eroding," in Zygmunt Bauman's formulation.[2]

Modernity is fluid, a condition recognized late in the century by, among others, philosopher Gilles Deleuze and psychoanalyst Félix Guattari. Deleuze and Guattari identified a state of permanent, ongoing dissolution where people are perpetually forced away from relations that make sense to them, that help them to make meaning of the worlds in which they live. Families are liquefied; places, ethnicities, and languages are shifted and erased as whole peoples are forced to follow modernity's flows of power and capital. Capital, not people, controls territory.[3] In exchange modernity offers increased global production and a new home in the brand, presented as ubiquitous and permanent—at least until rebranding. Capital offers new territory to people, but it must be rented and cannot be owned because it is infinitely flexible.

At the beginning of the twenty-first century we may be struggling with modernity's current incarnation as the information economy; people living at the start of the twentieth century in the United States had to contend with the disappearance of what F. Scott Fitzgerald typified in his 1925 novel *The Great Gatsby* as "the fresh, green breast of the new world." The agrarian world was being consumed by an age of mass urbanization, centralization, production, and consumption. In the United States such changes were exacerbated by fears about the vanishing West. As homesteaders in western territories like Utah and Wyoming neared California and rail lines connected the coasts, the frontier closed. Historian Frederick Jackson Turner proposed that the frontier had always been integral to American identity, writing in 1893 that, "frontier individualism has from the beginning promoted democracy."[4] What was to become of the American spirit without the perpetually receding frontier with its promise of infinite space for democratic experimentation and individualism?

Although it is a great simplification, it is also generally true that where modernity moved, a combined artistic, cultural, social, and political response followed. The surge of artistic expression was marked by anxiety, shock at change, and the need to understand a chaotic, speed-driven industrial world: what we call modernism. Daniel Singal notes helpfully that "modernism should be seen as a *culture* ... modernization, by contrast denotes a *process* of social and economic development, involving the rise of industry, technology, urbanization, and bureaucratic institutions."[5] Modernism is the cultural response to modernity.

Modernism didn't occur in one short period, on one continent, or in one single art form alone. Most accounts tie the beginning of modernism to the start of the machine's effects on large human populations. In the United States modernism can be seen to take shape as the Civil War ends and the post-war depression lifts in 1878. In France and Britain, which were ahead of the United States industrially, the beginnings were earlier (Mary Shelley's 1818 *Frankenstein* is often used as a quintessential marker of modernism). Germany seemed to lag mid century, but as Modris Eksteins points out, it had more than caught up by the First World War: "If Britain led the way in changing the mode of life on our planet ... Germany more than any other state took us toward our 'post-industrial' or technological world," obsessed as it was with what Eksteins identifies as the "cult of *Technik*," a fascination with process and early management science.[6] American modernism can be roughly broken into thirds: the first stretching from just after the Civil War to 1918; the second from 1919 to 1939, known as the interwar period; and the last, often called "high modernism," from the Second World War, particularly the two nuclear bombings of Japan in 1945, to a point either in the early or mid 1960s, or the final collapse of South Vietnam's government and the end of the war in 1975, or to a moment that has yet to occur (this latter position is rarely argued—generally, modernism is felt to have concluded).

Because it stretches across so many traumatic events (wars, revolutions, genocides, ongoing colonialism) that have shaped the late nineteenth and the majority of the twentieth centuries, it seems reasonable that one set of descriptors will not do justice to the term modernism. As I examine shortly, however, some contemporary critics would indeed prefer to tightly restrict the term's use. Modernism before 1900 might now seem tame, even quaint, to us. Explaining to a group of first-year students how revolutionary Kate Chopin's *The Awakening* (1899) or Stephen Crane's "Maggie, a Girl of the Streets"(1893) were can produce a groundswell of yawning about texts that seem dull, obvious, and preachy. Modernist American writers like Henry James, Willa Cather, Edith Wharton, and William Dean Howells were equally revolutionary, even if they have now become the old guard. Modernism as seen in the early-twentieth-century paintings of Gustav Klimt (typified by "The Kiss," 1907–1908) seemed to have more in common with the sweetness of much Art Nouveau, even the romanticism of the Pre-Raphaelites, than the harsh bodies painted by Egon Schiele, Klimt's friend and contemporary.

Modernism can be considered an overall project involved in struggling to come to terms with what Singal emphasizes as "the *process*" of modernity. As the twentieth century ground on through the First World War, the art became more rebellious, dangerous, as grim and chaotic as the world from which it emerged. When I use the word "art" I mean every possible form of human artistic expression, including but not limited to music, opera, ballet, theatre, film, sculpture, novels, poetry, and extending to include a number of forms that until recently have been considered to be low culture or commercial trash—comic strips, animated films, packaging, advertising and poster art, children's book illustration, quilts sewn for home use, pottery, textile and fibre art of all kinds. Käthe Kollwitz's drawings of people starving in Berlin immediately after the war existed in the same cultural moment as the savagely grotesque work of George Grosz and Otto Dix, whose painted scenes of sexual murder and battlefield slaughter can be difficult to tell apart.

It can be helpful to have a few names from across the countries to work with before coming to a short summation of modernism. In the United States, George Luks, George Bellows, Jacob Riis, and the entire Ashcan school of visual artists forced high culture to shift from looking at society's wealthy and powerful to urban poverty instead. Georgia O'Keefe, as with Emily Carr in Canada, looked away from people and attended to nature more carefully than any Caucasian artist had before, not Audubon in North America, not Gauguin in Tahiti, or Van Gogh in Arles. Seeing clearly and representing truths had changed drastically from creating sentimental images of rural life. While many artists began experimenting with new media (radio, film, animation, photography), a few had enormous impacts on media and culture. It would be to Georges Seurat that decades of painters would owe their understanding of light's operation in the world. Time would be anatomized by Eadweard Muybridge, Étienne-Jules Marey, Émile Cohl, George Meliés, and Winsor McCay, all of whom broke motion into pieces and knit it together again using photography, animation, and film. Frank Lloyd Wright and Mies van der Rohe would stretch space into new configurations, and musicians like Igor Stravinsky and Arnold Schoenberg would reject the familiar and find new harmonies in discordance.

Naming artists, an endless process, is only partial help. It is the multiple revolutions both in form and content that connect so much modernist expression. The narrowing of time and space around human beings, their jailing by industry and its new products (including a fully industrialized war—more than 57,000 dead or wounded British in the first day on the Somme in 1916), evoked art that broke with the past. Gone or badly damaged were the agreements about class, gender, and race, as well as much of the Victorian ideal of high romanticism espoused by Wordsworth, Shelley, and Keats and best visualized by the Pre-Raphaelite painters. As historian Jonathan Vance has shown, however, romantic ideas and social forms persisted despite enraged artistic responses to them.[7] Art became deliberately provocative, an irritant or overtly insulting to the upper classes who, prior to the First World War, were mostly its patrons. It was often ironic, deeply enraged at the machine's encroachment, sly, witty, playful, grotesque, chaotic, grimly serious, and "realist," reflexively discussing the process of making art itself, and with that reflexivity undoing (or as in Marcel Duchamp's case with his "readymades"—placing a urinal in an art gallery—outright trashing) previous aesthetic ideals handed down by royalty, the church, and the ruling classes. It was also earnest, focused on the plight of those at the bottom of the social order. Interwar modernism, particularly, was filled with "inventive gestures, daring performances," as Michael Levenson characterizes it.[8] Modernism has been called a project, an experiment, but to the artists working through the time, it was both alive and a way of living.

For some, aesthetic philosophy extended into every part of life. The Bauhaus considered its first task to be architecture, but its design ideals extended to colour use, textiles, furniture, and household industrial design items like kettles, cutlery, even toys. Directed at workers, the Bauhaus' concern with manufacturing techniques and materials came from the designers' conviction that ordinary people should benefit from industry, should be able to afford well-designed and -made, durable, pleasing artifacts that functioned perfectly. It was design that drew no borders between artistic, ideological, and material practice. Modernism is jammed with energy and surprise, with the willingness to shock the audience out of a sort of bystander's passivity and into active political engagement. Some artists wanted nothing to do with the audience or the masses (Stravinsky was one of these) and others felt the work failed if the masses weren't immediately charged with political will (Bertolt Brecht in Germany, Clifford Odets and Upton Sinclair in America). There was a loss of faith in faith and a concomitant dedication to the abstract, surreal, and absurd. The artist became the new guide, often a leader in new ways of understanding what Mark Seltzer has identified as both the panic and exhilaration of life near, under, and often inside the machine.[9]

As decades of cultural protest continued, an ongoing storm of change fuelled different groups. The Italian futurists put speed and war at the centre of their beliefs; cubists broke images into moving planes of space in time; Dadaists used collage, chance and juxtaposition to see afresh; these are a few of the hundreds of movements and groups working from the beginning of the century to the start of the Second World War, all united in what Roger Griffin identifies as "the bid to achieve a sense of transcendent value, meaning, or purpose despite Western culture's progressive loss of a homogeneous value system ... to create culture, to construct utopias, to access a suprahuman temporality, and to belong to a community united by a shared culture."[10] Each part of modernism is an attack on Victorian and then Edwardian, monarchic, aristocratic archetypes of what makes art great, or in the words of Matthew Arnold, "the best that has been thought and said." Instead art became a commitment to making people see clearly, to have them be shocked into an awareness of the world as it is and could be.

The end of the Second World War and the start of a newly terrifying nuclear present with its imminent apocalypse saw modernism shift again, becoming "high modernism." Experimentation turned inward, represented by the intensely personal images of Jackson Pollack and other abstract expressionists, who painted for reasons and toward ends that might or might not be accessible to, or understandable by, the public. But Pollack was only part of the story of an urban elite. For David Harvey, the opacity of much post-war art originated in "the belief 'in linear progress, absolute truths, and a rational planning of ideal social orders' under standardized conditions of knowledge and production .... The modernism that resulted was 'positivistic, technocentric, and rationalistic' at the same time as it was imposed as the work of an elite avant-garde of planners, artists, architects, critics, and other guardians of high taste." High modernism was ineluctably connected to rolling out "a benevolent and progressive 'modernization process' to a backward Third World."[11] My focus here is on modernism in the interwar period both in the United States and in Weimar and then Nazi Germany, and it is to the specifics of each of these eras and cultural moments that I now turn.

The Second World War radically destabilized meanings in part because superimposed on the physical battle was a war of images, a palimpsest produced by elite art overlaid on corporate, popular, and folk cultural responses to and visions of modernity. Beneath the layers of images was an ongoing nostalgia for varieties of nineteenth-century romanticism. In examining whether wartime images in both the Second World War-era United States and Nazi Germany were fuelled by the same modernism, I've found it necessary to reconsider the debates around modernism and how it might or might not be constituted, and whether such a word can bear the load all its attendant meanings have deposited on it over the decades.

Familiar compressed narratives of modernism tend to define it as a form of cultural rebellion against a stable existing traditional order: it's characterized as a series of artistic revolts that swept across forms and media, producing new ways of seeing in keeping with Ezra Pound's exhortation to "Make it new." But modernism in both the interwar United States and Germany is flexible, complex, confused. Like the people who lived in it, it was many hybridities, rarely one thing. In the United States, high culture could explain by example, creating a script written by

Ernest Hemingway, Zora Neale Hurston, and F. Scott Fitzgerald, illustrated by Edward Hopper, Charles Sheeler, Georgia O'Keefe, Edward Steichen, and Diego Rivera, set to a soundtrack composed by George Gershwin, Samuel Barber, and Cole Porter. The film itself could be shot by Buster Keaton, Charlie Chaplin, or Orson Welles. German modernism could equally produce a multimedia event scripted by Thomas Mann or Ernst Junger, with lyrics by Bertolt Brecht, music by Arnold Schoenberg or Kurt Weill, all of which would then be filmed by Fritz Lang, Friedrich Murnau, and Leni Riefenstahl. The biggest problem with navigating modernism by pointing out important landmarks and the people who created them is that such a view of culture seems all too close to the great man [sic] (in this case "great artist") theory of history: that human life, an otherwise shapeless mass of often random-seeming events, is formed by great leaders who channel human energy in particularly effulgent directions. Swallowing that explanation for human behaviour thumps closed the door on the quotidian's complexity, the way a countless thousand million mundane decisions incrementally shift a culture and its multiple underlying worldviews. Short summaries of modernism can be excused if they omit various artists—that's to be expected. The nature of such summaries' failure is more grievous: it's the very identification of particular artists, often specific works (*To the Lighthouse*, *Ulysses*), that pushes such outlines over into the great artist fallacy.

I start out, then, on a wide circle in order to return to the eve of the Second World War, the late interwar period after the Nazis forced themselves into power. Even a quick trace of interwar modernism's roots could carry my narrative back to a post-Civil War nation badly divided between an industrialized Northeast and a largely agrarian South wracked by Reconstruction. I argue that modernism cannot be limited to high culture narratives like the fictional collaborations between the now-canonical creators

I mention above. Modernism was more various than a discussion between elites. It was deeply tied to populist impulses like the Grange movement, and brought with it "significant democratization of diverse American traditions; a leveling of local and regional legends; and a far more inclusive social repository for American memories."[12] The populist imaginary includes powerful resistant texts from the world of the farm, like L. Frank Baum's 1900 *The Wonderful Wizard of Oz*, a magic story about the lure of gold, the importance of the silver standard for political figures like William Jennings ("the Cowardly Lion") Bryan, and threats to the worker, personified by the Tin Man, rusted shut and deprived of his heart by robotized labour. What Michael Kammen calls "an extraordinary dialogue" in the culture can be characterized as a struggle with fearful issues, often reduced to the antagonism between modernity's machine and the workers caught in it.

That machine, a dynamo, identified actually and metaphorically by Henry Adams in his 1901 *Education of Henry Adams*, represents a new kind of unstoppable force. Thomas Hardy's 1892 *Tess of the D'Urbervilles* stared bleakly at the destruction of whole worlds and peoples by the machine, where "families, who had formed the backbone of the village life in the past, who were the depositories of the village traditions, had to seek refuge in the large centres; the process, humorously designated by statisticians as 'the tendency of rural populations towards the large towns', being really the tendency of water to flow uphill when forced by machinery."[13] Terry Smith extricates the discussion from a simple binary of machine (modernity) and human aesthetic response (modernism), seeing in modernism an organic process that "exists essentially in the play of flow and blockage between imagined futures and echoing pasts."[14] Each vision of the day's ills with potential for future nightmares (H. G. Wells's *Time Machine*) or wonders (David Butler's 1930 film *Just Imagine*, or Edward Bellamy's utopian *Looking Backward: 2000–1887*) is created by a confluence of pressures, fads, enthusiasms, beliefs, and doubts that advance and retreat chaotically. Worlds as diverse as those envisioned by Dos Passos and Steinbeck coexist and may even be grouped together as belonging to the same cultural project because all is in uncertain motion, simultaneously productive, terrifying, exhilarating. To be engaged in and by modernism is, in Marshall Berman's view, "to find ourselves in an environment that promises us adventure, power, joy, growth, transformation of ourselves and the world," even when those changes are relentless.[15] For all of Berman's optimism, loss, dissolution, and disaster are as likely to be modernity's results when engines not only drive human water uphill against agrarian tradition, but forever alter the family's history, its sense of time and place. Lewis Mumford's 1930 characterization of industrialization as "only a subsidiary function of life" that has nonetheless overwhelmed us and "predominates over every other function [such that] it is a sign of cultural emptiness" would have found Hardy in agreement.[16]

Modernism arguably at once recognizes and further intensifies these shifts, adding discomfort to distress, answering changes in living conditions and physical and psychological landscapes by fracturing old forms and vomiting up incomprehensible new ones. Rather than retreating into romance, modernism pushes ideas up to and, for many experiencing it, beyond incoherence. But whether a 1913 audience caused a near riot at the first performance of Stravinsky's *Le Sacre du Printemps* is not the issue; rather, it's about the way we characterize modernism to ourselves, depicting something urgent, forceful, altering, but most of all, a positive surge that released artistic expression from its previous cultural performances. In finding modernism good it has also become traditional to align it with what in the twentieth century might have been styled as Western freedoms.

Peter Gay, defender of canonical modernism, argues that, "in order to flourish, modernism required the support of social and cultural preconditions. Thus—to take a single instance—it is too obvious to require demonstration that modernists needed a relatively liberal state and society to function at all."[17] Gay's defence of this position is lengthy and well supported. It's a pleasing conceit that liberal states have produced what we look back on as modernist high culture, where presumably less liberal states have been proportionately less effective. Is modernism, in Gay's formulation, the artistic payoff for democracies that resisted fascism, authoritarianism, totalitarianism? Is modernism another proof of Western culture's strength, another demonstration that by opting for an apparent free-market economy in which corporations organize life and encourage consumption, the West hit the cultural jackpot? Gay's argument that modernists have been lured by the ideal of perpetual resistance (which he calls "heresy") seems, ironically, reasonable. But to suggest that modernism requires freedom, a term even more hotly contested than modernism itself, is to close the door on other forms of powerful artistic expression. Gay's assertion that it is "too obvious to require demonstration" makes it all the more pressing that we examine cases other than those regularly offered as examples of liberal modernism. When it comes to analyzing the world of military heraldry in the interwar era, modernism and its assumptions prove to be elusive, phantom, intriguingly fluid.

One of the ways of making the fluid concrete is to separate modernism into two broad forms that originate in either the head or the heart. Setting aside for the moment that such a division must first overcome the argument that modernism is inherently the work of outraged hearts in rebellion, we would then push modernist work and artists into two opposing piles. One would be comprised of layers of cool, cerebral, illuminating works. There Sheeler's new landscapes of power would hang in Mies van der Rohe's functional cubes, with poems by Pound and Eliot engraved on steel plates in building lobbies. Heaped on the other side would be Georgia O'Keefe, Frieda Kahlo, and Diego Rivera's impassioned paintings, performances by Josephine Baker, the heated surreal novels of Zora Neale Hurston and Richard Wright. No matter the temperature, all the work meets the modernist requirements of freshness, surprise, shock, and revelation. Terry Smith considers this famous partition of modernist work, where one side evokes and often praises "the new industrial age," while the other celebrates the "multiplicity of life ... the right of all to satisfying experiences of work and leisure, the democratic openness of the usually unpainted workers, a call to struggle, an avowedly Communist artist."[18] Smith then astutely rejects the simplistic dichotomy and its accompanying assumption that the less emotional work is uninvolved or apolitical.

A short example of the problems may help. The struggle could involve a fight over whose portrayal of industry, Elsie Driggs or Charles Sheeler's, is more dispassionate. Driggs's famous 1927 depiction of a Pittsburgh steel mill's smokestacks (*Pittsburgh*) could be compared to what Leo Marx has called the new pastoral narratives of Sheeler's 1930 *American Landscape*.[19] Does Driggs's work capture the dark satanic mills Blake saw, where Sheeler shows new meadows of production? Is Driggs's work political because it paints industry fouled by a grimy haze while Sheeler remains politically uncommitted because he shows a clear calm day, as do so many of his Detroit paintings? If these two paintings, closely related in subject and time, can be thrown against each other and cause a fairly strong debate, must we then go case by case, frame by frame, and contrast each painting with its cousins? Would the central looming darkness of Hopper's 1946 *Approaching a City* be more or less political than Driggs's work? Hopper's work would seem to be of the cool, distant camp, but when compared to Sheeler's River Rouge series, which is the more distant and which the more passionate? If Hopper's landscape is at arm's length, does it get its political job done more effectively because corporations might be more accepting of art that is less challenging, and buy and hang such a painting in a corporate boardroom? Such questions point to the invidiousness of comparison and underscore its uselessness.

Simple divisions hurt more than help. Discussing key cultural terms like modernism requires our acceptance that they contain endless, irresolvable complexities. Careful auditor of the nuances running through modernism, T. J. Jackson Lears proposes that it's natural to find "modernist and antimodernist sympathies coexisting, often within the same individual."[20] A person's life is composed of overlapping zones, places where we assume different emotional, psychological, even physical, identities. In the present moment one likely curates those identities depending on whether one is in public or not, with family (by birth? marriage? extended?) or friends (childhood? co-workers?), or occupying a virtual space through a keyboard or other interface (audio, or audio and video? your voice? digitally altered or enhanced? still picture? of you or another person, animal, popular-culture character?) that may be further obscured by an avatar, screen name, or anonymizing software. Change will come to some of those identities more easily than others.

What we identify as the self will likely require stability. Other parts of the self that strike us as less central (not who we are when we're alone at home, the being in the mirror at morning and evening) could be more open to experiment. For some, home will be a place for reliability. For others, the very safety of home can make challenges to the way meaning is formed that much more tolerable. Ironically, one's worldview may be most malleable at the centre of that world. Staid surroundings produce a calm backdrop for disruptive, inaccessible art. Even revolutionaries have rituals—drinks they prefer, tea instead of coffee in the morning, kinds of tobacco or drugs, places to sleep, comfort food. Modernism includes understanding that modernism itself will be difficult, that difficulty isn't part of, but is itself the territory of the new.

Raymond Chandler's Philip Marlowe, having worked alone (naturally) on a chess problem finds himself at "three A.M.... walking the floor and listening to Khachaturyan working in a tractor factory. He called it a violin concerto. I called it a loose fan belt and the hell with it."[21] A collision of science (detection rooted in Edgar Allen Poe's August Dupin's bloodless ratiocinations), commerce (Hammett's ex-Pinkertons and trench-coated First World War survivors working for insurance companies detecting insurance fraud), and conscience (an unblinking witness to Hollywood's obscene interwar wealth and concomitant loss of manners), Marlowe always knows more than he lets on. He knows that he is a modernist icon; it doesn't impress him. He fends off modernism's cultural royalty, like the society queen he imagines who "is reading the *Waste Land* or Dante in the original, or Kafka or Kierkegaard or studying Provençal. She adores music and when the New York Philharmonic is playing Hindemith she can tell you which one of the six bass viols came in a quarter of a beat too late. I hear Toscanini can also. That makes two of them."[22] The blistering attack on a cultural elite that possesses arcane technical information exclusive to the well-bred moneyed cognoscenti aims in at least two directions. First it identifies how quickly the working classes are betrayed by forces driving culture. Modernism, so often sympathetic to the disenfranchised, is soon colonized by the very forces it proposes to resist; only those with significant money, education, and the time that comes with them can fully explore the meanings behind artwork that upsets the social order. Second, it addresses the reader who also must have sufficient cultural education to get the jokes, understand that Marlowe, in pulling off an insult involving Hindemith, six bass viols, and Toscanini, reflexively points to his own role as a modernist skeptic searching vainly for truth in America's new wasteland. Readers who laugh at the insult understand that they live in a complex circulatory system where products they consume speak of and to them. The pulp fiction audience reading about an antihero bearing a sixteenth-century British playwright's name is in on the joke, is also involved in the struggle over what modernism is and who it is for.

In historian Warren Susman's view, "the story of American culture remains largely the story of [the] middle class. There is a tendency, when treating this [interwar] period, for historians suddenly to switch their focus and concentrate on the workers, hobos, various ethnic minorities deprived of a place in the American sun."[23] Modernism is often presented as the product of outcast elites like Woolf, Joyce, Eliot, who engage in cultural exchanges with other estranged intelligentsia.[24] If one insists on claiming that modernism is elite, one must account for resistant work by artists such as Upton Sinclair, Susan Glaspell, Clifford Odets, and James Farrell, all of whom focus, exactly as Susman notes, on the displaced, disenfranchised worker or misfit who has been pushed to the culture's edges. As much as Gay dislikes the solution, it makes sense that in attempting to define modernism, cultural historians "have sought refuge in a prudential plural: 'modernisms.'"[25] If modernism is many, then while the struggle over who is and is not included can cease, the fight over whether modernism is inherently good ramps up. Formulating his own cultural map, Gay refuses "modernisms," locking into one meaning on which rests everything. Accepting Gay's assertion that modernism is necessarily symbiotic with liberal democracy, itself driven by a capitalist free-market economy, means that artistic expression (design, painting, music, film, industrial design, architecture) produced by non-democratic nations cannot be modernist.

Seeking a resolution to the debate's paradoxes and complexities, Daniel Singal proposes that "modernism should properly been seen as a *culture*—a constellation of related ideas, beliefs, values, and modes of perception."[26] But a constellation, a collection of related objects tied together by various forces, is still a vast unifying system. It's an attractive conceit, since cultures arguably have their own momentum, owing nothing to specific individuals. It could be a co-constitutive imaginary where like minds, after being attracted to the same core, fall into orbit around each other. Singal's proposition is paralleled by scholar Susan Hegeman's rejection of modernism as a movement of new forms characterized by "a seamless parade of jazz, cars, and steel." Materials alone won't tell the story of modernism any more than will lists of famous creators. Instead Hegeman points to "a perception of uneven development, and even friction" between places modernism visited; some places grew hot with it, particularly large northeastern cities in the United States, while others were, in her words, "touched less completely."[27]

Objects of popular or mass culture add another layer of complexity to the debate about modernism, something to which Chandler gestures when Marlowe scorns elite modernism. There's an ongoing cultural rumble between high and low, where inaccessibility is the elite's political badge. Marlowe concludes "the hell with it," he has no patience for such pretension. Even now popularity and commercial success doom artists of all kinds (craftspeople, architects, illustrators, singers and songwriters, dancers) to exile from the modernist heights. N. C. Wyeth's paintings of Blind Pew and Robinson Crusoe for Scribner's Illustrated Classics were and are beloved, but must live in their own gristmill in Pennsylvania's Brandywine museum, away from the great collections of American modernism in New York, Chicago, and Philadelphia. The Brandywine River Museum is one of the few spaces (the Delaware Art Museum is another) where high art and the popular share power without question. Seeing Andrew and Jamie Wyeth's paintings in the context of their father and grandfather's work underlines how much all have produced astonishing bodies of art. For the most part, though, a solid partition still stands between high art and narrative work, even as academics assiduously exhume work by accomplished, forgotten painters.

Outside illustration and narrative art circles, how many students or scholars know of Elizabeth Shippen Green, let alone the comic strips of Winsor McCay (*Little Nemo*) or Harry Hershfield (*Abie the Agent*). Much lionization of George Herriman's *Krazy Kat* has raised that strip's profile, but were it not kept in print by Fantagraphics Books, it too would soon disappear. I have yet to read an account of serious modernism, even popular modernism, that discusses genre work in the same terms as high art.

Krazy Kat benefitted from early support by Gilbert Seldes, who profiled the strip in his 1924 critical assessment of popular culture, *The Seven Lively Arts*. Herriman gained further cachet when, in 1931, Don Marquis asked him to illustrate the immensely popular and resoundingly modernist collections of free-verse stories about Archy the cockroach and his friend Mehitabel the cat.[28] Just because the contemporary world knows something about one modernist comic strip doesn't mean others of equal worth have been preserved, studied, or deemed worthy of canonization. The brutal, brilliant social satire of George Tuthill's *The Bungle Family* (1918), lightning surrealism of Clifford Sterret's *Polly and her Pals* (1913), eerie, shifting land- and mindscapes of Frank King's *Gasoline Alley* (1918), outrageous, pre-Marx Brothers insanity of Milt Gross's work (*Nize Baby* [1926], *He Done Her Wrong* [1930]) are known to an even smaller group of readers. These creators haven't been put side by side with those deemed to be serious visual artists of the time. None of the comics has received the slipcased hard-cover two-volume treatment that Modern American Library gave Lynd Ward's *Six Novels in Woodcuts* in 2010. When North America considers the German side of culture, it doesn't put Otto Dix's linear, often caricaturist, work in company with the early savage days of the *Katzenjammer Kids*, who were killers before they were domesticated by American newspaper syndication. These unknown, typically discarded, works possess the same urgent cultural acuity academics demand from canonical pre- and interwar modernist texts.

Lynd Ward's woodcut novels probably escaped the curse of being too popular because the model for his wordless books was German expressionist Frans Masereel's work: Masereel had made the form a serious part of post-First World War art. If N. C. Wyeth's powerful 1913 *The Wreck of the "Covenant"* wasn't compared to Winslow Homer's earlier *The Life Line* (1884), there was certainly no chance that J. C. Leyendecker, closeted queer artist who revisioned both fashion and graphic design with his Arrow shirt collar ads and covers for *Collier's Magazine*, would be recognized as a serious artist. Even as Leyendecker executed one striking graphic solution after another, month by month, year to year, his work wouldn't be accorded the same populist honours given to another successful modernist, Norman Rockwell.

Gaps in the modernist narrative widen when we further examine commercial success. What is the viewer to make of the Arrow collar ads that brought Arrow 96 per cent of the market share, wiped out a great deal of the competition, and almost by accident established a new model of urban male beauty in the US?[29] Was it simply a successful campaign for a staple consumer product? The stark elegance of Leyendecker's final Arrow collar ads of 1929–1930 echoed the flat-shape design brilliance of German illustrator and sometime Nazi, Ludwig Hohlwein (1874–1949). Hohlwein's pre-First World War and wartime propaganda posters smoothed the way for Leyendecker's visual starkness.[30] Arguments against claiming Hohlwein's work as modernist are familiar: modernism is supposed to represent the new, that which refuses to bow to corporate or societal forces. Leyendecker's ads, commissions to sell products, could hardly be classed with the *cris du coeur* produced by the Ashcan school. Even as George Bellows's paintings of savage, near-naked boxers engaged in blood sport were lauded, Leyendecker's polished society dandies were written off as corporate fodder. But checking into the social history around Leyendecker's images we find, according to fashion historian Carole Turbin, that they created an "elite representation of" a new group of men, an image that "resonated across class and ethnic lines."[31] Not all men were boxers, were heterosexual, rejected beauty, or performed modernism for an elite. As a queer painter, Leyendecker was already a cultural exile when he deciphered a way to make a living painting his own kind of resistance to the cult of masculinity championed by Jack London and Teddy Roosevelt.

Michael Kammen notes helpfully that "the crucial point is that the interwar decades were permeated by both modernism and nostalgia in a manner that may best be described as perversely symbiotic."[32] The shirt collar ads were the new edge of fashion in American art deco masculinity, but they also looked back to a history of dress that included detachable collars. Detachable collars were a way to extend the life of an old shirt; they came from a time when washing shirts was difficult and expensive, when water supply was unreliable and "labour saving" devices like washing machines, as the post-Second World War world would know them, did not yet exist. Modernity would eliminate shirts with detachable collars as the country invested in infrastructure, indoor plumbing, and ever more mechanized washing machines that made cleaning whole shirts, rather than snapping on a replaceable collar, feasible. The collar was a sign of transition, an indication that an age of expensive elegance for the few was passing, to be replaced by machine labour for the many. Clean collars meant dressing up and creating an evening-leisure as opposed to workday self. As Turbin notes, "the Arrow Man and his collar did not represent unmitigated newness": shirt collars, like other things sold in the interwar period and repackaged as modernism's cultural artifacts, promised a future but were indelibly about the past. They were hybrids. There is at once a deep sense of the familiar about this modernism, as well as the re-creation of urban masculinity: the first clears the way for the second, reassuring tradition opens the way for the new. If a halo of sentiment engenders the acceptance of homoeroticism, so be it.

Kammen identifies corporate actors like the Rockefellers, Ford, and the du Ponts who, engaged in destroying the past, had an almost perverse appetite for it. Ford particularly, with the 1929 establishment of his Henry Ford Museum and the wholesale creation of the nearby fictional Greenfield Village, was obsessed with putting behind glass a way of life his industrial processes and products were erasing. The determination to preserve "something of everything" from American life made, for Kammen, "a figurative dollhouse" out of people's lives.[33] If you are a relatively uneducated, powerless citizen, such infantilization could be terrifying. Your previous agrarian way of life was being eradicated, you yourself were directed to cities and industrial labour, while simultaneously, the contents of your home were tipped into a memory tank like colonial Williamsburg or what is now an eighty-acre curation of Ford's America.[34] One becomes a double prisoner, at once closed into a factory and its attendant living machines (cities and tenements), and also trapped in a representation of all that is lost. Ford's museum opened to the public in order to exhibit how it had, until recently, lived. In the memory archive you will find an image of your ghostly self, the dishes, furniture, and vast array of household items you might once have had. There, in that display case, is—no, was, your mother's churn. The Ford Motor Company owns it, your personal past replaced by America's collective generic experience seen from the perspective of its new industrial master. The Ford miniature village grew out of his own collection of artifacts that he bought up rapaciously like some frenzied Stakhanovite, consuming the whole of the disappearing past as if, Terry Smith suggests, in order "to own it."[35]

Ford's dual obsession with both past and future is common to much that is modernist. It is, after all, Chandler's Marlowe who, despite his skepticism and cynicism, is "not himself mean ... is neither tarnished nor afraid ... a common man and yet an unusual man."[36] Marlowe maintains antique values of chivalric honour even as he knowingly wades through the contemporary world's worst moral lapses, starting with a meaningless industrial slaughter in Europe. Not all modernism was Hindemith, bass viols, and arrogant *nouveau riche*; much of it was also sentimental and accessible. Gay points out that even though the upper middle class or fabulously wealthy supported modernism, "philistine taste continued to command the buying habits of the majority among the prosperous."[37] The line between highly cultured and more populist modernism could be blurred, expanded, and occupied by new mass cultural artifacts like newspaper comics, films, radio shows, and phonographic records. Advertising was itself both medium and artifact—a way of shifting an image from an obscure gallery or atelier to a mass-produced magazine, from a salon of elites to store frontage. Utility, as with the Arrow collar, could soften and make more desirable the new.

Art historian Michelle Bogart highlights the different jobs performed by elite and populist art, refraining from labelling the second as modernist: "Modernism might work for the 'sophisticated, bizarre and *small* class circulation field represented by Vogue and Harper's Bazar,' but it was illustrators like Norman Rockwell, J. C. Leyendecker, and Jessie Willcox Smith that exerted the most pulling power for the 'millyuns.'"[38] If popularity and accessibility aren't synonymous with modernism, then does popularity make a text less likely to be modernist? Is the perception of the text enough to alter the text's meaning? Does the accessibility and pleasure of listening to Prokofiev's "Peter and the Wolf" make the text less modern? Does difficulty in interpretation improve the quality of the message? Considering that Jessie Willcox Smith's and Norman Rockwell's paintings were so often domestic, does such a quality then exclude from modernism Mary Cassatt's astutely observant paintings of a maternal *ukiyo-e*-influenced world of the 1890s? [39]

Cassatt's paintings are subtler than Smith's or Rockwell's, but then subtlety isn't a useful measure of modernism, as Duchamp's wartime readymades illustrated. One signal difference between Mary Cassatt and Jessie Willcox Smith, Elizabeth Shippen Green, and Violet Oakley (the "Red Rose Girls," all trained in studio painting by the famous Howard Pyle, N. C. Wyeth's teacher) was that Cassatt was born into wealth and learned her artistic practice from Europeans in France, where Smith, Green, and Oakley developed and stayed in Pennsylvania.[40] While her pictures of children may be more illustratorly than Cassatt's paintings, Smith saw more closely into the domestic sphere of America's middle class. Comparing art by Cassatt and the Red Rose Girls supports the argument that modernism oscillated across the culture, where the messages about the new, "especially from the nineteenth century on," would be carried "by cultural middlemen who advertised, and profited from, their talents."[41]

Profit is the adversary of unbounded speech, goes the modernist dictum. Yet as the Arrow collar ads demonstrate, advertising, a crucial part of modernity and its symbiont, consumer culture, rapidly pushed new forms and images into public view. Ads did the heavy lifting of selling, capturing and holding the viewer's attention long enough to highlight, and eclipse, other brands. Art directors began adopting modernist forms in ads because "they thought these techniques would succeed in drawing attention. Indeed, many undoubtedly had personal motives for their experimentations. The artist and art lover in them believed that modernist styles were a more authentic mode of representation."[42] In Bogart's view, art directors weren't just imitating—they were also creating. To argue that only a handful of artists understood the modernist impulse is to ignore the tens of thousands of creative people of different genders, races, and classes working in crafts, trades, and businesses. Such actors were restricted by the need to make a living, weren't creating art for art's sake, and by a pure definition of modernism, weren't "mak[ing] it new." At the same time, advertising was and is a world that lives in speed. There isn't time for an ad, let alone a campaign, to bomb. Failed image strategies must be replaced without pause—the market is ruthless about unsuccessful experimentation. A savage quickness augurs against advertising producing "authentic" (unbounded) modernism. However the very speed in the creation and turnover of images suggests that advertising was and is capable of a kind of automatic writing which, when channelled by art directors, refreshes ideas until the item sells, the campaign runs out of money, or the business collapses. Bogart argues that adventuresome bosses who adopted modernist codes might wind up educating the mass audience, even if such education was not their first (or second) intention.[43] Inordinately obscure modernist work that required the viewer's deep patience and tolerance might not play with the masses. Nonetheless, Lears argues, adapting and making palatable much that was modernist was a reasonable goal: "it was possible to yoke formal innovation to thematic predictability and experimental techniques to familiar scenes—in short, to marry avant-garde with kitsch."[44] The assumption seems to be that the masses can accept the unusual if it has been deep-fried in bad taste (*weltschmerz, schmaltz*)—images greasy enough slide down the public throat.

The avant-garde doesn't have to be paired with kitsch for it to be palatable. Style that becomes faddish is as much capable of producing a look people accept. Cultural scholars Stuart Ewen and Miles Orvell, considering interwar patterns of the popular in America and the associated aesthetic drift in industrial design, suggest that the rise of streamlining is an example of risk-free modernism: it thrills without challenging the audience. The ubiquity of streamlining arguably creates a kind of kitsch, or what Ewen calls a "lubricated look," something fatty, empty, yet appealing.[45] The jagged and difficult is smoothed down and creates "a fetishism of the machine that transformed the look of everything from skyscrapers to toasters, evident in a vocabulary of electric angularities and zigzag designs connoting the *excitement* of the machine."[46] For both Orvell and Ewen, streamlining said more about what people understood technology to be than did the force of the machine itself. Cloaking the machine's brutal angularity in fairings and steel envelopes was mostly for consumers, not engineers and mechanics. Charles Chaplin's profound understanding of modernity and modernism is clear in his 1936 *Modern Times*. At the base of the atrocious feeding machine into which the Little Tramp is locked whirrs an insane collage of mechanisms. Only after it force-feeds the Tramp lug nuts and relentlessly pounds his face so that he is stunned, if not dead, does the factory director dismiss the machine as "not practical." Each time the device shorts out, its operators force their hands into the machine's smoking gears, the reality beneath its polished exterior. No such cover protects the Little Tramp from the speed boss's command to stay on station, even after the assembly line makes him monomaniacal, causes his temporarily insanity—everything in the world, even buttons and breasts, appear as two machine parts that need tightening—and sends him to an asylum. *Modern Times* reflects the mass experience of modernity which, as Terry Smith suggests, the American public could expect to come up against almost exclusively in "the factory, the trading areas, the secretary's and storage rooms, and the kitchen and bathroom of the home."[47]

The encounter had already started with the First World War. War, the production for, manufacture in, and execution of it, is one thing Smith leaves out of his list. If the American public had managed to somehow remain isolated from cities, rail, industry, steam- and coal-powered technology, the telegraph and telephone, radio, widely distributed rapidly produced newspapers, mass-produced clothing and consumer goods, as well as all the attendant advertising that drove those objects into the public's hands, the First World War ended that quarantine. In the war's massive wake were left enormous standing armies, the industrial forces, and their information-handling processes that had been developed to organize, equip, supply, house, treat, and transport them. The call of modernity, a speed machine now replicating itself through and across every discipline, brought a response from modernism that transcended elites and their chosen art forms. Human expression of all kinds, particularly design, produced at the behest of corporate and military forces, would reflect modernity's hammer blows.

And so we come around to the moment, the United States military in the late interwar period. Rapidly demobilized after the First World War, the military sagged drastically in numbers and funding. Only as the threat of the Second World War came closer did the military begin to get more attention. Everything the US military did in terms of design was as affected by the struggles in modernism and advertising, the corporate and public worlds, the nostalgic past and drive toward an exhilarating future, as anything else in America. In military heraldry, which includes all the visual signs an army uses to speak about itself (flags, insignia, medals, uniforms), there was as much turbulence as anywhere else. But just as the penetration of modernism across America was unpredictable and varied, and the expression of new ideas as likely to be popular as abstruse, there was less order to the military sign system than one might expect. Solutions to heraldic design problems faced by America's Army cover as enormous a range as do the design impulses representing masculinity reaching from Leyendecker to Bellows and Sheeler.

The Shoulder Sleeve Insignia, the specific patches that identify armies, navies, air forces, and all their many subdivisions, were created by artists who understood and believed in modernism's core philosophy, by those who mimicked the outlines of new forms because they found them intriguing, by another group who were blind to or uninterested in the new, and by still another that had no idea what modernism encompassed and, had they been informed about it, would have thrown it out directly.

Before venturing into heraldry, however, I pause here to rewind and create a parallel track that follows German interwar design expression. The familiar narrative about German modernism is that the Nazis shunned it in favour of antique forms taken from, among others, northern Germanic lore (Norse myths, gods, legends, and iconography). The Nazis became infamous not only for the purge of modernist intellectuals identified with the left (among them Theodor Adorno and the Frankfurt School; Walter Gropius, Mies van der Rohe, and the Bauhaus), but particularly for the 1937 Munich *Entartete Kunst* ("Degenerate Art") exhibit of over one hundred modernist artists. To recount the *Entartete Kunst* story is to reiterate that modernism only flourishes in liberal democracies. Once the show was over the offenders, already identified as Bolsheviks, Jews, homosexuals, insane, degenerate, enemies of the state, or all of these, would be deported and exterminated. The show proved conclusively that the Nazis were against everything the Allies were for, including artistic freedom. The story concludes that the United States accepted modernism, discord, and debate, while the Axis powers were retrograde antimodernist fascists who sought full control over public and private expression. I have just argued, though, that the story of American modernism is infinitely more complex, and I shift over to consider equally complex issues in Nazi design aesthetics, which contain broad strands of modernism.

CHAPTER 2

Macht Frei

The Paradox of Nazi Modernism

IF YOU HAD TO CALL UP AN IMAGE OF THE NAZI AESTHETIC other than the swastika, you could remember the Nuremburg parade grounds and then imagine them extended, multiplied beyond reason, and you'd be looking at Hitler and Albert Speer's design for *Welthauptstadt* (world's capital); or recall Leni Riefenstahl's depiction of fascist heroism in her 1936 *Triumph of the Will*; or maybe a world of outsize monuments, sculptures, and structures representing an updated neoclassicism, sometimes called "fascist stripped classicism," marked by the absence of decorative gestures common to Greek and Roman architecture. As for German modernism, you could whistle Bertolt Brecht and Kurt Weill's "Mack the Knife," or remember the *Entartete Kunst* show, displayed in wretched conditions, artwork jammed floor to ceiling onto the walls. Still, roughly two million Germans crushed in to see it, over three times the number that attended Hitler's official Nazi art show.[1] The public's apparent hunger for cubism, Dadaism, and the avant-garde supports the notion that, despite themselves, Germans could reject fascist authority, could connect with the show's inherent cultural revolution. The Germans, as much as the Americans, had fallen prey to modernity as machine, efficiency system, consumption engine, producer of a generalized anxiety that drove the *Volk* from their stable homes and lives on the land they had tenanted or owned and into the gears of perpetual debt. Modernism was the artistic brake to consumer capitalism's runaway machine; modernism, particularly as practiced by social realists pushing for improved living and working conditions, represented the best expression of what it was to be human. Relatively helpless citizens of the second industrial revolution might be tortured and elites might have to speak for them, but at least that speech would be free and justice would one day arrive.

However, as with America, there isn't one story of the Reich's attitude to modernism and design: there are stories. It might be helpful if we step over to Italy for a moment and consider the Italian futurists. Filippo Marinetti and his fellow futurists were some of the most astutely prophetic modernists. Their understanding of the role of speed in war, manufacture, and communication has, as Paul Virilio has investigated at length, had drastic implications for late-twentieth-century and early-twenty-first-century thinking about machine perception and the elimination of space by time. Renato Bertelli's *Continuous Profile (Head of Mussolini)* is a futurist microcosm because it is a repeatable portrait of a charismatic, a picture of an elite leader who sees the new world (even if it's fascist) and leads the masses there. Bertelli's sculpture is utterly unlike anything that has come before—static busts of past heroes. Here is a piece that stares at everything all the time. Looking like an artifact from a lathe, that quintessential industrial tool, the profile could have been drawn as one line and then rotated through space and time, carving out a new identity. Few works sum up as many core ideas so succinctly. These same inclinations existed in Germany. Gay's position that "it is too obvious to require demonstration that modernists needed a relatively liberal state and society to function at all" constructs a narrative that obscures the complexity of cultural existence.[2] One might be offended by the suggestion that the Nazi state was ambivalent about its cultural politics, but this is no salvage operation. Roger Griffin, deeply shrewd investigator of fascism, initially seems to agree that "the genocidal crimes with which its cultural policies are indelibly associated make it even more difficult to conceive Nazism as hosting anything genuinely modernist, a term that still tends of have progressive or liberating connotations."[3] Difficult does not mean impossible. The *Entartete Kunst* exhibit makes a slow plump target: the show was a very public part of the Nazis' reaction to modernism, but it was still only a part. Scholar Jeffrey Herf defines what he calls "reactionary modernism," which "also deserves to be described as an aspect of cultural modernism, as [Daniel] Bell and [Jurgen] Habermas have described it."[4] In Herf's formulation, reactionary modernism was as much a revolution and contained as much innovation as did the cultural stew boiling in Britain, France, and the United States. It was a kind of modernism that not only co-existed with Nazism, but was propelled and supported by it.

As the Nazis rolled up Europe and collected famous art in their drag net, they focused particularly on gathering and preserving modernist pieces. Concern with images originated with Hitler, the snubbed would-be artist twice denied access both to the Vienna Academy of Fine Art and the world of the aesthete. Hitler never let go of art and architecture, taking further instruction from Goebbels that vision and visibility were key to successful propaganda campaigns. And while as early as *Mein*

Kampf (1925–1927) Hitler attacked modernists as being "lunatics and degenerates," who once "would have been sent to the insane asylum" but had so far escaped that fate, for at least another ten years German modernism continued to thrive, arguably feeding off the conflicts between the Nazis and the remains of the Weimar Republic.[5]

The struggle over the image in the Reich is usually typified as an ongoing battle between sentimental populist *Völkisch* art, given full-throated support by Reich Minister for the Occupied Eastern Territories Alfred Rosenberg and Joseph Goebbels, one of the Reich's most powerful supporters of modernism. Steven Heller, American graphic designer and design historian, expands on the image war: "the [Nazi] conservatives took for granted that their historical Germanicism would become the country's official style, while others who leaned toward modernism presumed that the Nazi revolution would emulate Italian Fascism in adopting the new style."[6] Futurism was stuffed with rage, speed, and action, a combination that seemed to fit a regime that embraced new technologies and forms of combat (the newspapers' coinage of *blitzkrieg* to describe manoeuvre warfare could have come straight from Marinetti's "Manifesto del Futurismo"). The Reich's rise to power, while an old story of political usurpation, was a promise of a new world that would finally and completely erase the Weimar's history of loss, grief, and poverty.[7] As the fictionalized Jewish First World War veteran, amputee, artist, and art dealer Max Rothman says in Menno Meyjes's 2002 film *Max* about both the war and its legacy: "I've seen the future. Believe me, it came straight at us. There's no future in the future." His comments are all the more painful since his role in the film is that of Hitler's art dealer. Rothman is a modernist, but certainly not a futurist.

Just as the First World War shook American notions of what the battlefield was, the sheer scale and reach of industrial slaughter on European soil could not be ignored by the Germans in the

depths of a severe post-war depression. Herf notes that the collision of cultural and scientific forces in Germany was particularly
unusual: "Although aesthetic modernity and the cult of technics
existed elsewhere in Europe and in the United States, nowhere did
modernity and tradition meet in such unmitigated confrontation
as in Germany. Nowhere else did the reconciliation of romanticism and modern technology become a matter of national identity."[8] The divide over what images were to represent the Reich can
be characterized as one between the familiar and reassuring, what
SS reports later called "home-cooked, bourgeois art with little
dynamism," and the shockingly new.[9] The preference for *Völkisch*
art would certainly have been reassuring to a dictatorship that
couldn't tolerate resistance of any kind. Art would be decorative
and pleasing, but not aesthetically revolutionary. This was not,
however, the whole story.

Determining what was truly modernist seemed to be a great
deal of the problem. While Hitler could eliminate both art and
artists he considered to be lesser, the cultural condemnation by
others was less certain.[10] Of the hundreds of works in the *Entartete
Kunst* show there were, predictably, those by Archipenko, Braque,
Kandinsky, Matisse, and Schwitters.[11] At the same time Goebbels
supported and argued for German expressionists Emil Nolde,
Ernst Kirchner, and Ernst Barlach, each of whom refused to
sanitize the world or create the neoclassical kitsch the *Völkisch*
supporters lauded.[12] While we may identify the sterile paintings
of Adolf Ziegler, Albert Janesch, and Gisbert Palmié, as well
as the enormous sculptures by Arno Breker as Nazi neoclassicism still, the forms were unexpected. Breker's sculptures were
so Brobdingnagian that they shot right past their classical origins
into their own surreal universe of nightmarish grandeur.

German expressionism is the kind of modernism we associate
with the left, with an attack on capitalism's subjugation of the
citizen. Accepting for the moment that Ziegler and Janesch were

engaged in remaking neoclassicism, it is also arguable that they sought a future that wasn't either steeped in *Völkisch* sentimentality or defined by the vigorous fracturing (cubism, Dadaism) of previously recognizable forms. They sought a new aesthetic that would be recognizably a Nazi one, but also radically different from what had come before. Adolf Ziegler's art would have been equally unacceptable to Wilhelmine Germany as anything by Franz Marc, although the objections would have been different. As Jackson Lears points out "If one defined one's modernism solely as formal innovation, then modernist experiments could be used to promote just about any sentiment at all."[13] Pound's command to "make it new" didn't proscribe the anatomization and reconstruction of new wholes from older parts. Nazism was caught up in a familiar modernist struggle between the old world of the garden and the new, apparently progressive, landscape of the machine: all present were the strains of "romanticism, of utopianism, of casting aside the past in a zealous race into the future, of messianic redemptiveness, of social cleansing and the desire to begin again culturally."[14]

Modernism could look like something other than the Ashcan School's 1908 New York exhibition by The Eight. Had Charles Sheeler's industrial landscapes, classified as cerebral, cool, rational, been painted in Germany in the late 1930s, they would have been taken as praise for the Reich's progress. Roger Griffin clarifies the wider discussion when he "presents modernism as capable of not just collaborating with socio-political movements, but of expressing itself directly in them unmediated through art, and liable to manifest itself in the values and politics of the Right no less than the Left."[15] Divorcing the art from our political expectations of it renders the territory infinitely more complex, and makes it possible for us to explore an array of grey shades that compose any picture of war. Existence in the Third Reich's twelve-year span was as violent as its creation, an object in perpetual motion: "the Nazis operated in the subjunctive tense, experimenting, reordering, reconstructing, and it is this spirit of renovation that qualifies National Socialism as modern."[16]

Because Nazi actions and decisions were uniformly horrific, it is hard to see them as a group engaged in deep conflicts and disagreements, being pulled in varying directions dependent not only on different leaders and their personal ambitions, but on the lower ranks' mixed tendencies. Rather than there being a solid block of beliefs, there was, in David Welch's phrase, a "mosaic of conflicting authorities *and* affinities."[17] Not all modernists ended up sentenced to artistic and actual deportation to the camps. Some, like Ludwig Hohlwein, were already Nazis, and others were sympathizers. Some not only accepted, but gloried in fascism, as did Marinetti and his futurist colleagues Gino Severini and Umberto Boccioni. As Taylor and van der Will point out, "various artists and intellectuals during the period of Nazi culture were attracted to Fascist doctrine while at the same time remaining stylistically Modernist in inclination or expression."[18] Our past expectations that modernism is inherently about freedom and equality would force us to conclude that Hohlwein, Ziegler, Severini, and the others necessarily couldn't be modernists. Their work might appear to be modernist, but if it were rooted in oppression the modernism would be an appearance only. What begins to break is the assumption that the Nazis had one way of seeing. Jan Nelis argues that there was no "black and white situation in which 'modern' art was banned and the abstract notion of 'Nazi art' was elevated to an absolute level," reopening terms that have long been closed to debate.[19] He continues by taking on the *Entartete Kunst* show, the apparently irrefutable piece of evidence about Nazis and modernism, arguing that "there was a lot of confusion and arbitrariness in the use of the term *Entartete Kunst*, which up until today has not been unambiguously defined."[20]

As in America and its varieties of modernism (*pace* Peter Gay), the Reich's notions of modernism were manifold, contradictory,

divided between the lure of the past and future, recasting classicism in such a way as to render it recognizably modern. As
comfortable assumptions about modernism and liberal democracy
sag, so must the conclusion that Nazism legitimized one and only
one expression of art. In examining philosophers, writers, and
industrial designers, including Spengler, Junger, and a number
of engineers he profiles, Herf argues these intellectuals were yet
more reactionary modernists celebrating "beauty and form as
ethical ideals in themselves. In so doing they shared affinities
with the modernism of the avant-garde as well as with technical innovators."[21] Our historical view has been relatively late in
accepting the differences and conflicts that existed.[22]

Roger Griffin's complex and deeply thoughtful scholarship
vastly expands Herf's concept of reactionary modernism, arguing
that what the Nazis were pushing toward was beyond even modernism and was a "deadly serious attempt to realize an *alternative*
logic, an *alternative* modernity, and an *alternative* morality to
those pursued by liberalism, socialism or conservatism."[23] The
war is typified by the Allies as a struggle over the politics of
freedom; it can also be framed as the opposition of two corporate
forces in a battle over the right business model of managerial
efficiency; or two forms of nascent operations research, soon to
become management science and complex modeling of real world
situations; or two approaches to scientific development where one
sought to extend known technology (explosive devices that could
be carried across massive distances by rockets instead of artillery
shells or aircraft, or were even autonomous) and another based its
plan on entirely unknown science. Similarly, studies of modernism
understand the war as a struggle between modernist and fascist
art. The first is recognized, canonized, and taught across university
curricula—the martyrs of the *Entartete Kunst* exhibit paralleled
by American voices that shouted life into theatre, music, painting,
ballet, film, giving speech to those who, in all their anguish and

rebellion, had not yet been heard. The second is rarely seen, or is shown as a frightening example of what the Nazis got right (the inclusion of Riefenstahl's *Triumph of the Will* in film courses and discussions of propaganda is one example). But what if?

What if the corporate war won by GM, Ford, Standard Oil, and Hughes Aircraft had instead gone to I. G. Farben? The deep anxiety about what might have become of the Allies had they lost has possessed novelists who have conducted their own thought experiments, picturing a post-war Reich in America or Britain. Novels like Philip K. Dick's 1962 *The Man in the High Castle*, Len Deighton's 1978 *SS-GB*, Robert Harris's 1992 *Fatherland*, Harry Turtledove's 1994–1996 *Worldwar* series (the author carried on his fascination with the Reich over another eight alternate Nazi histories), and more recent fictions like the French *Block 109*, a six-volume *bande dessinée* series by Vincent Brugeas, Ronan Toulhoat, and Ryan Lovelock, where we join the Reich in the mid-1950s. Further explorations appear in the video game franchises *Wolfenstein* and *Call of Duty* (repeated user requests that they be allowed to join *Call of Duty* as Nazis or Wehrmacht have been refused to date: one can, however, fight as the Axis in *Day of Defeat, Codename: Panzers, Blitzkrieg*). Such fabulations have continued to intrigue the allied nations as we reflect morbidly on what might have been. All the texts point to a different modernism, but one that we have imagined relatively poorly—a caricature of Nazi modernism that engages in only tentative, stereotypical extrapolation.

The dangers of toying with Nazi culture are clear—the reasons for our persistent attraction to it are less obvious. Horror stories across the genres demonstrate the power of gory taboo-breaking narratives. Nazis have become such a horror staple that they even have their own spoof films (Timo Vuorensola's ongoing series *Iron Sky* [2012] and Tommy Wirkola's Nazi zombie series *Dead Snow* [2009] are some of the more recent examples from dozens made over the decades). For a while it seemed that Nazis were the worst thing the culture could imagine, a Rubicon that has long since been crossed. The author who explores Nazism seriously and finds things to praise there can still expect to be shunned culturally as someone sanitizing or legitimizing hate speech; the only proviso is that the texts may be permitted to pass if they declare themselves from the outset to be complete schlock, in which case they escape into camp. A deep exploration of what Nazism might look like ten or twenty years after an imaginary victory might be quite discomfiting. If we take Fritzsche's argument seriously that the Nazis were in constant motion, "experimenting, reordering, reconstructing," then assuming the Reich of the 1960s could be directly extrapolated from what it looked like before their military defeat would be a classic error in forecasting. Frank Spotnitz's 2015 adaption of Dick's *The Man in the High Castle* avoided that mistake and made a serious attempt to envision how the Reich and imperial Japan would look culturally in 1962. The series' wild success demonstrates that the public is quite prepared to entertain stories about how Nazi futures might have looked.[24]

The fight between Rosenberg's *Völkisch* forces and those sympathetic to modernism extended beyond high art into the popular. The dreadful sentimentalism at the heart of *Völkisch* expression produced a world of unalloyed bad taste—kitsch. It's unfortunate that of all the things lost or ruined by the war, kitsch wasn't one of them.[25] Kitsch, a term whose origins and meaning in German have never been completely clear, is sometimes defined by pointing to items: painted concrete garden gnomes or Disney figures; the African-American "lawn jockey," still a familiar sight in my youth; plastic bobble-head figures of Jesus—all representatives of what in 1934 an irritated German doctor called "small household atrocities," except his would have been "thousands of articles decorated with swastikas, including wrapping paper for soft cheese; silk pillow cases ... embroidery patterns with Hitler feeding deer." [26]

Such unintentionally hilarious abominations included working designs that were central to the Reich's aesthetic expression.

Graphic designer Steven Heller points out that difficult-to-decipher black-letter typefaces associated with medieval Germany like "Fraktur and Schwabacher [were] part of the antiquated past. Paul Renner, designer of the quintessentially modern Futura, who wrote a book titled *Kulturbolschewismus?* (*Cultural Bolshevism?*) that attacked Nazi anti-Semitism and medievalism in art, found unexpected allies in these [student] Nazi modernists."[27] American architect Louis Sullivan's famous dictum that "form follows function" (equally taken up by the designers at the Bauhaus) meant that while Fraktur might aptly express the Nordic origins of the Nazis' Aryan fantasies, the form wasn't functional enough and had to be jettisoned in favour of legible typefaces. Heller notes sardonically: "Fraktur was impeding the plan of world domination, and so—with their usual efficiency—the Nazis moved summarily to a new graphic scheme."[28] The Nazis' revised typography was committed both to modernism and modernity. Futura, an example of Renner's design genius, remains a gold standard of clarity, elegance, modernism.

Goebbels sustained modernist artists, collected their work, and spoke up for them until, as Petropoulos observes, those actions threatened "his powerful position atop the cultural bureaucracy."[29] Strong as Goebbels might have been, and as emasculating as Nazi military failure in the east was for Rosenberg, still Goebbels had to cede his culture battle.[30] Even after the political water boiled over, there continued to be a division between what design historian Gert Selle identifies as the "official" and the "popular" forms of art.[31] Some Nazis demanded a world made new, others one that aligned with different pasts (an antique Germanicism; Norse origin myths; belief in the occult), but all pursued their ideas of newness with "utopian zeal ... reminiscent of the Modernist urge to redeem and improve, to create the blueprint for a future society through artistic forms that could be uttered today."[32] Letting go of the axiomatic ligature between modernism and freedom, and accepting scholar Andrew Hewitt's contention that fascist modernism is "not a quirk nor an exception," means that we face a much tougher job in separating artists and designers and their toxic politics.[33] Following T. S. Eliot's conviction that the artist was ahead of, wiser than, and prophetic about the culture means we must struggle with the problem that art and design can be gorgeous for all the wrong reasons.

Art may be touching, brilliant, influential, and also morally and politically repulsive. The person apparently more culturally sensitive than we are may also be deep enough into race hatred as to be sociopathic (French modernist Louis-Ferdinand Céline is one example): do they still represent our best selves? Further, when art's entanglement with politics is dismaying, what happens when the work in question is commercial art and design done in the corporate, national, and transnational marketplace? When a different language enters the discussion, where the bottom line (sales, popularity, market saturation) can be equated with success, how will that affect our understanding of what constitutes "good" work? A design may be problematic, but if it sells millions of units, does it require our closer consideration, or will we just write it off as good design done in a bad cause, adopted by the misguided?

Steven Heller, award-winning designer, author and editor of over one hundred books on design, a lead art director at *The New York Times* for over thirty years, co-editor with Seymour Chwast of the influential Push Pin Editions book list, renowned teacher at the School of Visual Arts in New York, editor of the *AIGA Journal of Graphic Design* (the official publication of the American Institute of Graphic Arts), cannot let go of the idea of modernism as being, in its essence, a force for good. Heller's attempts to salvage modernism as an ideology are clearest when he confronts artists like Nazi Ludwig Hohlwein, a designer and illustrator as influential as Parrish, Rockwell, and Paul Rand in America. About Hohlwein Heller proposes that "it is incorrect to say definitively that Hohlwein invented National Socialist Realism, but his work was the paradigm."[34]

Hohlwein's images, elegantly spare solutions to a wide array of design problems, and their concerns for First World War veterans, point to the social realism Heller identifies. But Hohlwein's art was not limited to brave toilers working for the good of the state: there was more social realism in Diego Rivera and Thomas Hart Benton's work than in Hohlwein's, whose commercial work declares him to be an elitist along the lines of J. C. Leyendecker. To see Heller struggle is to watch a cultural savant deny the unpleasant fact that brilliant design doesn't make for good human beings, that art is not in itself a redemptive force, nor does it prevent the self from acting out of ignorance and hatred. Looking at 1930s German poster art Heller offers that the work is "so minimalist that it could easily be confused with a modernist design."[35] There is no confusion: it *is* modernist. The idea that the text is almost modernist, or could "easily" be confused with modernism unless one knows better, suggests two things: first, that there's an infinitely fine set of balances determining what does or does not weigh as modernist; and second, that Heller alone can read those scales. Is it the art or the artist and the context that determines the piece's artistic heft?

Looking at Hohlwein's famous body of work, Heller evades as best he can.[36] His move to ostracize Hohlwein from modernism aligns with the post-Second World War narrative the Allies have built about modernism, otherwise why push so hard to rid the design world of one of its luminaries? Particularly intriguing is Heller's choice to ignore Hohlwein's powerful work in support of First World War veterans, often shown as heroic walking wounded (Hohlwein's limited palette and stark designs make the appeals about veterans hard to ignore). Heller has struggled with the conscience he feels design should have, particularly in his 2008 book *Swastika: Symbol Beyond Redemption*? Others are sympathetic to his position. Assessing Hitler as artist and orchestrator of spectacle, art critic Peter Schjeldahl notes that while we "must remain vigilant," still, "we should regard beauty as the fundamentally amoral phenomenon that it is."[37] Such a statement continues an ongoing conversation about the nature of human perception and artistic complicity. Heller engages in the same contortions as do some film critics and scholars forced to admit that Leni Riefenstahl was an filmmaker of astonishing—and poisonous—films. Riefenstahl's history requires that her odious behaviour (most recently her denial of any involvement with the fate of the Roma and Sinti she drafted from and returned to death camps in the making of *Tiefland* [1954]) be rehearsed, causing important, painful, and familiar discussions about art and politics.[38] Riefenstahl's case is made worse by her perpetual ferocious unwillingness to accept a crumb of responsibility for wholeheartedly signing on to Nazism in all its practices.

History gets more, not less, complex. In 2002 art historian Gregory Maertz found his way into what he calls the "German War Art Collection." The collection includes, according to Maertz, 9,250 unique canvasses that were kept by the U. S. military at the end of the Second World War. Maertz has nothing kind to say about the German Wartime Art Project unit (parallel to the "Monuments Men" [MFAA]) which, under the post-war direction of Captain Gordon W. Gilkey, engaged in the illegal looting of hundreds of paintings that were then cached in three different locations by the Americans. Getting access to and documenting the nearly 10,000 images convinced Maertz that "certain types of Modernist art not only survived in Germany after 1937, but that 'Nazi Modernism' was produced under the official patronage of Adolf Hitler and the *Oberkommando der Wehrmacht* [Alfred Jodl]."[39] There was more bad news for modernist idealists:

seeing such a mass of images shattered Maertz's notion "of the complete ideological incompatibility of the National Socialist aesthetic with Modernist painting."[40]

What's important about such an archive is that it "raises fascinating and, for some, troubling questions about how much National Socialism actually imbued the art of the Third Reich."[41] Not only do the works suggest that there was more variety in the Reich's public and private art collections than we have been given to believe, but that much of the work recruits "recognizably Modernist idioms."[42] Newness, one of modernism's key features, was also something to which Goebbels was dedicated: creating "a new national culture" that would be "required to solve the problems of modernity."[43] These solutions could not come from blind reassertion of neoclassicism. Goebbels spoke out in praise of modernism (and served on a committee organizing a 1934 exhibition of Italian futurism); some large part of the regime saw to it that German expressionists like Emil Nolde and Ernst Barlach continued to thrive well into 1937.[44] Maertz proposes that the "master narrative" about twentieth-century German art is that modernism perished once the Nazis came to power and only the restoration of democracy brought its return.[45] But in the newly revealed collection Maertz finds "unmistakable features of Expressionism, post-Impressionism, New Objectivity/Verrism, and other subgenres of Modernist Realism."[46]

Stepping aside from painting and sculpture for a moment to consider, if briefly, other forms of art and design, it's important to recall that just as the Nazis were "experimenting, reordering, reconstructing," they were also embracing innovation and high technology. Nazi suspicions about the loss of the pastoral world didn't prevent them from producing or using machines to create a new world of objects.[47] Gay notes that Nazi Germany was committed to full industrialization, concluding that the Nazis "took technology to be a humble but valued servant; they celebrated modern inventions like the automobile and the airplane and used them ostentatiously as agents of military preparedness."[48] New technology required equal acceptance of new forms dictated by new functions. Powerful cars required high-speed roads. For Goebbels to soak the country in his version of reality, radios (the famous 1933 *Volksempfänger*, and in 1938 the smaller, cheaper *Deutsche Kleinempfänger* or "Goebbel's snout") had to be rolled out in sufficient quantity with simple designs and new materials (Bakelite) that were cheap enough to produce so that the masses could be coaxed to take them home. These objects were hardly free of politics, certainly not free of design, just as houses and apartments constructed in the interwar environment would reflect the adoption of new building materials and methods.

German industry was one of the few beneficiaries of the First World War, enough that it could be said that "industrial modernity was victorious."[49] Even the Nazi rejection of the Bauhaus came late in the Reich's short span. To read Gay's description of the *"Bauhäusler* [who] wore the badge of poverty with pride and ingenuity," as teachers who drilled their students "with terse maxims about the fundamentals that had brought them together: Tradition is the enemy. Mass-manufactured objects can be as good-looking as an artisan's unique product," is to hear more than an echo of the Spartan zeal espoused by both the military and Goebbels. There was an overall drive for efficiency and functionality in the Bauhaus that was also crucial to any war machine preparing for battle.[50]

The Bauhaus's polished reductive style was visible everywhere, even in "low-cost housing projects [that] provided more common ground for the left-wing branch of the NSDAP and those with promodernist sympathies."[51] Nazis pushing the remilitarizing state for high technology where function determined form and improved both had unhappy design allies in the *Bauhäusler* who championed mass-produced furniture made of common manufacturing materials like steel tubing. With even more irony, the Bauhaus, shut down in 1933, saw its chairs and pieces of furniture accepted as classics and put into official state exhibitions.[52] Even Heller concedes that "the Nazi rejection of modernism was not immediate, even though modernists in Germany, including the Bauhaus, were ideologically associated with left-wing parties (and seen as Jewish sympathizers by right-wing anti-Semites)."[53] The Nazis didn't demand radios, cars, roads, desk furniture, or household goods camouflaged as elaborately carved Wilhelmine furniture complete with dust ruffles to hide unsightly, potentially erotically charged, legs and naked feet. If the cheapest, most efficient way to make things was to use newly available materials like early plastics and dispense with ornament, the Nazis seized on it. If the new design aesthetic was to reveal the structures holding things together, they took it. Technology would be another partner in ideology and politics. These reminders of the interwar modernist landscape in the two nations are designed to prepare for a discussion of the ways in which the two nations signified power when they went to war.

Looking back from here, considering the many things that modernism was, we can see modernist designs beginning to influence military design. Like most things, military design has a history. The approach of modernist ways of seeing to what is typically thought of as a stodgy, reluctantly shifting organization like the military is one not so much of a collision as of two lines that appear to be parallel gradually narrowing the gap between them. The two lines run, occasionally touching, then connecting more often, and under the pressure of the speed, time, and heat of war, becoming one. The story of the two lines begins with the topic of heraldry. Heraldry began with wealthy and powerful families declaring their identities, first on battlefields, then in courts, then on paper, through the law and in corporate structures. Military heraldry is the overarching system of signs that is particular to militaries that must identify who and what they are to themselves, their allies, and their enemies. Behind heraldry is not only a deep history of how to indicate one's position in regard to power, but also the need to reflect cultural changes taking place.

CHAPTER 3

TRUE COLOURS

How American Heraldry Broke the System

HERALDRY WAS INITIALLY A SYSTEM FOR DESCRIBING relations between family members and collections of families together. What was once a program crucial to explaining how power worked in detail had, by the early twentieth century in the United States, become an antique holdover used by businesses to lend authenticity, age, and pedigree to products. American heraldry has become another way to demonstrate class anxiety, as one heraldic scholar notes: "The chances are that the automobile you drive displays a coat-of-arms," as does your cigarette package (e-cigarette logos have more in common with health product advertising: curling stylized clouds and graphics you might find in medical information pamphlets about asthma), your "professional association, a political organization, or an athletic club," are all likely to bear some kind of coat of arms.[1] The faux heraldic emblem is a persistent sign that it's better to have fake roots than none at all. If you personally haven't chosen to bear arms, that is, to adopt a family coat of arms, then your "corporate dwelling often does" for you. The "plethora of apartment houses that call themselves the This-or-That Arms, each of which pitifully displays some colourful and nondescript device" has the same quality of genuineness to it as does a Las Vegas Elvis wedding.[2] Coats of arms, with their tribal and military origins, have been governed in Britain and Europe with increasing strictness over the centuries. Heraldry, sometimes "armigery," the world of arms-bearing and study, is called both an art and a science by those who practice it—the laws governing heraldry and flags are interrelated, which I come to a little later.

Like any human sign system, heraldry is arbitrary. The rules have been formed in sedimentary layers over the last eight centuries by self-appointed guardians of systems dedicated to maintaining status and power. When heraldry scholar J. A. Reynolds points out that the "language of heraldry is heavily encrusted with terms and constructions that derive from the Norman French, or Anglo Norman," it is the word "encrusted" that best indicates how much the coat carries historically, culturally, and artistically. From the top down, the full coat of arms, known as "the achievement," may include some or all of the following: the banner and motto, the crest (often an animal or bird), a crown (usually on top of the helm), the helm (often a knight's steel helmet), the mantle (around the shield's upper edges, or shoulders), the shield itself with two lateral supporters (traditional examples are Britain's lion and unicorn), the motto (sometimes displayed around the edge of the shield, sometimes on the top banner, sometimes on a scroll or bottom banner), the compartment on which the supporters stand, the bottom banner (often unfurling), and finally the bottom mantle. The shield itself is often divided variously into quadrants, horizontal or vertical thirds. The crest (used erroneously to refer to the entire arrangement) is one small part of the design.

The older the achievement, the more history comes with it, the more complex the terms for each difference in type, placement, and colour of the various items. It is in part this deep historical complexity that causes heraldists to claim their work is a science. The desire to have a human-based sign system defined as a science, particularly an arbitrary one that has meaning only in the context of the culture that gave rise to it, one that is not tethered to some set of outside laws (like the physical sciences), betrays the anxiety heraldry scholars have about their work. If it is a science then it will also be necessary to survival and reveal foundational truths about the nature of existence. As old and beloved by its practitioners as the sign system may be, there is no science to it. There is an art to the design and a science to the organization of colours based on the physics of colour theory and the workings of the human eye. Otherwise, the rest is cultural. In specialists' eyes heraldry is critical to the formation of the civilized world, a point marking a transformative social contract between tribes that began to organize into armies united by common causes. Heraldic scholars argue for armorial literacy with some fierceness, seeing in it the ongoing Enlightenment project of politesse, history, and education.[3]

Implicit in recognizing and reading a coat of arms is knowledge of heraldry's semiotic codes. To know and read a coat of arms is to understand a language of force spoken at a familial level. The coat of arms divides those who have one from those who do not: to have one suggests one has also been schooled in power. To be an armiger, in the sixteenth century form of the word, is to hold position (like a knight or lord) and have the right to bear a coat of arms. Heraldry is an ongoing process of identification not only of how groups define themselves, but also how they measure against others. It is a system of inscription that fixes people into jobs and classes. The piling on and protection of heraldic rules is similar to the accumulation of laws that govern behaviour. Each coat of arms is a sign for an entirety and is "a symbolic design ... not [a] *curriculum vitae* of the [military] unit."[4]

First though, heraldry served a basic function. Troops recovering from battlefield chaos and searching for family, friends, and allies needed quick ways to identify each other. Early systems were the most basic, comprised of colours painted on an armoured shield (still a term we use), or sewn onto the armour's surplice (which became the coat *over* the arms, eventually the "coat of arms"). Both were fast ways to organize small numbers of people, to gather soldiers together "under their own officers."[5] Given the human predisposition to decorate, or in this case literally embroider on an idea, what were initially rough identifiers of allegiances soon became indicators of three things: the combination of coat, colours, and shield "has denoted rank and station, a man's skills and trades, and finally his loyalty to service, arm or regiment."[6] The tendency to pack an ever-increasing amount of information onto the achievement's shield means that a great deal of family history can be understood in a glance. The shield's information signifies using colour, shapes, patterns, and position, each of which has specific meanings. Such a language has been largely neglected or treated cavalierly in the United States.

Heraldry, like the trademark, logo, and brand, all of which I will argue serve the same core function, relies on good design to make its point. If heraldic marks are supported by performance as promised, where the family involved acts as it signifies on the achievement, then those marks will be accepted at face value. To describe a shield's colour, the direction of the figures on it, their placement relative to the different grids that can divide a shield's composition, is to anatomize what kind of enemy or ally one faces. Stabilizing the language of heraldry in countries like England and Scotland has meant that the signifying practice can be interpreted and used for organization. The deep history of armorial signs in Britain, where there are specific icons for sons, wives, daughters, and additional clan members, means the coat can be read exactly. The result of such deliberate one-to-one signifying is that "a heraldic decoration upon note-paper, for instance, at once reveals the position of the writer."[7] When heraldic scholar Eugene Zieber says that "the system is so perfect, when rigidly carried out," he identifies that the reason for the first is because of the second. Only when watched over and policed methodically can such a system make itself clear in one look. There is no frivolous interpretation in a proper coat of arms. Even if the family lies about its accomplishment (here used technically—that is, the whole of the heraldic work), still the accomplishment itself is a denotative sign system.

At least that's one story. So much heraldry is based on a distant unwritten past that arguments about what shapes and colours mean can come in for heated debate. Centuries ago when access to printing presses was unlikely, and in an early move to standardization, heraldists devised written descriptions for common graphic elements. In order to identify and reproduce a coat of arms without painting it in colour, a range of hues and positions were named in both French and Latin. The seven common colours, officially called "tinctures," start with the two metals, *argent* (silver) and *or* (gold), and continue with *gules* (red), *azure* (blue), *vert* (green), *purpure* (purple), and *sable* (black). There is a long list of descriptors indicating placement and orientation: a "charge" is an object, like a lion, which appears on a field, where its orientation (dexter, sinister) lets you know which way it faces. The description of a coat, called a blazon (creating a graphic representation of a shield is to "emblazon" it), begins with the shield's basic colour, then describes the charges, their colour, material (fur, metal), and position.

Apart from the tinctures and positions objects may occupy on a field, there are roughly fifty common patterns of shields including those with bars running horizontally, vertically, diagonally. Each of these fifty has its own name, although all are known as "ordinaries" because they recur so often. The ordinaries themselves further have subfields. There are another eight-hundred-some terms in heraldry that can be used to precisely describe the shield's qualities, charges, colours, and specifications. Since colour printing has been expensive and unreliable until very recently, there are black and white graphic patterns for each colour, an encoding system devised in early-sixteenth-century Italy by one or both of Silvester Petra Sancta and Marcus Vulson de la Colombiere. The method allows accurate diagramming of an achievement without recourse to any colour (standardizing hatching and various dot patterns allow a shield to be produced by someone with a quill and one ink colour). Because of all the terms, directions, tinctures, rules (metal never goes on metal, colour on colour), and the wonderfully obscure jargon that festoons heraldry, determining a shield's meaning is possible if one has had significant amounts of education and memorization.

Even in a relatively clear denotative signifying practice where the seven colours are understood, still their meanings are in dispute. As famous heraldry scholar Arthur Fox-Davies argues passionately: "That an argent field meant purity, that a field of gules meant royal or even martial ancestors, that a saltire meant the capture of a city, or a lion rampant noble and enviable qualities, I utterly deny."[8] It might help to have a small example of how complex just a description, not an interpretation, of a shield (not a whole coat of arms) can be. A partial blazon describing the shield in Canada's coat of arms (*omitting* the Crest, Supporters, and Motto) is as follows: "Tierced in fess, the first and second divisions containing the quarterly coat following, namely, 1st Gules three lions passant guardant in pale Or, 2nd, Or a lion rampant within a double tressure flory-counter-flory Gules, 3rd, Azure a harp Or stringed Argent, 4th, Azure three fleurs-de-lis Or, and the third division being Argent three maple leaves conjoined on one stem proper; An annulus surrounds the shield, being Gules edged and inscribed in letters Or with the Motto of the Order of Canada, DESIDERANTES MELIOREM PATRIAM, meaning 'They desire a better country'; The Royal Crown proper ensigns the full achievement of the Arms."[9] A bit of diligent reading makes sense of the language if the achievement is in front of you—the shield has been divided in three (tierced) horizontally (in fess), where the first two divisions are again divided, creating four squares at the top of the shield. The description then tracks left to right across the squares describing, in the first, a red (gules) ground with three gold (Or) lions crouched, faces turned to the viewer (passant guardant), and in the second quarter, a gold ground with another lion (this one in red) on his hind legs but in profile (guardant) inside a double bordered box (double tressure) with flowers inside and outside (flory-counter-flory), and so on. The precision of the description is impressive and particularly descriptive enough that one should be able to perfectly create the shield whether or not one is looking at it.

If in rigid armorial systems meanings are contested, as Fox-Davies's outburst shows, then when such a system came to America where there was no fifteenth-century College of Arms as there was in Britain, the results were predictably chaotic. Although fleeing a monarchy, new republicans didn't automatically unhook from issues of class. The young democracy had a wealth of one thing key to the establishment of a heraldic title: land. The vast availability of land meant that owning it no longer conferred aristocracy—the desire for land and class increased people's readiness to claim both. No surprise that by the late nineteenth century there was a fever for heraldic titles (in *The Adventures of Huckleberry Finn* [1884] two confidence men, the Duke and Dauphin, represent Twain's disgust with America's ongoing infatuation with royalty). There were also plenty of people to sell Americans what they wanted, no matter how fake. Scholars who supported the development of heraldry published books intended to educate the armorially illiterate.

One of these boosters was Eugene Zieber, who published his *Heraldry in America* in 1895. Zieber's book is a deeply enthusiastic argument for and introduction to heraldry. Knowing that his subject would stir up contentious discussions of genealogy and class, Zieber takes refuge from the charge that what he's doing may ill befit a democracy by suggesting that any American deserves to preserve the past "for himself or his children, the heraldic devices which were borne by his ancestors, even though in his own land such devices have no governmental recognition."[10] Further, Zieber understands that many of his readers (the fact that they must be literate, let alone have disposable income for expensive books or memberships in lending libraries, narrows his audience and efficiently eliminates unlettered workers) may "be deterred" from seeking their heraldic pasts "by ignorant or malicious criticism."[11] His book is a self-help guide for the postcolonial American hungry for legitimacy, who may strike his (less likely, her) fellow citizens as an ambitious social climber trying to sidestep the laws of "natural" ability. Modernist American texts like Edith Wharton's *House of Mirth* (1905) and Henry James's *Daisy Miller* (1879) and *Washington Square* (1880) address the middle class's deep anxiety over social standing, depicting a grim outcome for those who waste time trying to improve their rank positions.

Had Zieber's book been the sole plea for a restoration of armorial history it might have been benign. Unfortunately it was accompanied by fake genealogists who seized on the insecurities of those looking for meaning in their pasts. Michael Kammen documents the rise of interest in heraldry as well as the attendant parasitism by advertisers and con artists on potential buyers. He also notes the appearance of apparently official boards of genealogy in many major US cities. The huckster's shrill promise can be heard in a 1938 essay espousing the "blessings of American democracy ... that [brings] genealogy and pedigrees and an escutcheon within the reach of the common man .... It is only in America where the butcher, the baker and the bookstore-dealer may aspire to genealogical distinction."[12] Of course it will require money to do the research and reproduce (or fabricate) the "original" coat of arms, but the ordinary person's desire for heritage and social importance seems to be enough to cause people to pay for genealogical spelunking.

The idea that each "common person" possessed some noble lineage is precisely the kind of paradox that typifies interwar America. The impulse to reject all that has been is accompanied by a deep sense of loss and longing for a vanished past as well as a history that will anchor a fearful present and produce reassurance as the Depression, and the worldwide push to militarism in Spain, the Soviet Union, and Germany, set sabers to rattling. It's deeply ironic that the very things that caused original colonists to leave their home countries and seek a place where land-based classism wasn't the rule would now entice those same people. Keeping and discarding, looking only backward (and forward), rejecting and embracing, wanting the past and disposing of it as convenient, turns out to be a description of interwar America as well its attitude to heraldry. Heraldic scholar J. A. Reynolds notes that while American heraldry "derives predominantly from that of the British Isles," still Americans have "chosen, almost from the beginning, to disregard most of the sacred cows of the British Systems. We Americans are an independent-minded people: if we use heraldry, we'll use it our own way."[13]

Writing in the early 1960s, Reynolds had witnessed the chaos that engulfed American heraldry during and after the Second World War. His conclusion that Americans would make their predictably independent way through this design world, rewriting heraldic rules as they saw fit, is tolerant and forgiving, especially in an art that demands adherence to multiple codes. A contemporary assessment of the heraldic situation is much less phlegmatic. Heraldist David Boven notes sharply that "Armorial practices in the United States of America are largely unregulated. There is no American institution analogous to the College of Arms in London, the Court of the Lord Lyon in Edinburgh, or the Bureau of Heraldry in Pretoria."[14] If Americans had chosen to remake a historical medium, it would hardly be the first time. Why should shifting ground in heraldry make anyone unhappy? It's true that if meaning in heraldry is already blurred, as Fox-Davies suggests at the beginning of his massive armorial catalogue, why worry if the signifieds come that much more unglued from their signifiers? If meaning begins to drift and the interpreter gains the upper hand, taking power away from a central hermeneutic authority, what does it matter?

I'm not engaged in saving or arguing for American heraldry but in examining how the American military, as it moved through one world war and toward another, made design decisions about its heraldic problems. In America, "no heraldic Gregg or Pitman has arisen to systematize these [heraldic] devices uniformly throughout the services."[15] DuBois's naming of two formative experts in efficient information handling is prophetic. The solutions the growing American military would need, particularly once the Second World War broke open, would be driven more by speed, necessity and utility than history and tradition. While interwar America was deeply invested militarily in the Philippines and South America, there was relatively little concern for military heraldry that could be used to establish what we would now call America's "brand" as a rising global enforcer. America's eccentric history meant that as the Second World War approached, those trying to create a heraldic American present not based on Britain's past were thrown on their own resources. The governance of military heraldry finally came to rest in the Quartermaster Corps, which didn't begin studying the problem of army signs until "the end of 1941."[16] The United States Quartermaster Corps, in conjunction with the Transportation and Ordnance Corps, handles all the logistics and supply for everything an army needs in the field, which is to say, everything. It's safe to say that without an effective quartermaster operation, no mass army can function for even the shortest time.

The result was quintessentially modernist. Where other countries were either governed by their pasts or hoping to rekindle them (as in Germany and Italy's case), America discovered that it barely had one, let alone a legacy of signification. It was free of the seven centuries of design tradition straitjacketing the British. The Reich, too, would find itself choosing selectively from a much deeper military past than America's. However, in America's case the outcome of little or no tradition was the creation of a new form entirely: "The US armed forces, notably the Army have the distinction of being the originators of the unit patch."[17] The unit patch, known officially as the Distinctive Unit Insignia (DUI, sometimes just "DI" and mistakenly called the "crest" or "unit crest"—for the sake of brevity I will often refer to it just as a "patch" or "insignia") has arguably become the most significant ubiquitous form of official graphic communication the military uses, although there are times when it is the Shoulder Sleeve Insignia (SSI) that is better known. I draw mostly from the latter. It and smaller versions of it appear as pins or embroidered badges on the front and sleeves of the uniform, shoulder tabs, and headgear.

The insignia is the formal utterance of the United States military, containing both official and many unofficial significations. The patches are open to interpretation, but as with most signs, cannot be made to mean anything. The creation of unit insignia was neither planned nor structured: early patches were rough and hardly serviceable. They also received bare official recognition, where "in many cases, the army chose to look the other way, depending on where and on what uniform item the insignia were attached."[18] There was a pure functionalism at work in the young military's post-Civil War years: establishing battlefield order trumped the particulars of signifying, let alone whether those insignia and other identifiers followed centuries of standards.

The consequence of having few or no heraldic standards in the United States is that "there are probably more *Assumptive Arms* borne in that country than anywhere else," and those bearing such arms are at the mercy of "unscrupulous self-styled Heralds."[19] Such usurpations continue to the present, with the most recent celebrated case being Donald Trump's wholesale theft of the Joseph Edward Davies' family emblem, bestowed legally by the British College of Heraldry in 1939. Amusingly, in the process of knocking off the emblem, Trump changed the motto from "Integritas" to the more predictable, if entirely heraldically unacceptable, "Trump."[20] Although the Davies family considered suing Trump, a family member and lawyer familiar with Trump convinced his cousins not to waste their time and money. Interwar unit design carried on with no knowledge or understanding of the semiotic traditions of European heraldry. Some units were left alone without insignia, and "each department and group was responsible for its own choice of emblem."[21] As it turned out, the apparent lawlessness of design produced some of the best: "The designs and patterns adopted between 1941 and 1945 have enjoyed great staying power, with few changing form between the end of the Second World War and the present."[22] But that was later.

First came patches that had only local meaning specific to the places, times, and myths significant to the unit. The accumulation of unconnected art created interpretational chaos that allowed its users (mostly soldiers) to construct the stories they pleased. Colonel Robert E. Wyllie, a heraldist writing in 1921, recounts one explanation for the progression of rank insignia worn by

American officers. A junior grade lieutenant wears a single gold (or "butter") bar; a lieutenant first grade wears a silver bar; two silver bars for captain; gold oak leaf for a major and silver oak leaf for a lieutenant colonel; followed by a silver eagle for full colonel (hence the colloquial expression "full bird colonel"); followed by the one through four stars for generals. Wyllie uses his book as a corrective, shredding the traditional narrative that had the young officer entering "the forest in the lowest position with the universe above him, the forest symbolizing the regiment," then climbing the "lowest bar of the fence [in order to see] ... [then] needing a better vantage point climbed into an oak tree," finally transforming into an eagle, then a star that rules over all. Such hermeneutic excess is a testament to the human proclivity to produce complex mythological tapestries from the thinnest fibres. Wyllie scoffs at such locally imposed meanings, noting that it "is pretty sentiment but unfortunately it has no historical basis," then goes on to complain that the interwar "system was not the result of a careful study at any one time, it simply grew like Topsy, each step being forced by the conditions which existed, and each time the action taken was that which would make the least disturbance of what we already had."[23] Wyllie's reference to Harriet Beecher Stowe's *Uncle Tom's Cabin* is a perfect example of the tension between the high and the popular, the pretentions of the classic (the practice of heraldry), the political past (Stowe's novel in all its antebellum popularity and problematic depictions of African Americans), and the difference between contemporary American practice (modernist refusal of the past) and the deep habits of the past inheritance from Europe.

Heralds like Zieber and Wyllie were determined to convert American heraldic malpractice into good doctrine, a program that would require the inculcation of heraldic literacy in both citizens and government. Zieber argues that knowledge of armorial laws is "indispensable to the architect, artist, and author, and to lovers of the fine arts and literature. How many blunders in our art and absurdities in our literature might have been avoided had not Americans of a certain class assumed lofty indifference to a science they had taken little trouble to understand!"[24] Zieber, Wyllie, and Reynolds agree that there is something intrinsically American about the determinedly disorganized growth of what had until then been a predictable language. But a serious military would demonstrate itself by speaking the formal, international language of force signification. For a contemporary armorial historian like Reynolds, American heraldic graphical anarchy produces displays that "are shoddy and perform a genuine disservice to the institutions they represent. Inept and unknowing (*uncouth* is the technical term here) in design, they have a commercial quality that belies the social nature of the institution."[25]

What's interesting about Reynolds's displeasure is the differentiation he makes between the heraldic sign and corporate identity. Even in the post-Second World War era, Reynolds sees the military primarily as social, attacking the connection between the commercial and national. As we will see later on, Reynolds is not alone in linking new forms of heraldic signification to marketing in late-nineteenth-century and early-twentieth-century America. Marketing, another of modernity's creations, was intimately joined to the then new science of psychology when in 1921 Dr. John Watson, one the first of the behavioural scientists, entered advertising. American heraldry was stretched between two forces: on one side was nostalgia, chivalry, and tradition, and on the other the new, surprising, colloquial, modernist, and, inevitably, corporate.

Before the First World War basic identification was urgent. Civil War troops tied strips of cloth (that is, rags) around their arms and legs in order to identify themselves. One unit chose "the heart" as an insignia, but "the order was silent as to the size, the material from which the badge was to be made, and the part of the uniform on which it was to be worn."[26] Battlefield chaos would only be worsened by idiosyncratic, poorly made, coloured, placed, or shaped insignia. By the First World War the system was somewhat more sophisticated, as the famous story of the 81st Infantry shows. Vague orders from the staff gave the troops directions to choose some form of identification. When the division arrived in France it had adopted the insignia of a black cat on a green disk, giving the unit the nickname "the Wildcats."

The roughness of the design reminds the viewer of its antiquity. Here is a patch that has the texture of a nineteenth-century colloquial artifact, with its bad rendering of the cat, its unlikely profile and open mouth, misplaced eye and ears, and ill-proportioned legs (individually some of the details are accurate: the lynx's upright ears, the short tail from which the "bobcat" gets its name). There's little visually pleasing about such an insignia, but it reflects the speed and informality of its creation, in itself an item of pride. The 81st was the first division to get its own device, to declare itself a band of wildcats who were all individuals yet paradoxically united in a common cause. Even as command tried to rescind the patch's legitimacy, the troops had adopted it so thoroughly that the military backed away from the issue, instead ordering other units to follow the 81st's example.[27]

Figure 3.1 US Expeditionary Force 81st Infantry Division: Bad luck for design and command.

Few acts underline the American forces' expediency more than their creation of the unit insignia for the 33rd Division. Unit colours were "chosen because they were the only paints available when it became necessary to mark the equipment in Texas."[28] Embracing taxonomic chaos became the military's First World War operating rule as American pragmatism axed hundreds of years of heraldic genealogy. Paul Fussell adds sardonically, "before you get into a war, it's best to be certain of your uniform supply—and resupply."[29] That supply (a Quartermaster issue), extends to paint for signs and material for banners, as well as badges and metal pins to be worn on uniforms. Heraldic experts missed the parade during the creation of the famous 14 × 10 cm patch for the 1st, 2nd and 3rd Cavalry that seems to have been instigated by a cavalry "officer's wife at Fort Bliss" who found the old shield hard to see through "the dust kicked up by horse-mounted cavalry," and demanded highly visible, large, yellow insignia instead.[30]

Expediency and horse sense became the rule in design decisions as exemplified by the development of the 2nd Division's insignia, created by a driver who "painted the device on the side of his truck."[31] There's an intriguing lack of concern about decoration and style in these examples. What was acceptable for an initially small First World War army that perforce allowed colloquial expression in 1917 would vaporize at the interwar period's close when millions of new military personnel arrived.[32] When America entered the First World War, the Army numbered 100,000 troops. Eighteen months later it had a fighting force of four million. By the Second World War the military at full force numbered eight million soldiers. Fussell puts the combined numbers at sixteen million. The age of battlefield recognition would give way to corporate signification so lamented by Reynolds.

It was in part the economy of scale that put the Quartermaster Corps in control of American military heraldry such that it alone became "concerned . . . with the heraldic semiotic and representational arts: that is, the arts of designing and emblazoning heraldic emblems."[33] Organizing the mass of humans and materiel required to fight the Second World War required the science of planning that became operations (sometimes "operational") research.[34] No job on the planet had ever been bigger than or required the logistics necessitated by the Second World War. The staggering list of needs to be satisfied included the generation of the patches for an entire army, making these early war years "an important formative time for the three services and their badges and insignia."[35] The war's scale precipitated a cultural, technological, and sociological shift that Paul Fussell characterizes as a move from "light to heavy duty."[36] The early, naive ideas about the war are typified by grimly funny instances of how unprepared the entire population was for the imminent carnage. Spike Milligan, justly famous British comedian, writer, actor, and musician, recounts a story of his artillery unit being ordered to stand by their guns and yell "bang" because of the lack of ordnance with which to practice.[37] None could predict that within a few years grease guns, saturation bombing of open cities, the genocide of multiple populations, and one-shot weapons seemingly capable of destroying the planet would have become the new standard.

The war had the same heavy-duty mass effect on insignia, uniforms, and their decorations, where the sheer volume of wartime use meant that "55½ tons of brass were needed each year to make insignia."[38] The 55 and a half tons of brass the men wore as they fired other pieces of brass at each other are inextricably entangled. The issue of "the brass" is crucial for the resentful amateur soldiers of WWII who referred to their leaders by the one thing that marked an officer's uniform—the amount of brass on it. Just as robotized assembly-line workers came to be known metonymically by their most important feature (factory hands), so were their class superiors signified by the metal that separated them all. The insignia cannot be abolished without an enormous deleterious impact on specific unit identity, and with it, troop morale. The bigger the standing army, the more units, and the more each unit strove to distinguish itself from others—the grind of humans pushing for recognition as individuals inside enormous groups. If the men in a unit couldn't be seen individually, uniting might gain them a sort of larger corporate recognition and success. An individual lost through the motions of the enormous military that has broken, absorbed, and reformed the self has become, as Fussell knew too well, "really nothing."[39] Immersion in an endless sea of others makes the unit, with its history, birthday (some, like the United States Marine Corps, have their own particular and much-celebrated "birthdays," which are celebrated without irony), place of origin, creation myths, songs, and mottos, all captured by the unit flag and distinctive insignia, a place of familiarity (if not safety) in the war world.

The unit is bigger than one death or—more importantly— hundreds of deaths. The unit is the repository of pride, the force that reincorporates the vanished self and encourages identification with the corporate body's endeavours. The most compressed, eloquent summation of that new being is the insignia, a perpetual reminder on the shoulder, headgear, and blouse that one's family has accompanied one to war. The military learned just how important unit signification was when the men went overseas. In England and on the continent, American soldiers arriving with badly manufactured patches soon discovered that they could have their insignia and uniforms remade locally, often beautifully. The tendency to decorate, improve, make the mundane more glorious, may not have been the Army's first concern, but it was obviously on the minds of its soldiers. The push from the troops was for more complex, striking badges, comprised of metal threads (silver, gold, or if necessary aluminum wire) that could be "masterpieces of embroidery."[40] Now in countries like Britain, Italy, and Germany with deep heraldic backgrounds, Americans didn't ask "for authorization from the War Department," but instead had their insignia refashioned, a "practice [that] became widespread from the winter of 1944–5 until about 1947, and thousands of these insignia were made illegally all over the world."[41]

The mythological apparatus that breathes life into the uniform has preserved the unit motto, although it likely doesn't appear on the insignia. The oldest and most famous of these mottoes are so fogged by tradition and ritual that they have no more authenticity than any apocryphal narrative. That very lack of reliable record strengthens them: they are the new truths from which the unit creates itself. The 501st Airborne's motto, "Geronimo," may or may not have been yelled out by a soldier on his first jump; what matters is that the unit seized on and deployed the myth.[42] The days of arbitrary military signification were over: the motto is a nucleus around which a corporate identity collects. American heraldry is recognizable in the way it attaches itself to the local and colloquial: "Each of these insignia tells a story that memorializes people, places, or heroic deeds—moments in history captured in cloth that reveal the history of a nation."[43]

Heralds who study military arms, often themselves military personnel, believe wholeheartedly in their adopted sign system as a force that creates meaning and purpose. For one military commentator, the unit patches "symbolize commitment; a reminder to all that every army organization is committed to accomplishing its mission of protecting America's freedom."[44] The insignia is metonymic of the unit's mission, the military, the country, its values and future. Every patch is inscribed with the whole narrative evident to the viewer, should you know the code. Assumptive though the arms may be, they are worn with enthusiasm bordering on fanaticism, appearing on every article of clothing, including but not limited to hats, shirts, infant's sleepers, yoga pants, pins, embroidered patches, decals, or magnets for the car. As far as an experienced heraldic scholar like Rosignoli is concerned, "being able to wear such a badge is as primitive in its own way as the initiation rites of a tribal group. There is, in the collecting of such badges, a sub-conscious element, in which the civilian owner possesses some of the magic that these badges exert in the military environment."[45] The military's lure is not limited to the uniform and the implicit social authority it bestows on its wearer; there is also the promise of reassurance, if not pleasure, people will experience in joining and drawing power from the group. Behind the patch is the promise of the mass force that backs it. If this unit member is killed, others loyal to the same principles will be along shortly

The patch, the worldview writ small, becomes totemic, invested with the sacred. However the desire to be recognized as an individual doesn't vanish. Paul Fussell muses about the "paradox of uniforms: each person senses the psychological imperative to dress uniformly and recognizably like others, while responding at the same time to the opposite tug, the impulse to secretly treasure and exhibit occasionally a singular identity or 'personality.'"[46] To confront the army patch is to face the problem of the role of the state in the personal, the purpose of the individual's life in the politics, both large and small, of the nation that bears arms. The insignia is a challenge to identity: what does it mean to join such a group? If one sacrifices part or all the self and subsumes the solitary in the power-giving mass, there must be a promise of more. The patch becomes a marker of belonging and possession, of unity and alignment. It offers a cover for the self which, although it may be exposed to metal rain on the battlefield, is protected in the army's corporate memory. There is permanence, strength, and above all, immortality that transcends the body's destruction, something that understandably consumed soldiers on the industrial battlefield, witness to the worst atrocities that could befall the body. Religious studies scholar Mircea Eliade points out that "the crude product of nature, the object[s] fashioned by the industry of man," here, the insignia, "acquire their reality, their identity, only to the extent of their participation in a transcendent reality."[47] The patch is the node of exchange: it is a ritual marker that leads directly to the centre of being, meaning, and purpose on a battlefield where none of these things exist. It isn't a promise of salvation—wearing the patch has already guaranteed it.

The importance of the uniform proves itself by its absence. When in 2014 eastern Ukraine was invaded by troops with no official markings on their battle dress, the question of legitimacy could not immediately be thrown back on any particular government. Whatever power, presumed to be the Russians, sponsored the troops was paying for them to be deliberately unmarked. The very lack of signification was a serious political act.[48] A similarly deadly event was witnessed by a group of five Australian journalists present at the 1975 Indonesian invasion of East Timor. Before all five were killed by the invaders, they recorded Indonesian troops making landfall near Balibo, East Timor. The troops were dressed as civilians until they began fighting, at which point they shed their outer clothes to reveal Indonesian military uniforms. The Indonesian impersonation of East Timorese rebels was eventually discovered decades later when the Australian and Indonesian governments admitted the journalists' murders had, like the uniforms, been covered up.

Central to heraldry is the flag, a sign system related to but separate from the achievement, one that has its own formal and informal rules. Vexillology, the study of flags (the Latin for "banner" is "vexillum"), is ruled as much by composition (geometric organization) as it is by colour theory and the physics of light. Masses of colour appear differently to the eye than do small points of light—differences caused by the function of the human perceptual system. It is at this particular edge that science enters the discussion: the way things appear to and are interpreted by the human being are, some claim, transcultural and transtemporal. Support for the view that visual design may have a set of rules common to most human beings comes from a field related to heraldry—brand marketing. If there are innate human responses to colour and form, it behoves the herald and marketer alike to have and exercise that knowledge. Marketers and brand analysts Riesenbeck and Perrey argue that brand management is "*art, science,* and *craft,*" where the "*art* is in endowing the brand with a superior brand proposition," the science is in gauging the brand's market performance, and the "*craft* is managing the brand rigorously."[49] (Keep in mind one heraldic scholar who speaks for the group when he says: "Heraldry is at once a science, an art, and a set of social practices."[50]) Rather than suggest humans share the same codes when it comes to interpretation, it is the study of brand reception that the marketers argue is a science. Similarly a successful flag designer will use the art of design, the science of observation of test subjects, and the craft of managing the image in order to develop a successful armorial image. Good heraldry, whether the entire achievement, the shield alone, Distinctive Unit Insignia, pin, badge, or flag, will establish and hold its place as a visually striking graphic in which people perceive the key value Eliade identifies: a transcendent reality.

Many flags bear the heraldic achievement and stop there. The creation of new flags that go beyond reproducing the coats of arms is as delicate, as difficult a design job as there is. According to vexillologists, at the philosophical centre of every flag is the precept that "you cannot identify a flag unless you know it already."[51] A good flag, then, will need to be seen only once to be remembered and will be so well designed that it will already feel familiar—not because it's like another flag but precisely because it looks only like itself. The flag, achievement and brand, each a different medium with different design demands, encapsulate a paradigm and provide the audience with a preview, "a sort of prejudice, in the literal sense of a prejudgment. Like all prejudices, it will seem unfair to the people who are on the wrong end of it—in this case, the less well-known competitors of the big brands."[52] Only if you know the system will you understand the import of a particular flag and the coat of arms tied to it. To see a coat of arms and recognize it (whether it includes or actively excludes you) is to take part in a network of political meaning that answers questions about loyalty, identity, belonging, definition of character, and beliefs. Vexillologists may not be often called on to produce new national flags, but it's a good idea to have them around when you do. In 2004 the United States directed the redesign of the Iraqi flag, resulting in a largely white flag with a blue sickle moon and three stripes (alternating royal blue and yellow) running across the bottom border. It

Figure 3.2: One possible Iraq: A flag of a different colour.

immediately put viewers in mind of the similar colours and design of the Israeli flag (two strong horizontal blue bars boxing in a Star of David).

The startling shift from the traditional combination of green (for religious reasons a preferred colour in Islam), red (Arab nationalism), and white and black (historical colours

Figure 3.3. Another Iraq along the historical spectrum.

of Islamic battle flags) that represent many Islamic countries (among them Jordan, Palestine, Sudan) to the white, blue, and yellow immediately produced commentary from outside vexillology circles. When asked, the designer and well-known architect Rifat al-Chadirji, an Iraqi living in England, said simply, "Political opinions don't concern me. I approached the design from a graphic point of view."[53] It was a fair comment from a purely visual context, but Chadirji's brief reply belied the extensive design work he had already done. He had produced six different flag designs, the first of which not only used familiar colors (red, black, green) and a sickle moon, but was also a powerful statement of unification.

Now ninety-three (he was seventy-seven when he was asked to propose the designs), Chadirji has existed immersed in the design world and historicity of a flag that goes back to Gertrude Bell and the British colonialist formation of Iraq itself. Seeing both Chadirji's first and final designs suggests that there was a wide range of possibilities available to the American-backed interim Iraqi governing council.[54] Everything made by humans exists in the context of its creation, a situation that is necessarily alive with politics and meaning. Of all of these objects, the flag, one of the most visible forms of speech, cannot possibly escape its context, the ideas it represents, the people united under it, and so, in every way, its cultural gravity.

The colours alone were enough to sink the design. Chadirji's notion that the two blue bars represented the Tigris and Euphrates rivers might have worked if no other flags for the region had ever existed, but the context prompted some deeply sarcastic comments from, among others, Wayne State University Center for Peace and Conflict Studies' Frederic Pearson, who cracked, "This flag will symbolize mostly the view that an illegitimate U.S. occupation has produced a flag"; to journalist Chris Allbritton's concise: "Damn, that's an ugly flag."[55] The discussion orbits the problem that one cannot produce a flag for a people who do not yet have a concept of themselves as a whole. Flags are concentrated nationalist statements, "Rorschach blots on which people project their hopes and fears, loyalties and hatreds," says designer Michael Beirut.[56] The flag may be a site for unconscious desires, but it must also represent at least some of the country's consciousness as well. The flag's usage requires that it be a shared object, one that makes itself recognizable to its adherents.

The problem of the flag is similar to that of the brand where, as brand consultant Hayes Roth puts it, "you have to understand the target audience, the core message and brand promise."[57] The flag cannot escape its position at the eye of a Venn diagram of design aesthetics, cultural expectation, tradition, political utterance, multiple stakeholders, and past and current struggles. Chadirji's comments reinforce the wishful notion that art and design somehow exist outside the mundane world, that because they originate from the imagination they can be even slightly removed from politics. But no image, particularly in this enormously politically sensitive milieu, can live free of significations on a topic that could not be more publicly anguished. Setting aside the cultural context for a moment, the flag is also aesthetically weak, particularly when compared to Chadirji's initial proposal. One sure test of design is to pair it to with another from the region, in this case the black flag (sometimes called the Black Banner or Black Standard, whether or not it bears the *shahadah*, or profession of faith) flown by various Islamic groups.[58] The black flag, with its strong white script, is a stark piece of undeniable power.

The rules for vexillology are useful for those in heraldry as well. When it comes to the flag, the main rule is to "Keep It Simple: The flag should be so simple that a child can draw it from memory."[59] In keeping with the idea that you cannot understand a flag you don't already know, the flag must make instant sense, be available to the viewer who will seize the compressed message immediately. By the same token the shield, the central part of the achievement of the coat of arms, must function with forceful simplicity for it to be memorable. Heraldist Lieutenant Colonel Stroh's advice about the insignia sounds identical to vexillogical ideals: "Shields should not be complicated or cluttered, but simple contrasting colours and capable of satisfactory manufacture in embroidery for textile items and in metal and enamel when reduced in size not exceeding 1½ inches for Distinctive Unit Insignia Badge to be worn on a uniform."[60]

The human propensity to choose one colour over another raises a debate about social construction and innate understanding. Colours appear to be at once socially bound, as in the case for Iraq's proposed new flag, and also determined by the eye and brain. The claim that certain colours are understood similarly across cultures and time persists and has been made by semiotician and vexillologist George Pasch, who puts biology first in the human understanding of colour: "the general characteristics of human vision, like the esthetic appreciation of colours, are largely dominant over particular considerations of choice and over peoples, races, governments, religions, cultures, and so on."[61] But Pasch is no essentialist fool when it comes to social determination of meaning. He has written carefully and convincingly about problematic cultural assumptions, particularly in his discussion of African flags, where he attacks the idea that Africa is united by the many African countries' common choice of red, yellow, and green for flag colours. Examining how each colour is understood by different countries, Pasch demonstrates just how identical signifiers produce wildly different signifieds (for instance, Pasch discovers that yellow represents, across various African countries, "le sol, la richesse, le sable, la pureté, l'amour et la victoire de la Revolution," pausing to add, "C'est trop!").[62]

One thing that connects flag and insignia design is the need to identify each object rapidly and with certainty. Pasch argues that the human eye and brain, permitted only brief glances at an object, face significant limitations: "humans have a natural aptitude for seeing three colours as a whole; four colours demand an effort of memory," leading to his conclusion that good, certainly memorable, design will favour fewer colours, simpler forms.[63] The brand market is no less severe about the constraints imposed by memory or millisecond glimpses afforded to ads and logos by viewers.

The fight for eyeballs on the web and in the marketplace seems as intense as on the battlefield. According to brand manager Marc Gobé, both are fraught with colour "associations" that are "much more complex ... [where] the subtle variations are endless."[64] Gobé argues that brand rules governing the spectrum can be summarized with some assurance: "true orange is friendly, pastel tints are gentle, yellow orange is welcoming, pale blue connotes calm, navy blue symbolizes dependability. Gray is generally perceived as a professional colour, and often implies qualities of seriousness and anonymity."[65] These claims, however, are inextricably bound not only to their present cultural moment in the Western world, but to their genealogy. Is navy blue dependable because it has been adopted by the US air force and commercial airline pilots, or did the colour have its own internal merit, was understood to represent steadiness, and was adopted as a uniform colour for aircrew who require steady nerves to perform? If blue is a signifier of steadiness, why would not surgeons' gowns also be a deep blue? The discussion of the cross-cultural ideas about colour is so complex that I cannot do it justice here except to mention the debate triggered by the World Colour Survey, conducted by Brent Berlin and Paul Kay, and published as *Basic Color Terms* in 1969 by University of California Press. Since that time, the survey has been vastly expanded and its conclusions greatly disputed by those who argue against the legitimacy of drawing universalist conclusions about colour. I argue that understanding colour is almost entirely culturally bound and that colours and their meanings are generally co-constitutive, where groups of nations (and by extension millions or billions of people) may agree on how they "see" colour. The ubiquity and reach of a definition doesn't change the fact that these are social constructions. I return to this discussion further on in relation to the use of red on flags and insignia.

One final piece of the achievement that survived the American butchering of the United Kingdom's heraldic tradition was the motto, often incorporated on the unit insignia. Since unpredictability is the rule with American heraldry, the motto may or may not appear and may be in English or Latin. According to Stroh's foundational guide, "the motto should be appropriate and of an idealistic or exalted nature and must not include anything of a sordid, malign or malevolent character, implying animosity or partiality towards any nation or groups of nations or peoples or which stresses the destructive nature of warfare."[66] The first statements are intriguing enough, suggesting that there are rules to be followed and military decorum to be observed. It's the end of the sentence that is most curious and revealing, showing how much armorial practice rejects the reality of industrial warfare, even though the one has broadened because of the other. Heraldry takes the high road, especially when it comes to the motto, because the military and civilians who support it refuse to surrender the idea that war is an art, an exchange of differences between foes who at some basic level respect and honour each other. Patches that, according to Stroh, should assume the moral high ground run smack into the reality of insignia for things like a strategic thermonuclear bomb wing. Where the older 91st Strategic Missile Wing's motto is a genteel "Poised for Peace," abiding by an optimistic good-neighbour policy, the more informal and sardonic motto for the 741st Strategic Missile Squadron is the abrupt "We Deliver."[67] Such a motto, with its combined laconic threat, promise, and statement of plain fact about the Squadron's purpose, has little geniality about it. Mass death in a variety of forms is going to be hard for a cheery motto to redeem.

Even more difficult to countenance are the units whose sole job it is to deliver barrages of intercontinental thermonuclear

missiles, after which point presumably the unit's job, and everything else, will be finished. The 341st Strategic Missile Wing
("wing" is somewhat misleading as a unit like this one consists of
people sitting at the bottom of missile silos waiting for the launch
command) operates with the motto "Pax Orbis per Arma Aeria"
("World Peace Through Air Strength"). The repetitive hammering at peace (the Strategic Air Command's famous motto "Peace
is our Profession" is shown to particular ironic effect in Stanley
Kubrick's *Dr. Strangelove* as two different American military units
engage in close combat directly below a sign displaying the motto)
underlines precisely "the destructive nature of warfare" that Stroh
says should be avoided. Euphemisms can be crueller than the bald
"We Deliver" of the 741st. Treating the final word in industrial
warfare as if it were a polite round of jousting makes it easier to
understand nuclear forces' willed blindness. Working as a nuclear
missileer wearing a patch declaring the job to be one of peace-
keeping requires ongoing acts of cognitive dissonance, resolving
conflicts by compartmentalizing them. Economist John Kenneth
Galbraith has long since identified the corporate equivalent of
cognitive dissonance, what he calls the "approved contradiction,"
which consists of an implicit understanding about the way the
world works being covered by a shared, pleasant myth about corporate behaviour. Galbraith gives the example of corporations
that don't publicly drive for profit maximization but instead speak
about working for the public good, meantime operating according
to the corporation's own goals—it's a contradiction that everyone
accepts.[68] Heraldry is one massive approved contradiction, maintaining that there will be decorum on the battlefield, reinforced
by the military's rules of engagement, that genteel traditions will
be maintained despite the indiscriminate slaughter that has characterized twentieth- and twenty-first-century warfare.

The relationship between military heraldry and one of the
waypoints in this book, a discussion of propaganda, may seem

slightly hazy from here. What we've seen in the development of the system of family power, represented by an achievement and the massively information rich shield at its centre, is what in today's world we'd identify as a brand. The brand accomplishes a lot of the same jobs as the heraldic crest, although usually with a great deal less specificity. Before going on into that world, however, and in order to keep the parallels between the Americans and Nazis in view, I look now to the development and operation of the Nazi system of heraldry.

CHAPTER 4

Instant Classic

The Nazi Brand

THE FORMATION OF THE NAZI RITUAL APPARATUS WAS in some ways as arbitrary and improvised as was the American military's Second World War heraldic expression. Around the black sun of the swastika orbited a system of flags, banners, armbands, pins, rings, belt buckles, and ceremonial knives (particularly the highly prized SS *Ehrendolch*, or "honour dagger"). According to aesthetics scholar Malcolm Quinn, there was a boardroom tussle over the swastika-as-logo, where the "final scheme of the Nazi flag was thrashed out in committee discussion and by sifting through various drafts [that] recalls the process by which the contemporary corporate identity is designed, as does Hitler's expressed wish to find a sign which could be used to compete with the 'market share' gained by communism in Germany."[1] Hitler would later state that he was solely responsible for the swastika's final form because there was only ever one struggle—his. If Hitler was to retain the role of prince, then everything must be understood to originate from and return to him, whether or not it actually did.[2] Once the design was set, it had always been Hitler's: "I sketched it myself and gave it to the master goldsmith, Mr. Gahr, to execute. Since that time, this Standard has been the symbol and field-badge of the National Socialist battle," even though it was known that the dentist Friedrich Krohn originally designed the flag.[3] Hitler assumed ownership of the Nazi promise.

As I continue with this discussion of Nazi heraldry, I recruit the language of brands and marketing, continuing to relate the worlds of heraldry, military signification, and corporate image and brand strategies. However in the interwar period, particularly immediately following the First World War, the connections between these diverse fields might have seemed tenuous.

The failed Munich beer hall putsch of 1923 made mythologization of the Nazi flag and swastika relatively easy. The death of sixteen Nazis and four police officers as well as Hitler's subsequent imprisonment turned out to be a publicity gift to the then small movement. Propitiously for Hitler and Goebbels, one man of what came to be known as the "old guard" bled onto a Nazi banner, thereafter known as the "*Blutfahne*" (blood banner), which was collected and "piously preserved."[4] The bloodletting became a crucial moment to establish, and renew annually, a ritual of authenticity, to create what marketers would now call an "instant classic." The process of canonization requires time, something the Nazis didn't have. A number of authoritative cultural stakeholders will have gradually come to a consensus that a given object has lasting worthwhile qualities: it is well made, holds up to repeated interpretations, has complexities in it that speak to shared human—as defined by the particular worldview—struggles, has some ineffable property representing core beliefs and values. It has been measured against and outlasted its competitors and become an accepted representative of its genre.

Declaring something to be an instant classic is a game played in the contemporary worlds of marketing and spin, but the Nazis understood the need to confirm beliefs directly, to imbue objects and practices with indisputable power. All successive Nazi flags had to be consecrated by being ceremonially touched to the bloodied swastika flag. Original acts of creation that took advantage of events were common with the Nazis, who seized on Hitler's famous phrase in a public letter "*SS Mann, Deine Ehre heißt Treue*" ("SS man, your honour is loyalty"), adopted it for the SS's motto, and inscribed the words on the SS *Ehrendolch* blades. These Solingen daggers are now some of the most highly sought after Nazi artifacts that collectors pursue. As of this writing, depending on their condition and how infamous (the worse the better) their previous owners, they command market prices ranging from a few to tens of thousands of dollars. Eliade identifies some commonalities about these kinds of authenticity rituals: "As the first step, the 'reality' of the site is secured through consecration of the ground ... then the validity of the act of construction is confirmed by repetition of the divine sacrifice."[5] Genocidal words and acts about "blood and soil" ("*Blut und Boden*") would be supported by these new rituals. The idea of not only creating an instant classic but putting it to immediate mythological use shows the Nazis' canny understanding of how to conflate marketing and magic. They knew not to let something so ripe with potential languish, putting on continuing *Völkisch* "Blood and Soil" art exhibits in Munich from 1937 to 1944.[6] The very recent dead, killed in a few moments of a street brawl, become heroic martyrs who magically protected the regime.

Rituals that establish mythological origins, unbound by linear history and directly connected to what Eliade calls the sacred centre of the world, are common across militaries. Just as the Nazis clutched their *Blutfahne*, the Union army held on to the eagle Old

Abe, the bird that apparently became the inspiration for the 101st Airborne's screaming eagle, about which more later. The desire for something genuine drives the instant classic syndrome—paradoxically it doesn't seem to matter how questionable the creation's circumstances. The massing of new work suggests that the Nazis weren't solidifying a brand as much as a worldview. For a recently broken national power attempting to remake the whole world, the blood flag would have to convince new initiates that what they were joining was immensely more than themselves and their mundane concerns. Roger Griffin's reading of the anointing of the new standards by the *Blutfahne* is, as others have suggested, that it was not just one of "countless newly invented rituals" but also the creation of "elaborate 'political religions' presided over by Mussolini and Hitler."[7] The assemblage of flags at the Nuremburg rallies (the *Fahnenweihe* or "flag consecration") was recapitulated by the Soviets at the end of the war in their June 24, 1945, victory parade. In a well-planned photo opportunity, hundreds of Nazi standards are shown being carried parallel to the ground, and in a beautifully choreographed series of motions, tossed like junk onto a fast-growing pile of hundreds of flags complete with poles and gilt finials. Just as Hitler knew the power of the blooded flag, the Soviet Union understood the importance of showing the Reich's glory, hundreds of colourful flags, being thrown down presumably to burn—at least metaphorically. It's likely that many of the standards survived and were kept on public display by the Soviets. The camera surveys the shamed military wreckage, its gaze coming to focus at last on the Nazi eagle topper common to all the *Standarte*, with the box containing the regiment's name—Hitler's. Having scanned the pile of fallen standards with their bourgeois colours, tassels, gold headings, fringes, and Teutonic heraldry at odds with the uniformly dark-green Soviet uniforms and sea of black helmets, the camera lifts and moves on, finished with the Nazis.

Figure 4.1: From blood flag to mud flag: A dead sign system—or just a temporarily dormant one?

The *Reichsadler*, or Reich's eagle—another piece of carefully reworked Hitlerian design (the Reich's eagle faced left; the Nazi *Parteiadler* faced right), wreath, and swastika with regimental name box is, Littlejohn notes, "somewhat reminiscent of the ancient Roman military banner,"[8] massively understating the direct references made by Nazi heraldry to the Romans' infamous laurel-wreathed header with its initialism SPQR (*Senatus Populusque Romanus*, "Senate and People of Rome") proclaiming the imperial will of the Roman state, its designs, reach, and hold over the peoples of the world.

The swastika in its white circle on a red ground was fully complete. Unlike other complex designs, it required nothing else. It was as readable and powerful from the size of a nail-head on a dagger handle, the silver-dollar-sized party pin, on the armband, to the indoor or parade-ground flag, and finally the two- or threestory-high banner, hanging against the grey stone of Europe's aged buildings. Hitler understood too well that the "new flag had to be a symbol of our own battle and have a striking poster-like effect."[9]

What made the exterior banners so astonishing was their ability to capture and immobilize the eye. Nothing else like them existed on the drab streets. Artists, designers, and advertisers in the Reich may not have had to compete with the visual noise the inhabitant of current consumer society finds so familiar, but the immense banners that matched the outsize kitsch buildings and artworks made famous by Albert Speer and Nazi sculptor Arno Breker (Breker's gargantuan, hilariously awful neoclassicist pieces look like any number of Marvel's or DC Comics' more grotesquely muscled characters come to life, particularly figures like the Hulk), beat other signification into submission. On a background of nearly achromatic stone buildings, whether on the streets of Munich or Berlin, or in the stadia like the Nuremburg rally grounds, the red stripe with its white eyeball and perpetually turning *Hakenkreuz* was unavoidable and "stood out against the drabness of everyday life in the Weimar Republic. It was a splash of bright colour on the subdued background of post-war Germany."[10] Focused on the sign's aesthetic impact, scholar Frederic Spotts points out that the party made sure there was only one visible image: "Swastika flags festooned every possible space—including the sky, some pulled across the heavens by aeroplanes and dirigibles."[11] The swastika, ubiquitous and uncontested, created a world.

The swastika flag was visually arresting enough that it didn't need to explain itself to the viewer, but its authors still had plenty of intended meanings for the image. Taylor and Will argue that the form arose in part not just from canny design, but from an understanding about "mass-psychological effects."[12] As if posting a plaque beside an artwork in a gallery explaining his creation,

Hitler commented in *Mein Kampf* on the purpose for each piece of the design, seeing in "the red ... the socialist ideas of the movement; in the white, the nationalistic; in the swastika, the mission of the fight for the victory of the Aryan man ... [and the] victory for the creative work of a culture, which was anti-Semitic."[13] Hitler knew how to choose. Commenting on colour in vexillology, Jilek notes that in languages that distinguish between dark and light (many North Americans would render those as black and white, but not all cultures do), there is "always ... a term for red. This is true even if there are no terms for any other colours," as determined by the World Color Survey.[14] Establishing what each colour means has everything to do with socialization and acculturation, but the designer must still contend with what attracts the human eye. As brand maven Marc Gobé notes, "colors with long wavelengths are arousing (e.g., red is the most stimulating color that will attract the eye faster than any other) and colors with short wavelengths [blue] are soothing."[15] Gobé's point is not that the physiology of the eye necessarily defeats all other factors, but that such organic issues cannot be ignored.

Gobé does warn would-be branders who want to institute new global brands that colours are invariably culturally bound, and that "selecting colors is complex, and the interpretation of color independently of its product or without the guidance of a color designer is ill-advised."[16] Jilek believes that red is transcultural, arguing that since red is the colour of blood and fire, is apparently "the first color to which infants react," excites the central nervous system either for good or ill, and whose appearance is "accompanied by a transient increase of blood pressure and pulse rate," red will always be important.[17] Even artists determined to break previous aesthetic, social, political, and moral codes, could not deny the importance of red. Pieces of a shared aesthetic heritage between Western industrialized countries are built into language: people colour-blind to red are known as "protanopes," those colour-blind to blue and green are labelled respectively deuteranopes and tritanopes. The prefixes refer not to colour but the importance of colours as ordered by the Greeks, who put red first (proto), and green and blue second (deuter) and third (trit).

The power of the physical objects (brassards, pins, banners) but also the "Hitler salute" with its accompanying "*Sieg Heil*" ("Hail victory") is representative of the Reich's limited but widespread signifying practice. Studying the force of the hail, Tilman Allert argues its ubiquity and frequency were diagnostic of a personality cult. It was also a daily, sometimes hourly, reminder to remain a believer. Until its military disasters and victories (the siege of Stalingrad and battle of Kursk became as famous as Rommel's desert war), and apart from its dreadful effectiveness in conducting genocide, the Reich could point to few lasting accomplishments. Like any structure determined to invent itself mythically, there was a constant need for miraculous successes and more instant classics, like Heinz Guderian's contribution to tank and manoeuvre warfare. The repetition of the Hitler salute reaffirmed the Reich's continuing health and existence.[18] The danger with repetitive signs is that their signifying power can burn out. Monomania can turn even the strongest signal into white noise. Overplaying a piece of music as unusual and striking as "The Ride of the Valkyries" would do worse than empty meaning out of a foundational myth like Wagner's Ring Cycle—it would become a grating, loathed event. In Gobé's view, the sign that pounds at the viewer relentlessly "is sort of like having an ongoing conversation with someone who says the same thing again and again. We tend to eventually tune them out!"[19] Reformatting or replacing signs can cause even more difficulties, a test the Reich never faced because it didn't survive. The brand, however, has been kept virulently alive by various stakeholders, from white supremacists to hobbyists and re-enactors, as well as conventional media companies producing feature or documentary films, novels, histories, and photo books. All have kept Nazi signification public. Gobé's parting advice to the corporation experiencing brand fatigue is "to think like a consumer and to attempt to view your brand's presence from their perspective."[20] The Nazis were adept at thinking like their membership, although at times the fetish for the image became extreme, even for them.

Paul Virilio recounts the story of Goebbels's intention, following the Führer's wish, to replay the 1940 battles between the Germans and Allies at Narvik, Norway, in front of Veit Harlan's cameras in order to produce the film *Kolberg*, intended as a reminder for the Reich of its victory there. Harlan was hardly of Hitler and Goebbels's view that "such a film was more useful than a military victory."[21] A potential photo opportunity (driven by what Welch calls "Goebbels' continual obsession with dramatic effects") became a likely disaster when Britain learned of Goebbels's plans and only half-ironically offered to send along the fleet for a proper re-enactment of the battles, suggesting this time the outcome might be different. Harlan noted, "to die for the fatherland struck [Admirals Raeder and Dönitz] as more logical than to die for the cinema!"[22] Staging a mock battle was one thing, staging an actual slaughter of one's own troops was too much, no matter who was asking. The admirals had to personally intervene with Hitler to convince him that using the original site in Norway was far too dangerous. The production of *Kolberg* continued with Hitler putting the Wehrmacht at Harlan's full disposal. As the film wrapped, the territory fell into Soviet hands, causing one witness to note bitterly about the ruined town, "Back then, this was all props; now it is a horrible reality."[23] If Goebbels and Hitler had difficulty determining the difference between dying for film or Fatherland, the people involved had no such problem.

Successfully being refreshed without losing power is the perpetual nightmare facing brands gone stale. The military, I will argue shortly, a corporate entity, confronts the paradox known as Theseus's Ship, sometimes more familiarly as "Grandfather's Axe." Both are physical artifacts that have deep enough histories such that they have become part of a collective identity (the crew recognize the ship; the family knows precisely what tool is meant by "grandfather's axe"). But in the course of use parts have been worn out and have had to be replaced. At different times the thwarts, hull, mast, sails, oars (or haft and axe-head) have been patched, swapped out, or entirely rebuilt so that little or none of the original material remains. How then are we to know we're looking at the same item? All that remains unchanged is the object's name. The irony of a campaign intended to make a virtue of the newness of the product is it can as easily kill as recreate the item, as happened with the famous 1988 Oldsmobile project with the tagline "This is not your father's Oldsmobile." It turned out that the one thing the buyer wanted was exactly their father's car: the new model sank, taking the brand with it.[24] In the current climate of irony, meme, and virality, what was a classic failure has become enough of a social trope to become a brand itself ("Not Your Father's Rootbeer," "Not Your Father's Barber"). Recasting without losing brand identity is the story of Theseus's ship afloat on a consumer ocean.

If brands are to perform the magic brand aficionados believe they're capable of, maintaining a perfect balance of sameness and newness is critical. Ongoing brand maintenance requires finding the perpetually new in the familiar. One solution proposed by brand manager Simon Anholt is that the brand builder focus on the "good stories about" specific brands, stories that are rich "with symbols and rituals that these people enact to create a place in people's minds."[25] That's another way of suggesting one use consumers to remake the brand in their image. Each person will have a different experience with a brand, but overall there will be enough commonalities for them to recognize Theseus's ship: "Brands are patterns, too. They are also memes, containing specific and differentiated ideas about companies as well as their people, products, and services"[26] The brand is a zone where users share their mutual understanding of the world. Using the brand, repeating its slogan with levity, irony, or high seriousness, place one on a spectrum of belief. Although all will use the same sign, it will not always signify the same things. Allert ponders the Hitler salute's true use, wondering if it was "really a greeting" or whether it operated as many more things: a "communicative practice that merely took the form of a greeting as a means of disguise, a verbal armband, a membership card."[27]

The brand exists in the mind of each user, but is also a common space into which one's fellows must be welcomed. Thinking about the standard pre-Nazi greeting "*Gruß Gott*" (many common salutations reflect a god's protective presence: "adieu," "adios," "addio," "goodbye" ["God be with you"]), Allert speculates that the phrase reassures both parties that there will be "a peaceful encounter by including the other person within the moral sphere defined by a supernatural authority. A third party—in this case, God—is therefore entrusted with maintaining the symmetry of the interaction and 'bringing the other to speech.'"[28] For Allert, however, the Hitler salute replaces a communal wish for blessing with an abrogation of communication that he calls state-sanctioned "social radicalism."[29] Perhaps one of the signal differences here is that the Nazis were intent on making new not only their society, but the terms of membership: new rituals made for new relations.

The salute is another instant classic, a daily wish for a different, if entirely genocidal, future. Writing in a post-Second World War France more than ever run by large corporations, theologian and philosopher Jacques Ellul argued that, "as in all propaganda, the point is to make man endure, with the help of psychological narcotics, what he could not endure naturally, or to give him, artificially, reasons to continue his work and to do it well."[30] The salute, like other pieces of the Nazi appearance machine, refreshes the cultural rituals that reinforce belief, tamp down doubt, and remind individuals that they exist in a matrix of true believers content to do as they have been told. As with much spectacle, the image becomes the new real, installing itself in place of the thing it once represented: "What Hitler provided was ritual in place of belief, or ritual *as* belief."[31] There need be no actual belief when ritual occupies the space once accorded to it. If belief need not be consulted because the eyes and mind have been kept occupied with perpetual brand maintenance, then repetition becomes the new salve for anxieties about the present and terrors over the future. Repetition is compulsory to survival.

The repetition of the Hitler salute reassured people sharing both the burden and the excitement of the new world they'd been promised that everywhere there were partners, people joined in a special relationship fuelled by a living presence, not some imaginary force that might be found in a church. After a certain time those repetitions gain their own power, the strength of habit, of common use, reliability, sameness. What was new becomes a new tradition. Hitler and the Nazis were by no means the first to understand the coercive strength of a recognizable visual system. As we've seen, families and their militaries had learned it, and family legacies that became corporations knew, too, that this system of identification worked in their favour to build pride in shared experiences of consumption. They didn't appreciate, perhaps, just how important that identification, closer now to a brand than ever, could possibly be.

CHAPTER 5

ONE PUNCH MACHINE

Corporate Logos and
Military Identity

BEFORE ARMIES: FAMILIES. STRONG, WEALTHY FAMILIES
that survived political and military struggles developed their own
identities and, using the language of the heraldic sign, concisely
defined how their histories were to be recorded, inscribing images
on the achievement in order to determine what was to be remembered. The coat of arms was the outward presentation of power in
what Jurgen Habermas would call the public sphere. While the
family might have been the planting ground for corporate seeds,
that new creation set aside both family and familial heraldry
in exchange for an inordinately more compressed statement of
identity. Within a generation most American corporate parents
of the late nineteenth and early twentieth centuries had become
brands: with a few exceptions the names that created big industry—Carnegie, Rockefeller, DuPont, Disney, Ford—faded into

the background as the corporate beings they'd spawned grew, integrated, merged, and grew again. Steven Heller puts the origin of "the modern corporate logo ... in Germany shortly after the turn of the twentieth century, the direct descendent of burgher crests, coats of arms, trade and factory marks."[1]

The corporate logo is the machine's herald, a one-shot punch that, like a hallmark, left an indelible stroke on the world. Just as modernity and modernism are interwoven, and modernity is contiguous with some of modernism's most influential new media (photography, photolithography, film and high-speed cameras, high-speed printing, wax and lacquer recordings), so corporate identity created new forms of communication and signification. Consumption would bulk up advertising volume that in turn would demand speed and concision. Identity marks had to say everything at once and, like a good flag, be memorable enough to be redrawn by a child. The increasing speed of machine production, the organizational philosophy inherent in scientific management and efficiency systems that led operations research (and digital computing) to create enormous simulations of engineering, logistical, and societal problems, provoked the cultural criticism we know as modernism. Modernism's complaints were powerful because they questioned the legitimacy of the machine as a way of life, disputed that national and industrial health were necessarily the same, and criticized the idea that technological and scientific progress were equivalent to societal and human progress. Just as modernity created modernism, so corporations created logos and, more complexly, brands, which this chapter considers a little later.

Family history had to exist to create heraldry; similarly, companies that made or traded in goods first had to establish themselves. Early identifying marks might have been accidental or considered relatively insignificant, but ultimately the company name became the guarantor of its business's quality. Marks like company crests might take more space on the product than one had, or might be distasteful to those who didn't want to advertise. The result was the "reductive trademark," credited to "members of the Bauhaus and the *Ring Neuer Werbegestalter* (circle of new advertising designers)."[2] The reductive trademark, soon to be recognizable as a logo, initially seemed synonymous with the branding iron's creation of a permanent burn or the metal punch used to stamp a hallmark on goods. For a time the words brand and logo appear to have been interchangeable. However the way brands have come to be understood today, they are vaster by far than any logo, which is primarily an identification device.

The shift from maker's mark to brand occurred largely in the interwar period with the result that "by the end of the 1940s, there was a burgeoning awareness that a brand wasn't just a mascot or a catchphrase or a picture printed on the label of a company's product." Instead the corporation developed a unified meaning, what Klein traces as the beginning of a "corporate consciousness."[3] The corporation was the planet's new life form, bearing its own individual sigil and signature in words and graphics. While this language now illuminates miracle miles leading into urban centres in North America, streams of logo speech in primary colours organized around the grammar of the car and superhighway, the landscape between those centres is littered with the ruins of an industrial empire that seemed immortal. What once were taken to be lasting signs of strength on the massive scale of the mid- to late-twentieth-century industry (enormous plants and mills that owned or seemed to compose whole towns, complete with water towers bearing company brands) became rust belt ruins.

The monuments may have fallen, but they were merely physical. The corporate identity, that "was designed to last forever and look appropriate in any context as a true reflection of the conservative values of the time," created spectacular factory sites. Such identities have become infinitely more fluid and are "multisensorial expressions of not only what the company thinks it is, but also reflections of how a company wants to be perceived by people."[4] Branded water towers may have fallen, an image Michael Moore used metonymically in his 1989 account of General Motor's betrayal of working Americans and the collapse of life in small-town America, but the GM brand survived.[5] No matter where it is used or what the scale, the logo remains the announcement to the world of the company's existence and intent.

As with a flag, our responses to a familiar logo are rooted in our experiences with the corporation, its overall behaviour and politics, and the level of our agreement with or concern about the brand as entity. Myers traces the development of the brand from its early, hard reality as a representative of things, considering its "radical evolution from commodity, to product, to experience, to relationship, to this book's current usage—the interdependent living system of stakeholders."[6] Meyers describes an entire culture's development. What starts out as a relatively simple object that is presumably, but not necessarily, essential to life, becomes the repeatable experience of a manufactured product, then a transcendental quantity, then a series of interlinked presences, until we enter a complete ecology, an "interdependent living system." It's hard to imagine what could escape the gravity of a system so comprehensive that it presents itself as a totality. What began as identification has become a world or, for some, universe. Logos are disciplined works of energy that capture all that has come before and promise an improved future.

Among those with a genius for the logotype, the twentieth century's new heraldry, was Peter Behrens, famous then and now for his AEG (a German electricity company) logo, and designer Wilhelm Deffke, known for dozens of famous signs including the Henckels's Twins. It was Deffke who produced the swastika's penultimate form in 1920, although he later argued the sign was hijacked by the Nazis. Like many of the designers he knew and identified with at the Bauhaus, Deffke made an art form out of precision, understanding at some deep level how to create what Heller calls the "reductive trademark," using striking, elegant geometric forms that were subtly complex. Heller's term "reductive trademark" is itself a compressed term. All trademarks are by their nature reductive. To talk about a reductive trademark is to describe the quintessential piece of design that renders the idea of the corporation such that it hits us as natural, inevitable, irreplaceable, and most of all, irreducible. It is a logo's logo. Deffke not only produced logos, he wrote about their larger meaning, arguing in 1920 that, "trademarks acquire their real worth and significance only through adequate usage," and that when used persistently, "the trademark will be the most likely to establish an inseparable bond between the user and the manufacturer."[7] The logo pierces the fabric of the consumer's life and sews together the user and corporation. The result transcends selling and passes into emotional spaces coveted by brand developers. It isn't just money that transforms the trademark from corporate logo to identity to brand, but belief in a sacred icon.

Deffke realized that "a pure mark void of superfluous ornamentation could communicate directly with the public like few other business tools."[8] The logo was no longer to be hidden, stamped on the bottom of a piece of goods, but absorbed into the design where it would be prominent. Deffke wasn't alone in his understanding: "German trademark design of this period was the most advanced of any Western industrialized country. Graphic designers, including Peter Beherens, Karl Schulpig, O. H. W. Haddank, Lucian Bernhard, Carlo Egler, Valetin Zietara," all saw the power of this new corporate form.[9] It was the swastika that shut out all other logos. Even now the swastika with clockwise-facing hands (the South Asian good luck sign that is enormously popular generally has counter-clockwise hands) is forbidden as hate speech in many countries. It has yet to be outdone in cultural clout and taboo. In Steven Heller's mind, "no other mark—not even variations of the cross or, for that matter, the Nike swoosh—are as graphically potent."[10] The swastika's story is, in small, one of power.

Hitler's background as a would-be artist and his ongoing fascination with art sometimes eclipses what are thought to be his designs for the Nazi brand. He makes claims to the creation of much design. He is thought to have sketched an early, near-perfect image of the Volkswagen hood in profile. He is reliably thought to have "devised a party badge, party stationery, the masthead of the party newspaper and even the official rubber stamp, all bearing an eagle with a swastika in its talons."[11] He borrowed what he needed to, including the German imperial red, black, and gold. The gold migrated to the braids, laurels and eagles visible on the party headgear after 1933.[12] Hitler takes responsibility for the whole vexillogical effort: "after countless attempts, I had finally drawn the final form. It was a flag with a red background, and a white disk with a black swastika in the middle. After many experiments, I also established a balance between the size of the flag and the white disk as well as the shape and thickness of the swastika lines."[13] His dissatisfaction with the previous Reich's eagles caused his creation of the streamlined, modernist *Parteiadler* and *Reichsadler*.

While we don't know precisely who sat at the drafting table, it seems likely that Hitler was the final arbiter. Deffke produced the penultimate form of the swastika and was responsible for thickening it and giving it more force; it was the dentist Dr. Friedrich Krohn who produced the final logo, with Hitler reversing the arms' direction.[14] Krohn disappeared in the Nazi fog, as did, until very recently, much of Wilhelm Deffke's work.[15] Both Heller and Simmons argue convincingly that Deffke's imprint is clear when one compares the swastika to his other 1920s design work.[16] Simmons credits Deffke with modernizing the swastika "the same way that he did for the trademarks of Krupp and other heavy industries."[17] The final bit of design genius was to take the swastika, usually seen grounded and stable on one of its square sides, and tip it up on a corner. At that moment the emblem became completely new, perpetually turning, always on the rise. Because the arms don't quite touch, the eye struggles to form a square out of the whole and resolve what was known as the *Hakenkreuz*, or hooked cross, into solidity. But the eye and brain labour in vain for the "principle of closure" derived from the "Gestalt principle of *Prägnanz*": the space between the end of one arm and the back of the next carry the eye on an infinite roundabout, seeking completion and finding none.[18] What was a square has become an endless disk of both motion and stability, a moving force of the future. Refusing the eye interpretative closure is also at the heart of the hammer and sickle's genius, where the gaps are just large enough "in these not quite circular figures ... to be suppressed by the observer's perceptual apparatus. As a result, the quasi-rotating figures create an impression of dynamic motion. The emblems, appearing first to be closed, then open, thus become a source of tension to the observer, who feels compelled to focus attention on them—not unlike the hypnotized subject focusing on the hypnotist and his induction device."[19] The mesmeric sign is accompanied by similarly incomplete but promising messages to a select audience about possible alternate worlds that will be accessible if one fully surrenders. Those included dream a collective dream; the excluded are exterminated.

The logo's appearance near the beginning of a global industrial near-total war, and its acceptance as an institution during the second of those wars, is no coincidence: "Logos and their colors—whether expressed as symbols (like Nike), logotypes ... or a combination of both ... have been an essential part of all major branding strategies since the middle of the last century." [20] By "logotypes" Gobé probably means corporate signs formed entirely by the company name in a particular font and colour(s), like Xerox,

Coca-Cola, and FedEx—these are a subset of logos known as wordmarks. What was new about logos was that they granted corporations an identity, something that has led contemporary corporations to fight for legal recognition as people. In the last ten years the corporation has gained ever more ground in obtaining what is called "corporate personhood." Two recent cases pushed the corporation further along this path: the 2010 case of *Citizens United v. FEC* and the more recent decision in favour of Hobby Lobby against the Obama White House, *Burwell v. Hobby Lobby* (2014). Both Supreme Court cases bestowed the rights of personhood on corporations: the first awarded corporations the right to free political speech; the second agreed that corporations are capable of holding spiritual beliefs.[21]

Because the logo is the corporation's face, severe damage to the corporation may require revision or deletion of the logo. When the logo conjures unwelcome associations, rebranding is not far behind. Whether the rebranding is matched by change in the corporation's behaviour is something else. One such recreation happened to the private military contractor Blackwater USA, which, following war crimes perpetrated by Blackwater soldiers in 2007, replaced its signature bear paw print surrounded by a sniper's scope red crosshairs with a large black X, as if in an attempt to cross out the besmirched past with an incoherent present.[22] Rebranded first in 2009 as Xe (pronounced "Zee"), the overly large X (like a reversed Greek letter Chi) contained a smaller inset lowercase "e." The meaning of these signs, if any, was never clear. The company's legal problems, however, continued until it was once more rebranded in 2011 as Academi, complete with vague logo that might (or might not) be three overlapped shields, all of which was the equivalent of a visual euphemism for something—it was never clear what.

Where once Blackwater USA used its threatening brand aggressively (one graphic designer noted, "The old logo suggests that they're targeting people. The new logo is a more ambiguous, more safe corporate logo."), Academi has survived largely by becoming invisible in the marketplace outside mercenary services.[23] If the logo and company's fate are one, then Blackwater was forced out of its bloody macho adolescence and, after committing murders and other crimes, groomed to maturity when it was swallowed by the much larger supplier of private armies, Triple Canopy. The logo, like a monarch's signet ring, is an "expression of a corporation's culture, personality, and products or services it has to offer—the very symbol and signature of the values that should inspire trust with consumers, employees, clients, suppliers, and the financial community."[24] Even the signet ring's power pales beside the logo. One human, no matter how powerful, even if representing a kingdom or religion, signs once. The corporation signs simultaneously hundreds of thousands of times and affects hundreds of millions.[25] Corporate signing by Coca-Cola is infinitely louder globally than any single human signature can be. That is because Coca-Cola's logo is a sign of a worldview captured by the whole of the brand.

The brand has become an existential construct around which corporations are organized. Hajo Riesenbeck and Jesko Perrey, brand specialists at McKinsey, write, "Brands are mostly made, not born. They do not arise accidentally; their growth and development can be measured and predicted."[26] Their commentary is particularly useful in part because it comes from McKinsey, with its history as one of the oldest management advising companies in the world. In 1926, University of Chicago professor James McKinsey started the corporation to fix supply problems the United States Army Ordnance Department had during the First World War. McKinsey's rigid practices and politics made the company a leading brand of business consultants. McKinsey is the kind of company that should understand, if any group does, how to engineer a brand and transform it into a worldwide power. Riesenbeck and Perrey's statement that brands are fabrications, constructs that require managing, suggests that they are controllable artifacts that don't take on lives of their own.

There's more than a touch of evangelism about those who work on and write about brands. George Creel, an early brand believer, journalist, author, and wartime chief of the United States Committee on Public Information, wrote in his 1920 *How We Advertised America* that Americans had to have the "*war-will*, the will-to-win*" that depended on "no mere surface unity, but a passionate belief in the justice of America's cause that should weld the people of the United States into one white-hot mass."[27] Creel understands what most propagandists know: to be more than a limited success a brand must create a mythical narrative about itself. Once it transcends mere objects, people will take up its cause as their own and align themselves with the brand's aims. That the brand is a corporate product may get lost in the passion and rhetoric; in fact, it's probably necessary for any corporate brand to appear to be much wider than it really is. If people are going to sacrifice or be sacrificed for it, they have to know they have what Creel calls the "approval of the world" that produces a "steady flow of inspiration into the trenches."[28] It's a curious, almost religious, phrase suggesting that humans will be moved to behave obediently toward their government because great powers have breathed into them an understanding of their mission. Government, national, and corporate goals must be converted into personal beliefs not only for the soldiers who will go, but for the families and communities that risk losing them, must do without them for the duration, and support them while they're away.

Almost one hundred years later brand developers still use the same language: "Imagine a better world through marketing. Consumers are demanding it. Consumers, and some marketers, are already building it. If you don't help them, I will."[29] That's Max Lenderman, advertising creative director and brand advocate, whose vehement beliefs almost seem to threaten the reader. Lenderman argues that what he calls "experiential marketing" is the only way to save the world; if you're not marketing, being marketed to and buying your way forward, you're probably a naysaying critic. Precisely how consumption will bring about Lenderman's "better world" is his book's moral, but the explanation cannot be separated from capitalist consumerism: we will have to buy, literally and metaphorically, the politics of our salvation. Lenderman's goal is to sift the junk out of our heads: "a marketing experience that doesn't deliver an inherent benefit to the consumer—physically, emotionally, viscerally, or mentally—is not experiential marketing. It's just more white noise and clutter."[30] Since there's a war on for our attention in the current marketplace, winning the battle for eyeballs is insufficient. There's a disagreement about how many ads, brands, and labels one sees each day: Lenderman guesses that in the mid 1970s the consumer daily faced 560 targeted ads, and that one is now exposed to three to four thousand ads daily—more for heavy users of the web and social media.[31]

Lenderman's numbers may be high, but the general consensus is that we are exposed to one thousand ads and contacts with brands per person per day. One thousand, three thousand, at a certain point it hardly matters because they merge into an infinite blur of sensory garbage that overloads us. Lenderman's solution for the contemporary citizen looking for brand-free space is to convert junk input into meaningful signal. The idea of reducing the noise overall, passing laws that restrict advertising, doesn't seem to be a possibility. In agent provocateur Morgan Spurlock's *POM Wonderful Presents: The Greatest Movie Ever Sold*, Spurlock interviews long-time consumer advocate and political candidate Ralph Nader, asking him, "Where should I be able to go where I don't see one bit of advertising?" To which the heavy-eyed Nader responds laconically, "To sleep."[32] Lenderman's method puts experience first and makes the brand integral to a worldview.

Wholeness, sensations of wellness and pleasure, are secondary. A product will not so much create a particular feeling in us as lay out a road to a better life that will then have beneficial side effects. The logo should be a socially engineered turnkey, a preset piece of interoperational technology, a switch, that can be toggled anywhere at any time by a group of likeminded individuals, marketers, consumers, producers. The logo, an arrow pointing to a world of satisfaction, pulls us into the brand's purer, better environment. We willingly return to the brand's sphere because the experience has been a desirable one that we wish to repeat frequently. As Riesenbeck and Perrey put it, brands "save us time in that we do not have to check, challenge, classify, and critically weigh up everything before we make a decision to act": to connect with the brand is to be translated into the realm of the familiar, comfortable, and improved.[33] There we will meet others like us who share our values, sensibilities, and assumptions, and more covertly, class. If they, and we, have been properly programmed, brands eliminate anxiety and become direct, emotionally pleasurable experiences.

The brand may promise to save us time and angst involved in choosing, but it also promises us freedom. We are apparently free to leave a brand, to vote elsewhere with our money should the brand take positions of which we disapprove. We enter into a relationship with a brand: "branding bridges the gap between the provider and the receiver—between authority and freedom. It is about trust and dialogue."[34] Implicit is the idea that trust will be earned and maintained, with the user perhaps periodically surveying the brand's behaviour, then either continuing to authorize its decisions, warning the brand one is prepared to leave, or shifting to another worldview if the brand disappoints or betrays expectations. The user will have tolerances as to how many mistakes (if any), betrayals large and small, the brand will be afforded. Perhaps there is no limit on the brand. In case of a catastrophic break, however, one moves to another brand experience, not out of the brand universe. Recall Tillman Allert's proposal about the kinds of "communicative practice that merely [take] the form of a greeting," but are in reality disguised markers of recognition like "a verbal armband, a membership card."[35] It is Gobé's invocation of the power relationship between "provider and the receiver," who are engaged in the respective acts of "authority and freedom," that should get our attention. For Gobé the provider has only as much authority as the free agent receiver is prepared to surrender, about which media scholar Arjun Appadurai would comment, "these images of agency are increasingly distortions of a world of merchandising so subtle that the consumer is consistently helped to believe that he or she is an actor, where in fact he or she is at best a chooser."[36]

Marketers today who are evangelical about their mission and power to build "a better world" look well beyond mere brand recognition.[37] If approached about how to sell ideas that are not apparently capitalist (true green policies, politics of zero consumption), the marketers I discuss here wouldn't hesitate to argue that the same method applies no matter what is to be sold or communicated in such a way that the message is taken up. If we're going to have actual ecological policies, would argue brand experts like Lenderman and Gobé, it will be because successful brand campaigns will convince people to wholly adopt the idea of saving the planet, which would become the new product. Although it seems like the corporate logo and the swastika accomplish the same task, they have, argues historian Malcolm Quinn, "followed similar paths in the twentieth century, but to a radically different purpose." Quinn argues that the logo is part of a gift economy, where the swastika was part of a world of "injunction and law," a disciplinary system.[38] One could argue, as many have, that corporate control of the statehouse, courts, global communication systems, and key natural resources that humans require to survive (including but not limited to water, food, fuel for heating and cooking, medicines, medical care, education) make global multinationals more powerful than the Third Reich was at its highest point. Many have argued corporations don't desire genocide since it would be bad for the marketplace. But there are many ways to exclude people from life apart from outright genocide. A particular group may be chosen by class, if not race, ethnicity, or religion. The corporation cannot extricate itself from this discussion, particularly since corporations profited not only from the Third Reich, but from the slave labour it provided to some of its key corporate partners like I. G. Farben and Krupp.

While I. G. Farben and Krupp made arms and weapons systems, they were subcontractors to the Nazis who fabricated the war itself. Corporations were guilty of war crimes and of pressing the Reich for favourable terms—Saurer and Opel produced the vans used as mobile gas chambers—but it was the *Einsatzgruppen* that gave detailed instructions about how the vans were to be designed.[39] The logo in which Hitler saw the future became a full brand marketing scheme, aided by architect Albert Speer. It was Speer who was responsible for much of the Reich's famous spectacle, the displays that supported Leni Riefenstahl's mythologizing work. While Hitler scraped the swastika's final form off Krohn and Deffke's drafting tables, it was Speer who saw to the brand placement of the mammoth banners, initiating what "many regard … as the beginnings of post-war corporate identity schemes."[40] Photographs of city streets and parade grounds plastered with red banners make it clear that no other visual systems were permitted to compete with the Reich's. In purging the environment of all but a few designs chiselled down to their elemental units, Hitler and Speer curated a design monopoly that guaranteed the Reich the appearance of victory.[41] Few logos ever had such power, had been spread so deliberately and ubiquitously, were so committed to starkness and newness. The irony of using a sign already thousands of years old reinforces the Nazis' success of following Pound's dictum to "make it new." The logo was a modernist sign about modernity *and* tradition, an open saw blade cutting into the future. The Nazis rewrote the swastika's history using their brand backed by hatred, power, money, and industry. It was a sign of "the future tense" with a "discourse ... about objectives, missions and goals, rather than traditions and continuities."[42]

Naomi Klein points out the dangers "of advanced branding [which] is to nudge the hosting culture into the background and make the brand the star. It is not to sponsor culture but to *be* the culture."[43] The logo, flag of the brand's new world, flies over newly occupied territory that contains whatever the brand is intended to create. Still struggling with the implications of superb, successful fascist design, Steven Heller is forced to admit that "the design and marketing methods used to inculcate doctrine and guarantee consumption are fundamentally similar."[44] Better just to say it: they are not similar—they are identical. Whether the brand becomes identified with the publicly intolerable, as happened with Erik Prince's Blackwater USA, is not a function of branding. Brands can sicken and die, just as can the corporate "persons" who support them. Unlike a human being who can be held accountable, or not, for his or her actions (assessments of mental fitness would presumably follow), the brand is harder to locate, making it possible for it to escape dissolution. Historian Peter Batty recounts with some emotion the post-war arrival of the British at the Krupp plant in Essen. The newly appointed chief, whose job it was to wind down the Krupp *Werke,* told the few surviving workers that "no Krupp chimney will ever smoke again."[45] By the mid 1960s Krupp's chimneys were back at full roar. Even its actions during both world wars were not enough to destroy its brand in the eyes of the global economy.

Many would argue that there is no forced labour in today's free market, and certainly there is nothing comparable to work done by inmates at Auschwitz or Majdanek. However, determining who has and has not been coerced, and what conditions are survivable, can be more complex than at first it appears. Large corporations may engage companies that use cheap labour to make products for the North American market. If those workers face the choice of having no jobs or jobs in bad conditions, can hunger be considered a coercive tool? If the worker takes a job but is killed in a factory fire because the factory has no functioning safety requirements in place, who bears the responsibility for those deaths? If a gargantuan multinational claims not to employ slave labour or support murderous working conditions, who can police it to ensure the corporation fulfills its pledge?

One need look no further than the business practices of a corporation like Walmart to see whether fire safety in Bangladeshi clothing factories was of concern to it in 2012. Walmart had flagged fire risk at the Tazreen Fashion factory and determined that, while the factory was a dangerous place to work, "it is not financially feasible for the brands to make such investments" in ensuring factory safety standards are met.[46] When 112 workers were killed at Tazreen, Walmart refused to discuss the convincing charge that it "played the lead role in blocking an effort to have global retailers pay more for apparel to help Bangladesh factories improve their electrical and fire safety."[47] A year later when Rana Plaza, another such factory, collapsed, this time killing over a thousand people making garments for Loblaw's brand Joe Fresh, Loblaw denied all culpability.[48] There are enormous differences between forcing concentration camp inmates into factories and working them to death, and deliberate blindness or lack of diligence on a corporation's part about potentially fatal working conditions in another country's factory. There is, too, coercion involved. There won't be the self-declared hallmarks of authoritarianism that made the Nazis so famous, but the results exist along the same continuum: someone else suffers under, and may be killed by, systemic corporate practices because other people believe they have a right to a product, land, power, or some other equally attractive end.

The relationship between brand and nation has seemed to be clear: the first serves the second. But it's brand advocates, not detractors, who argue the brand can and will be supreme. The corporation exists across borders, can invest itself in people's lives and weave itself into cultural fabric, can withstand what a country cannot. Brand makers argue that "the brand approach offers America the ultimate prize if it does things well: the chance to be top dog and be loved. A superpower can't achieve this. A brand leader can."[49] Anholt's final manoeuvre reverses the dominance between brand and nation. It doesn't matter whether the United States chooses to be a brand leader—one will arise, globally, and will wield more force than any superpower.[50] While some brand enthusiasts are staunchly patriotic, and Anholt is one, there are others who, like Joseph Heller's Milo Minderbinder in *Catch-22*, know that some things have more of a future than others. The squadron's mess-officer-cum-CEO Milo Minderbinder finally establishes himself as a world business leader, using the end of the Second World War to unite the forces fighting for M & M Enterprises. Correcting Yossarian that the "Germans are not our enemies," Milo explains, "Sure, we're at war with them. But the Germans are also members in good standing of the syndicate, and it's my job to protect their rights as shareholders. Maybe they did start the war, and maybe they are killing millions of people, but they pay their bills a lot more promptly than some allies of ours I could name." He then complains prophetically (remember Heller wrote the novel over eight years in the 1950s and before America's deep investment in propping up the South Vietnamese government) to Yossarian, "Frankly, I'd like to see the government get out of the war altogether and leave the whole field to private industry."[51] Heller's acute understanding of the multinational's role during and after the Second World War follows "the rise of the brand [as it] is linked to the privatization of the economic functions of the state."[52] The brand is the *new* new being and "not just smoke and mirrors; the results [of branding] are often quantifiable because public awareness and brand loyalty can be measured by sales—or votes."[53] But why go through the difficult, unpredictable, rarely pleasurable process of voting when labour can be exchanged directly for brand power? Brand identity promises continuity, stability, strength, and longevity, if not immortality— all things that are enormously reassuring to short-lived human beings.

The next shift is a slight one as we look toward a brand environment that exists during wartime. War environments tend to heat things up and, following a physics metaphor, produce speed as a result. Brands at war become more powerful, more lively, and frighteningly ubiquitous.

CHAPTER 6

Loyalty Program

Brands at War

MODERNITY SHOOK THE CULTURE. IT DROVE PEOPLE INTO cities that had no infrastructure to support mass populations, reshaped labour practices, the trades, the concept of work, and created a world of overconsumption. It exacerbated anxieties to the point that the world seemed "increasingly on the verge or in the midst of apocalyptic disruptions," which was answered, in historian Warren Susman's view, by the image of "man as designer [who] was called upon to find some new order in the world."[1] The elevation of the designer to a place of cultural power is part of the traditional narrative of modernism. The designer, bluntly lionized by Ayn Rand, is not only an expert backed by a disciplinary authority like architecture, engineering, or psychology, who uses the language of rationalism to describe ways of creating stability in the wildly fluctuating new economic, social, and political orders, but is a creative intercessor who speaks to the machine on the behalf of humanity. Frederick Taylor focuses on getting the size of shovels right; Henry Ford smooths the production line into a fluid entity; John Watson leaves the University of Chicago and becomes an agent of consumer desires. The designer is the new celestial smith, one who understands and embraces progressive forces in production and creation, where machines make ever more complex machines and tools, no longer simple devices, are full of complexity. The designer is the next step on the evolutionary chain identified by Mircea Eliade that begins with the alchemist, continues with the smith, and carries on to the specialist: "He who makes real things is he who *knows* the secrets of making them."[2]

While experts pushed aggressively for change, societal forces looked on with alarm. Large-scale organization required planning, and perpetual technical innovation, with its attendant cultural shifts, "did not appeal to governments and corporations seeking stability; nor did it appeal to ordinary people who sought the familiar comforts of traditional life," resulting in the drive to calm the terrors brought about by modernity.[3] James Agee and Walker Evans's mid-Depression record of tenant farmer sharecropping, *Let Us Now Praise Famous Men* (1941), detailed the working poor's bitter living conditions. Agee and Evans gaze at length at the few pieces of colour, decorations the families put up in their bare shelters. They are advertisements, calendars for soap and farm supplies displaying cruelly ironic images of a land of plenty. Even as the most desperate victims of the machine sought comfort in art, businesses worked to erase evidence that humans, with all their weaknesses and desires, made corporations function. Ads for soap and other household staples had to be made by someone, but attaching names to artwork meant diverting power from the corporation. Artists who became too well known threatened the corporate author: "It was agency policy whenever possible to eliminate the artist's signature, so as to focus attention on the advertisement itself and to hold costs down by keeping the artist anonymous longer, maintaining him or her in a merely instrumental role."[4] Even as modernists engaged in enshrining the figure of the oppressed (usually male) artistic genius as an irreplaceable, unitary, prophetic force, corporations understood the threat individuals could pose to the nascent brand. *Collier's* and *The Saturday Evening Post* could not tie their fortunes to either Leyendecker's or Norman Rockwell's.

Watson immediately comprehended the risk individual identity presented to corporate longevity. He knew that the end result of an advertising campaign should not ever be the question "whose piece of copy is it when it is finished—who wrote it?"[5] There would be no author left but a corporate one, no personal ownership in the new entity formed by and under a brand. A similar ethos was at work in another collaborative medium—animated film—on which I'll focus more in the final chapter. Just take a second to listen to two of the most famous, authoritative twentieth-century Disney animators and historians as they consider the reflexive possession each worker feels when looking at the final animated film: the "actor who did the voice is saying, 'Well, I know he's my character because he's me; I did him!' And the animator nods knowingly, because no one can deny that he set the final model and brought him to life, and the assistant knows that without his work the character would never have reached the screen. The person who selected the colours, those who painted the cels, even those who carefully checked to see if this character had all his buttons; the cameraman who shot the scenes; the sound mixer who gave the special sound to the voice—to all of them, he is *their* character! This is as it should be."[6] There speak Frank Thomas and Ollie Johnston, two of Disney's so-called "Nine Old Men," master animators responsible for guiding, writing, animating, and directing the bulk of the studio's best known output during the years roughly covering 1940–1980. The line they trace passes through only a few of the many labouring hands that touch an animated film. Their labour matters—they themselves do not. What's indispensable on the screen is "Walt Disney," initially a signifier that referred to a human being, but within a decade one that had become a brand. In what became a standard deception, the creative work, whether a concept, piece of writing, film, music, or any of the multitude of things humans invent, was at once the creation of a nameless collective expected to take pride in the work, as well as the corporation itself. The collective has touched but never possessed the artifact: only the corporation owns it.

Many years ago on an animation studio tour I witnessed a Disney animator draw a character from one of the studio's then feature films. In the audience was a child in a wheelchair. When, at the end of the demonstration, a woman approached the animator to ask if the animator might not give the drawing to the child, the animator said that was impossible. When pressed, the artist admitted somewhat sheepishly they did not have the right to give away what was not theirs. What makes sense to a corporation's legal team may be harder to explain to a child in difficult circumstances, which is why there are gift shops at the ends of tours. The ad "agency," which in reality possessed the agency given to it by humans, ultimately did become the controlling entity: this was the bigger, more forceful answer to the angst caused by modernity.

Because corporations appear to behave similarly in countries embracing full industrialization and strategic planning, it can be hard to reconcile why some nations fully welcomed fascist forms while others did less so. How did it happen that signs for generally liberal policies failed so miserably, that the signification produced by "the democratic parties in Germany tended to be of inferior value as neuropsychological signals and also were much less skillfully utilized"?[7] Without plumbing the deeper history, I'm pointing not only to the immense interwar popularity of the Ku Klux Klan and other white supremacist organizations (including American

Nazi parties), but also to widely embraced national public figures like Father Coughlin. Why was there no swastika for the moderate party? Heller hopes to answer the problem of "why the audacious visual identity of Nazi Germany was so extraordinarily effective, and how it ultimately became a textbook example—indeed, a perverse paradigm—of corporate branding."[8] The very audacity that Heller touches on is a deep part of what makes fascist presentation in interwar Italy and Germany so strikingly modern. The Third Reich's nascent brand was refined over a decade, an enormous span in a design world where a year can be a long time.

The Nazis' intention to "make it new," as genocidal and pathological as that newness might be, was initially successful. But Nazi modernism was dogged by Rosenberg and Himmler's *Völkisch* aesthetic, accompanied by a familiar past full of young wanderers traversing a bucolic countryside, occasionally meeting up with Wotan cults engaged in Nordic rituals (the more avantgarde might perform Wagnerian operas). Hitler resisted Himmler and Rosenberg's vision of the future based in a cult of romantic legends because, Spotts argues convincingly, such an image "ran directly counter to his own intention of making National Socialism the religion of the Third Reich and himself the object of unique veneration."[9] Aldous Huxley condemned Nazi art by claiming that there "are no masterpieces ... for masterpieces appeal only to a limited audience": he made the mistake of looking for individuals in ateliers and salons, of focusing on the elites, instead of admitting that the street theatre being performed night and day *was* Hitler's art masterpiece. Of all people, Huxley needed to accept, as much as it might have disgusted him, that the brand with its militarized corporate partners and the newly remade ancient logo, was the new work. If he couldn't see the art in it, it was truly unfamiliar.

Widespread corporate force produced an enormous cultural levelling. So much of canonical modernist history is a dramatic account of the supreme peaks and terrible deep valleys played out in the lives of Picasso, Woolf, Fitzgerald, Kahlo, Stravinsky, Pollock. Despite those few spectacular stories, sameness was brought about by the "war machine," the force that "completed the monopolizing thrust of each of these two-sided drives [toward corporatism and utopianism], cemented the business–government alliance, smoothing the tensions that still marked the previous decade" of the 1930s.[10] Out of the joint collision of modernity, modernism, corporatism, and elite and popular culture came a world that should look familiar to us, one both immaculately planned but full of chaos, panic, exhilaration. Today, market analysts typically identify brands that they feel can be held up as exemplars of this new genre. In Gobé's case those would include "Coca-Cola, IBM, and Mercedes," not because their products are necessarily superior (although I suspect Gobé might well argue that) but because they "are examples of successful identity programs that have withstood the test of time."[11] Gobé inadvertently supports Smith's conclusion about the war machine in that each of these brands created stable forms of corporatism that convincingly spoke modernism. All of them survived, thrived on, global war.

Coca-Cola did brisk and increasing business in the Reich, winning over a nation of steadfast beer drinkers to the American drink, bottled in Germany by Coca-Cola GmbH, which remained a German arm of the American company throughout the war. The indomitable Max Keith, who took over from his American boss, pushed his salesmen to make Coke into a popular German brand, happily associating Coke with the swastika from the 1936 Olympics onward. Keith even followed Hitler into Austria during the Anschluss and built the company's Vienna wing. When the American supply of the syrup formula 7X dried up, Keith directed his Coca-Cola workers to devise a replacement that would be an ideal, a "*Fantasie*" of a new drink. The *Fantasie*, immediately trademarked as "Fanta," sold throughout the Reich during the war, and in the West after it.[12] It has continued to be a global best seller. Keith never joined the party, and the Coca-Cola plants in Germany were handed back to the American company at the end of the war, profits intact. Despite the occasional fraudulent ad (particularly one reading "ein Volk, ein Reich, ein Getrank," a play on the Nazi's "ein Volk, ein Reich, ein Führer" slogan), Coca-Cola ads show the drink was a popular part of the Reich.

IBM's first incarnation was as the Hollerith punch card machine manufacturer, Deutsch Hollerith Maschinen Gesellschaft (shortened to DEHOMAG), which was bought by the American Computing-Tabulating-Recording Company (CTR), finally renamed IBM by the chief executive officer, Thomas Watson (no relation to the psychologist and advertiser John Watson). The Nazis used Hollerith machines for tabulation during the deportations of millions to the death camps, with specific punch card codes for the various laager as well as categories for deportation (Jewish, political prisoner, homosexual).[13] Despite IBM's adamant blanket denial of these charges levelled by Edwin Black in his deeply researched *IBM and the Holocaust* (2001), IBM has yet to demonstrate its innocence. Although it claims, as do other corporations that are seen to be on the side of the good (Ford, Coca-Cola), that it lost control over its German business operations during the war, Black has come forward repeatedly with more proof that IBM, and Watson particularly, not only knew how the machines were being used, but established a Dutch shell company to enable IBM New York to continue to work with the Reich. In the years since publication of his IBM book, Black has concluded that "at a time when the Watson name and the IBM image is being laundered by whiz computers that can answer questions on TV game shows, it is important to remember that Thomas Watson and his corporate behemoth were guilty of genocide."[14] Gobé's final example, Mercedes, needs no annotation, although the design and technological elements that made

Mercedes and Porsche wartime powers also made them leading authors of both modernity and modernist design.

Gobé's examples are united by their common history of not only surviving but prospering during and after fascism. Fascism infused Coca-Cola, IBM, and Mercedes with power. Reacting to shortages and cut off from its American parent, Coca-Cola GmbH cloned itself and promptly created a drink almost as popular as the original, even though it lacked its signature flavour. The Allied blockade against Germany brought about more, not less, wartime and post-war success for the company. IBM's record in processing data for the fastest, biggest genocide seen on the planet to that point was a testimonial to the brute-force information-handling power of the predigital computer and specifically the Hollerith punch card sorting system, used worldwide for another four decades. Brands seem to be more capable than human beings of publicly surviving their dark histories.[15] Their pasts can be scrubbed through various legal manoeuvres, reparations can be made, although that involves admitting guilt. Corporations seem less likely to admit guilt than the humans who staff them. Time is on the corporation's side as the steady erosion of memory, the gradual silencing and death of survivors, helps to bleach unwelcome stains.[16] Indication that brands and the military establishment not only coexist but also coconstitute each other is nowhere clearer than in the 2002 launch of the US military's first official video game, a first-person shooter called *America's Army* (a first-person shooter [FPS] game typically shows only the arms and gun barrel, sometimes just a gunsight or reticle for the player involved: the gamer's point of view is in the first person, with the player inserted directly into the game environment). The game was available free to all, resulting in, according to *America's Army*'s information, some thirteen million registered players who have together racked up 260 million hours of gameplay.[17] The game uses realistic training simulations so that players who might be potential recruits will be familiar with various weapons and protocols.

For brand expert Max Lenderman, the US Army not only vastly widened its exposure with the game, naturalizing contemporary battle fields, but since the game's release coincided with America's invasions of both Iraq and Afghanistan, the game solved the immediate recruitment problem. Signing up was free, but for American citizens it required providing the military with addresses, emails, and phone numbers. Lenderman salutes the Army's accomplishment, noting that "nobody makes the game come alive better than the U.S. Army," in creating "an advergaming juggernaut, an empire that is looked to enviably by the rest of the advergaming nations."[18] Lenderman's typical marketing jargon and diagnostic portmanteau word signalling the demolition of traditional boundaries between advertising and gaming looks outward to a convergent media world where a game becomes a viral organism that will colonize television screens, the web, mobile devices, existing gaming stations, leaping to other media like comics. Winning the game will be accomplished when its young players are drawn into the military itself, where they will engage in simulated, then real, combat. The line between consumption of the game, with its combination of advertising and military "core values," and consumption by the military in whole or in part, blurs. The chain of acculturation and normalization is so long that by the time the player arrives in the barracks, there will have been no point along the way where the recruits noticed themselves being coerced. They were always players; they are players still. Without a shred of irony Lenderman exhorts "marketers ... to forget going after eyeballs; it's hearts and minds they should be after."[19] Lenderman calls it like he sees, or rather, experiences it, meaning that if he needs to quote Lyndon Johnson's colonial advice about winning the war in Vietnam, he'll do it. When the planning and execution has proceeded as it should, the consumer will have been, to quote science fiction author and Vietnam veteran Joe Haldeman's famous *The Forever War* (1975), "Born, raised and drafted."[20]

It's been something of a circle to bring us to this moment when we can start to connect the many modernisms, which in turn affected both interwar cultural worlds in the United States and Germany, with military expression. As modernism grew in range and power, so too did the initially small (in Germany's case, forbidden) militaries. The remaking of heraldic systems and their connection to brands meant that the newness associated with high art flowed into the marketplace, corporate identity schemes, and back to war. It's time to consider how the United States military, in this case the ground forces, adopted, adapted to, or refused to engage in modernist design.

CHAPTER 7

ON YOUR SLEEVE

American Interwar and Wartime Patches

THE UNITED STATES' INTERWAR ADOPTION OF DEVICES that become the new heraldic shield are most visible as the distinctive unit patch or Shoulder Sleeve Insignia. The patch is the American reduction of the achievement's shield to a single statement—a military logo. The United States military continues producing whole achievements for each unit, but they are rarely seen by the public, and are rife with problems. As with corporate heraldry, the patch's job is to deliver in one graphical stroke the entirety of an identity, tying together the unit's history with its future promise. Distinctive unit and shoulder sleeve patches may be memorable to untrained viewers (perhaps an occasional war film viewer might recognize a military patch like the 101st Airborne's screaming eagle), but what those patches signify is something else. Often the images are significant to their wearers alone. Heraldic scholar Eugene Zieber concludes that an animal or image might have been adopted through happenstance, not because there was a particular intention by the designer: it might be meant "to inspire terror in the minds of his enemies" or it might be "merely from caprice."[1]

Early coats of arms, like the 81st Infantry's black bobcat, were basic signifying practices intended to separate one group from another. The meaning in much early heraldry has been lost, so contemporary viewers must beware of assigning particular connotations to various animals or shapes that appear on the achievement's shield. In Zieber's view, a camel (it might or might not signify sloth) or a fly (always buzzing into people's affairs, the fly might indicate nosiness), have no fixed meanings. Zieber also warns the viewer about the problem of historicity. An image's meaning and context may have changed wildly over the course of decades, let alone centuries. To understand an image means that interpreter must know the complete historical context, the official and unofficial connotations of each object: "The real signification of these creatures is frequently hard to ascertain," because "in former times animals and their characteristics were looked upon in a way very different from that now customary."[2] As interwar America began to close on the Second World War, the devices became much more specific and were designed to have their significations decoded, understood, recorded, and remembered. This chapter examines first, under what authority the patches were produced, and I give a slight history of that contemporary organization, The Institute of Heraldry (TIOH). I continue by looking at a selection of patches from the interwar and wartime period. Doing that work caused me to wonder to what extent the forces and public were aware of what military heraldry looked like during the war, which I explore next. Finally, I consider where heraldry is in the contemporary world.

The historical complexity governing heraldry in Great Britain and Europe was replaced in America with semiotic incoherence.

The American military of the Second World War faced the problem not only of distinguishing service arm from service arm but also unit from unit. The growing military, no longer limited to an infantry, cavalry, navy, and fledgling air force, now needed to discriminate between military specialties—artillery, engineers, scouts, military engineers, demolitions. More specialties demanded more colours. The American military tradition, such as it was in the interwar period, generally gave light blue to the infantry, yellow to the cavalry, red to the artillery, and used dark blue for the air force. Some patches' design indicates the hybrid nature of new forces: the first, second, and third armoured divisions have for insignia triangles divided equally between red, yellow, and blue, because the tank supports infantry, is a piece of rolling artillery, and was the new incarnation of the cavalry (helicopters will add to the cavalry when they are weaponized during the Vietnam war).[3] Although these basic colour codes make sense, it should also come as no surprise that the rules were almost instantly broken, although there are times when shield colours follow the general force assignation. When it came to rules, few were left over from the First World War.

The interwar forces' disorganization and lack of standardization around heraldry can be read as diagnostic of the small professional military, one forced by the Second World War to form rapidly and with little regard for other militaries' deep histories. The military that existed as a ghost of itself a few years before 1943 now bulged across the nation and beyond to the globe, fought a two-front war, and supplied its allies with the necessary materiel to continue fighting. The military inherited a habit of making up its own rules, unconcerned about what European heraldic colleges would say. The United States was much less concerned with whether they were, in Reynolds's terms, "uncouth" or not.[4] It wasn't until much later that the heraldic offices were unified and organized as they are now. The post-war organization of United

States military heraldry casts light on what had been missing in the interwar period.

When the military dissolved many of the units and disposed of their insignia after the First World War, one would think some office was left in control of the system. But the interwar military was an unusual affair: "each department was responsible for its own military symbolism program," until the whole practice was centralized under the Office of the Quartermaster General in 1924.[5] The same chaos that ruled before and during the First World War continued after it. Heraldry, as reinvented in America, was directed by "no centralized authority" that would "register, record or regulate the design and use of military symbols, or insignia." [6] Responsibility for coats of arms and unit insignia was finally created by Public Law 85-263 in 1957, which gave the Secretary of the Army the power to create a heraldic service, and lead to TIOH's creation in 1960.[7] Since 1960 the institute has guaranteed at least minimal consistency across the forces. Presently there is a full-time staff of twenty-four, including designers, researchers, and illustrators. Given the United States military's size, the institute's funding is decidedly modest: in 2006 the budget for TIOH was $2.3 million, a tiny amount when one considers that it answers to the United States Department of Defense, one of the largest employers on the planet. It's even more surprising in an era that lives by brands.[8]

We might assume that by examining TIOH's history one could determine how different design philosophies have informed the creation of patches from Vietnam to the present wars. After all, major corporate bodies usually have large public relations, communications, art, and design departments that work to shape the corporation's exterior and interior aspects. Heraldic scholar David Boven concludes otherwise: "an examination of the pattern [of designs] shows that" there has been no particular variation from the institute's directors.[9] Instead, new patches follow a generic pattern and are badly composed, cluttered and vague. Certainly research is done, with the process including "a careful study ... of the history and battle honors of the regiment. Thereafter a proposed design is made and blazon and description are written. If approved, the design is transmitted to the commanding officer of the regiment for concurrence, together with an explanation of the symbolism employed."[10] That all sounds reassuring, but at the heart of it, argues Boven, "the training of heraldic designers at the Institute is not done in any structured way."[11] Some of the institute's employees indicate just how difficult it is to get the kind of specialized education necessary for heraldic work, noting that "you have to learn the language of heraldry," with some claiming in surprise, "It all has its own language."[12] Becoming fluent in such a language is comparable to, but less difficult than, the acquisition of what London's cab drivers call the Knowledge. Unlike the unofficial but rigorous preparation London taxi drivers undergo, potential heralds have little training at all. About learning the Knowledge, one writer notes: "Actually, 'challenge' isn't quite the word for the trial a London cabbie endures to gain his qualification. It has been called the hardest test, of any kind, in the world."[13] It's curious that the United States military doesn't have some equivalent system for the people who will brand one of the few global superpower armies.

Not only is it necessary to ingest and master the different heraldic dialects developed over the last 800 years, but also to understand the difference between acceptable and good heraldry, and most of all, what constitutes good heraldic design. Good heraldry and good design aren't coterminous. Boven adds that TIOH's lack of standards and "heraldic control" means that "the work produced for American military units varies greatly," from those that are clean, functional, and attractive, to those that are "barely even useful as identification marks."[14] Despite the unevenness in the institute's productions, they do follow basic rules in keeping with Stroh's concepts of gentility when it comes to armorial utterances: good patches don't attack others based on race (Stroh doesn't specify about gender or class, but presumably these would be off limits as well), or point out the unpleasant nature of industrial warfare, no matter where one serves (patches and mottoes for nuclear, biological, or chemical warfare arms are deliberately vague). The current director of the institute, Charles Mugno, has the authority to refuse "any image that could be considered in poor taste," as well as images that would become anachronistic too quickly, pushing for design that will "stand the test of time."[15]

Boven cannot, however, contain his despair at the current state of US military heraldry. He assesses fully a fifth of TIOH's designs as too cluttered to be readable. It's one thing not to be able to read a flag until you know it, something else again not to be able to read it when you do. He points to a seemingly endless list of painful errors, taking one example of an achievement's description that "misuses ... the term 'in fess' for 'dexter' and sinister ... described [a colour field] as 'solid white' rather than 'argent,'" and improperly adds a long explanation of the achievement's signification to the work.[16] Mistakes such as these reveal an ignorance and carelessness that reach back to the first pages of heraldic lore. Boven's solution, radical as it may seem, for this and myriad other equally jejune mistakes is to recall all unit insignia, have them vetted by expert heralds and redesigned or discarded as necessary. While Boven is prepared to accept a certain untutored wildness from American heraldry, he ultimately cannot "take America's home-grown heraldic authority seriously,"[17] a sentiment shared even by the forgiving herald J. A. Reynolds, who observes lamely that "the American system, if the word is properly applicable, is certainly the loosest of all."[18] After two world wars and other undeclared, protracted military struggles, the process of military signification remains in the eye of the untutored beholder who is innocent of design expertise.

Here's a final story about work done by TIOH. Proudly describing TIOH's production of the famous blue ovals used as backdrops for military media events, military journalist Meghan Vittrup explains: "Each oval was hand-crafted at the institute. Epoxy resin was used to create the White House and Pentagon castings, while the blue background was formed using foam-core board. The oval frames were constructed of wood. Then the ovals were hand painted."[19] Closer reading, invited when we're told the ovals were executed by a "master carver," tells us that a cheap one-time resin, not metal, cast was used, with the background being made out of a mounting material (foam-core) that is a sandwich of a thin paper wrapper around (as the name suggests) a stiff plastic foam centre. These products, typically used for window displays and children's grade school projects, are not archival. The wooden frames were presumably made with the help of a band saw, jigsaw, or computer-driven cutter (CNC), then painted by hand, as opposed having someone use a spray gun. If produced as described, these pieces will last exactly as long as the glue attaching them to the foam-core backer doesn't dry out, at which point the whole assembly will collapse. They are standard disposable props made for any television ad or film shoot, designed to last only as long as necessary and not a moment longer, after which they are broken down and thrown out.

The patches I've chosen to examine are some of the earlier ones or have achieved a high degree of visibility. I have focused on ground forces to the exclusion of aviation or nautical patches in order to keep the field reasonably tight. There is an enormous range of patches in use, although the interwar army was a great deal smaller than it is at present. The contemporary American military is one of the largest, if not the largest, employers in the world. With a few exceptions I've drawn patches from the early to mid-twentieth century, and have necessarily excluded the mass. I discuss a mere eighteen patches of some more than

4,000, which are for ground forces alone, leaving out naval and air forces. Because the range is too large, I have chosen many for their recognizability even for those with little exposure to or knowledge of unit identities. As well, I have made no particular differentiation between distinctive units and in some cases whole armies. The United States Army divides its commands, as do most contemporary militaries, into a field army (in the American system, numbered) composed of a number of Corps, each of which is broken into Divisions ranging from ten thousand to eighteen thousand soldiers. The Divisions are made up of multiple Brigades formed by a number of Battalions, then Companies, Platoons, and finally Squads of four to ten men. I have drawn some patches from the Armies, most from the Divisions. I have organized my discussion more chronologically and by the imagery used, rather than by service arm. This discussion doesn't pretend to be exhaustive, quantitative, or scientific, but is rather a cultural reading of badges created in the face of a second global war. Although I discuss special insignia briefly, the recent proliferation of special operations units like the SEALs is outside my focus on interwar modernist design in the United States.

In general, Second World War ground force insignia fall into one of five classes, and can be summarized as patches that: (1) are antique; (2) have visible influences; (3) appropriate other cultural or cultures' signs; (4) are mostly serviceable and functional; (5) are modernist. First come the patches that appear to be or are antique in design and reflect an army that had not yet encountered full industrial modernity. As with the 81st Infantry's black cat, the design is rough and represents a homespun aesthetic. Because I've looked at two of these, I set the group aside. Second are the patches that have visible influences and betray their graphic heritage, whether British, Anglo-Saxon, Franco-Prussian, East or South Asian. Third are the designs that overtly take motifs or signs from other cultures. Fourth come those that are serviceable but operate purely functionally and have little apparent design intelligence to them. Some, like the Second Army's massive "2", are more complex than at first they appear. But in most cases it seems likely the insignia were created in haste and were kept in place as dictated by force of habit or cost. Finally there are the patches that are clearly new, that are informed by a fresh graphic sensibility, that break sharply with the past. These graphical shouts are stark, but also capable of subtlety. They go well beyond communicating unit information and can be decorative without being fussy. They are clean, often colloquial expressions of interwar American modernism.

1. ANTIQUE. Having considered the 81st's patch, I want to begin by briefly examining the relationship between the military and Native Americans. Illustration historian Walton Rawls notes the first use of the head of a Native American tribesman on the American-manned French-organized Lafayette Escadrille's insignia, which featured a widemouthed screaming generic Plains Native in full war bonnet headdress composed, ironically, of the colours of the American flag, feathers streaming out behind him.[20]

Since in 1916 America was not yet officially at war and could not legally field a combat unit without joining the war, the squadron flew under the French air service where the insignia (technically it was a "device," that is, one of a number of elements on the achievement's shield), says Rawls, "was subtly but

Figure 7.1: Lafayette Escadrille (1916): Camouflaged by irony.

exactly what was called for when Americans, citizens of a neutral nation, could not blatantly appear to be taking sides before their country entered the war."[21] The word "subtly" cringes, for in 1992 when Rawls's text was published, the political implications could hardly have been more problematic than if the planes had flown marked by pictures of Jim Crow or Aunt Jemima (I take this up later). The image literally shrieked for attention, evidence that the American idea of proficiency in war was best represented by one of the many peoples Americans had vanquished in the process of marching across the land and closing the frontier. Pictures of Native Americans were useful if one wanted to signify both stealth and aptitude for war because a Native American wasn't a *real* American—a Native in war bonnet was a code for Americans hiding in view. Taming America's apparent savages and exterminating or reducing millions of human beings to tenant slaves showed the force of American determination and military will. Flying a plane with the appropriated skin of a Native American stretched over it allowed Americans of European origin to believe they were fighting incognito. In many ways the same thing would happen later when both Navajo and Choctaw were pressed into service code talking during First World War, which the Navajo did again in the Second World War.[22]

I've touched on the issue of signs that become too toxic to use, as happened to the swastika in Europe and North America. Once the public has made indelible associations with certain images it is usually impossible to undo such connections. In the minds of brand specialists Anholt and van Gelder, "images [such] as gold prospectors, the Alamo and cowboys and Indians have captured the imaginations of millions, and have become so intrinsic to the idea of America that it is impossible to imagine America without them."[23] The widespread wartime use of racist Native American stereotypes by the Walt Disney Company indicates how much the Native American was considered to be a friendly ally during the Second World War. I move on from antique patches now, largely because they poorly ape British heraldry and don't further the discussion.

2. VISIBLE INFLUENCES. One insignia that declares its influences is that of the 76th Infantry (known as the Liberty Bell Division because its number is the year of American independence), with its stylized tierced shield split between the blue top third (called the "chief") and red lower division that is a combination of the fess and base (the next two tiers). What appear to be white inverted crenellations are officially known as a three-tined rake. In heraldry such a device is called a "label" and indicates to any viewer that the shield's bearer is the household's first-born son.[24]

Looking at these and other American patches it makes sense that red, white, and blue will make repeated appearances. Red and white are also are famous for signifying the United States' nineteenth-century cavalry. The small, swallow-tailed flag (a guidon—"guidon" may also refer to the standard's bearer) flown at spear-point and carried by mounted units, was typically composed of two

Figure 7.2: 76th Infantry: Good old-fashioned boredom.

bands, the upper of red and the lower of white (vexillologists describe this organization as being "red over white"). The heralds who devised the 76th's shield might have argued that they were justified in using the rake, even though the sign has one very particular meaning in British heraldry. The 76th was the "first division of the National Army" formed by the 1917 draft and became known as the "First Sons of the Nation" due to its composition.[25]

The draft was conveniently obscured by the heraldry that proposed these men were the chosen few, each with the status of favourite son. The irony deepens when we examine the Division's official cry, "Onaway." "Onaway" was supposed to have been a Chippewa (really Ojibwe) word (the Division trained on what had once been Ojibwe hunting grounds). Although the official story says that "Onaway" is an "alert cry" (it has been mistranslated as "awake") in fact there is no Ojibwe word "Onaway," despite the halfdozen towns and lakes named just that. The 76th's pseudo-mythology can be traced to Henry Wadsworth Longfellow's 1855 poem "The Song of Hiawatha," where the line "Onaway! Awake, beloved" from Hiawatha's wedding scene "led to the assumption that 'Awake' was the English meaning of Onaway"—in the end it is neither the name of an Native American princess (as has been proposed), nor rallying cry, nor word for "awake," but something whose meaning is known only, it seems, to Longfellow.[26] In some tortured way it seems fitting that the drafted sons of the nation—the first sons would presumably have been volunteers—had foisted on them a similarly fake adoptive cry that was a colonialist appropriation of a mistranslated word taken from a suppressed people against whom genocide had been waged. The unit identity's myth crumples under the burden of all these misunderstandings, misappropriations, mistranslations, misuses of form. What remains is a graphically exhausted image that has little new to offer those forced to wear it.

For some older patches, like the 1925 design for the 9th Infantry Division, there are clear heraldic reasons for the insignia. Again there is the red over white tradition of the cavalry guidon. The 9th Infantry roundel repeats those colours and later used white for the numerals on the 9th's Second World War-era flag.[27]

The common "-foil" suffix used to describe flowers in heraldry is derived from the anglicization of the French "feuille" for "leaf." A quatrefoil or cinquefoil is a flower with four or five leaves, respectively. An indication of how fluid significations could be, this patch became known as the "flower power" (as well as the "psychedelic cookie") patch during the Vietnam war, turning the military's own signifying against it.

As the decoration's name suggests, the four-leaf design (here doubled), produces a flower. The eight petals are in this case called "brothers" to the central white bullet, the ninth of the Division's title. The pattern—clean, balanced, striking—has more in common with East Asian than Anglo-Saxon design. The flower possesses the directness and elegance of many Japanese *mon* or heraldic family crests. Most often framed in a roundel, *mon* frequently depict a natural object (flora, fauna, stylized

Figure 7.3: 9th Infantry: Leaves from another book.

elements like water, fire) and are almost without exception graphically attractive. Arguably the Japanese had already won the signification war before the Second World War started, drawing on centuries of sophisticated, disciplined, elegantly reduced graphical expressions. Heraldic scholar Guido Rosignoli concludes that the Japanese were (I would add "are") "masters of iconography," adopting "a series of simple, understandable badges."[28] While the 9th Infantry badge can be recognized for its Anglo-Saxon decorative heritage, with the quatrefoil suggesting the House of York's rose,

Figure 7.4: Saga prefecture flag: Same flower, different tree.

Figure 7.5: US Fifth Army: Old signs for new.

it is closer in spirit to Japanese signs that had existed for hundreds of years, ones not unlike the image on the flag of the Japanese prefecture Saga.[29] Saga's camphor tree flower has only six petals, but the design fundamentals are the same.[30]

There is equal irony in other designs, such as that of the Fifth Army, which caused some consternation recently.

The patch bears the silhouette of a sort of mosque, requested specifically by General Mark Clark, who wanted to reflect the Army's beginnings in French Morocco in 1942. The mosque occasioned some cultural panic when, during the United States wars in Iraq and Afghanistan, people wondered what a mosque was doing on a Christian nation's flag. The question drew a response from the blog Medium Cool explaining the image's history.[31] The generic quality of the mosque silhouette speaks to the overall lack of interest America had in Morocco. There is sufficient feeling in the form to make it recognizable to a westerner, who wouldn't see a problem with the confused architecture or shape of the dome. While the patch's colours again vividly represent the American flag, they are also close to being complementary, which makes the patch vibrate unpleasantly in the eye. Each colour generates its opposite: the orange red creates blue in the eye while the blue makes the same orange red. The result is that the edges and interior of the blue seem to shimmer and bounce erratically when looked at for any long period. It can be a headache-inducing problem.

One of the technical difficulties in tracing the origins of type styles that appear on the patches is that type books, which are like samplers of different typefaces, can be hard to find. Unless one has access to a large archive of type books, finding a specific typeface, let alone font, may be impossible. The same typefaces may appear in two places under different names and be of uncertain origin. It may be useful to recall some terms about type, starting with the difference between typeface and font. A typeface refers to a single design that is a unified vision of letters, numbers, special non-alphabetical characters both in upper and lower case, such as Helvetica or Garamond. The typeface is a whole family. Most popular typefaces have many iterations, called fonts. A Helvetica font is one particular fixed example of that typeface. As the word "font" suggests, letters were for hundreds of years cast in metal. A font taken from the forge would have had specific, unchanging characteristics. It would belong to a typeface (Helvetica), and have its line weight measured in points (usually between a minimum of five points—depending on the font the physical letter might have been a few millimeters high—to a maximum of about 72 points), with particular height, width, thickness, and orientation to the baseline (if it leans rightward to the baseline, it's probably italic). Specifying 12 point Helvetica regular (sometimes "book") is to speak of a font, a set of metal pieces, that are permanently fixed at 12 points in the regular Helvetica weight. Because the font is regular, it cannot also be italic or bold. An entirely different font would be required to set words in 12 point Helvetica bold italic, which would be permanently fixed with those characteristics.

Whether set by hand or machine (like linotype), the physical pieces don't change. Digital word processing has blurred typographic terminology. Gathering together all the varied Helvetica fonts in size (8 to 72 point), by weight (regular, bold), orientation (roman, italic) with special characteristics (outline, expanded or extended, condensed), these collectively compose the Helvetica typeface. Typefaces are also divided into serif and sans serif. The serif is the small flange or stroke that is added to the end of each letter's arm: those typefaces without that stroke are without (sans) serif. There are many subsets of each, including the so-called "slab serif," as well as "grotesque" fonts (typically plain, bold, modernist sans serifs), and the now rarely used gothic or black letter typefaces that recall medieval texts' complex, often unreadable, letterforms. Black letter typefaces are still used to give a newspaper (even a digital version) a sense of age. *The New York Times*, *L. A. Times* and *San Francisco Chronicle* all set their names in black letter typefaces.

The American Fifth Army patch shows a modernist typeface that is probably either Futura, released in 1927 by the famous German type designer and philosopher Paul Renner, or Twentieth Century, type designer Sol Hess's 1937 American response to Futura. No matter which, the patch creator modified the A's bar, raising it so as to make space for the design's elements (typically a large capital letter indicates the service—in this case, Army).[32] While each of the patch's devices is relatively clean, the overall effect suffers from congestion, with each piece squeezing uneasily over or into the other. The A presses uncomfortably near the mosque's peak, the 5 is too close to the A itself, and the two white figures seem unnaturally crammed inside the silhouette. If one drew the baseline through the A's feet, it would precisely divide the 5's bowl—an unsuccessful attempt by the designer to rationalize placement of the 5 (aligning scattered forms on an invisible grid in space is a common way of giving the eye an easy way to understand a complex image). The colours shout at the eye, and the shield's irregular hexagon causes the eye more confusion. While the piece reflects a number of modernist impulses, its graphic focus is on the mosque as seen by Western eyes—it's classic orientalism.

3. APPROPRIATION. One patch that caused distress during the interwar years was that of the 45th Infantry Division. It is one of a number that appropriate signs from other cultures' and peoples' religions, design histories, and sensibilities—in this case the swastika's thousands of years of Middle Eastern and Asian heritage as a sign of both sun and good luck. While we could argue that the Fifth Army patch is a graphic appropriation, the mosque's silhouette isn't a quotation of Middle Eastern design but is instead a caricature of how the West sees the East. To appropriate a Middle Eastern design would be to take, unchanged, some of the mathematically and visually complex, interlocking patterns seen in wall and floor mosaics. The 45th Infantry patch, however, with its clockwise armed swastika precisely like of the National Socialist German Worker's Party, meant trouble.

It's an intriguing failure of signification. The 45th's gold swastika was said to be composed of the four corners' states, with each arm representing one of Colorado, Oklahoma, New Mexico, Arizona. The similarity of the patch to the Nazi banner is striking, complete with rotated square (if not emblem) and red ground. By mid 1939 the Division admitted graphic defeat at Nazi hands and withdrew the insignia. It would be good to report that the Division took

Figure 7.6: 45th Infantry Division, interwar patch: One (in)appropriation for another.

a new tack, but it immediately moved to appropriate a thunderbird as the new sigil. The military's flexibility in handling the contradiction reflects its power: it might have been beaten, but there were few better ways of showing strength to a new enemy than by reminding an old one that it, its gods, rituals, and symbols had all been suborned for the conqueror's purposes. The stylized yellow thunderbird silhouette placed precisely where the swastika had been was more bad news politically.

There is a much larger discussion to be had about the way the American military appropriated and continues to appropriate Native American signs; I take on only a small piece of that here. Some examples are blatant, such as the Native American head on the 2nd Infantry's shield (similar to the Lafayette Escadrille's sigil), borrowed from the image on a five dollar (half-eagle) gold coin struck during Teddy Roosevelt's presidency—the patch remains unchanged today. Similarly the silhouetted tomahawk head merged with a peace pipe used by the XIX Corps replaced the original mission bell design derived from bells famous in the American Southwest. The third iteration of the patch, a different, black-handled tomahawk on a blue ground with a red feather attached, became the preferred insignia.

Figure 7.7: XIX Corps: Which man's army?

The mission bell was traded for the new tomahawk because Eisenhower requested a design for the XIX Corps that was particularly American. Without irony or reflexivity Stein notes that "the tomahawk is one of the most American symbols."[33] Few signs could be less about a country fashioned from new ideas and more about self-creation through genocide. Taking a defeated enemy's central cultural emblem and declaring it to be essential to one's own identity is a partial answer to the question of why American signification lagged so badly behind that of the Nazis. American brand-making was unfocused and riddled with internal conflict. Other signs are fascinatingly absent from the patches: the Pilgrim's hat, Civil War slouch forage cap, Liberty Bell, Conestoga wagon, flintlock musket—most of these never appear.

4. FUNCTIONAL. Some famous patches are simple and direct. However, simplicity does not itself make for modernism. These signs get the basic job done, serving as blunt battlefield markers. Many seem to be in keeping with the impulse to bare identification that had Civil War soldiers tying coloured bands to their clothing. The most obvious example of pure functionality is the insignia for the 1st Infantry Division known by its nickname, "The Big Red One."

The number is an unremarkable serif in red on an olive drab ground. All patches come in two versions: a brightly coloured parade ground version that appears on dress uniforms or in the homeland barracks, the other, known as the "subdued" patch, is used on what are now called battle dress uniforms (BDUs) meant to be worn in the field. These desaturated patches are intended, ironically, to limit

Figure 7.8: 1st Infantry Division: Basic math.

the amount they identify troops so as not to target them for the enemy. They render the original design in camouflage colours appropriate to the battlefield landscape—olive drab, black, dark green, khaki, grey, white. In Vietnam, American troops had to learn not to salute officers in the field, since doing so often resulted in their being sniped. The corollary was that unpopular officers were often deliberately saluted. Reducing rather than emphasizing hierarchy became the new form of camouflage. As well, shiny dog tags could endanger their wearers, not just because they reflected light but because of the telltale clinks they gave off in the jungle. The grunts' typical battlefield modification was to tape the tags together and rub Vietnam's red laterite soil on the tape, rendering the tags unreadable.

The subdued jungle or forest Big Red One patch is black on dark green. The number is the most powerful thing about the Big Red One, something emphasized by herald Barry Stein, who writes that the 1st Division was "the first to land in France, the first at the front ... first to attack, the first to make a raid ... first to inflict casualties."[34] The hammering "firsts" underscore how dangerous it was to be assigned to the Division. Where the patch wasn't initially notable, the Division's actions made it so over time. It became what its signifier suggests—the one. It is the original, where signifier, signified, and referent all come together. Because of the Division's bloody history (some five thousand dead during the First World War alone), the number also took on the sensibility of a wound. Soldiers bearing a permanent bloody patch became a perpetual reminder of the Division's history.

The mythic account of boys becoming experienced, veteran men through their wartime suffering is recognizable to readers of Stephen Crane's modernist *Red Badge of Courage* (1895), an observation about early industrial battle. Crane's Henry Fleming first loses then finds his battlefield courage by uniting with soldiers wearing bloody bandages. The Big Red One's patch similarly promises heroic personhood. In 1980 Second World War veteran and film director Samuel Fuller released his war epic *The Big Red One*; it seemed to be a cultural remnant from the war epics of the 1960s and 1970s (*The Longest Day* [1962], *Battle of the Bulge* [1965], *The Battle of Britain* [1969], *Patton* [1970], *Midway* [1975], *A Bridge Too Far* [1977]). The film told what in the post-Vietnam years looked like an anachronistic story about a cowardly young man, played by *Star Wars'* newly famous Mark Hammill, who undergoes *Red Badge of Courage* Henry Fleming's initiation into war trauma.[35]

I would argue that *Star Wars* (1977) nicely bridges the gap between the classic Second World War epics and a generation ready for newly redefined space operas and war films. *Star Wars* doesn't create anything that hadn't been seen in countless Second World War action comedy-dramas where the Nazis, with the exception of their psychotic leader, are all gullible fools, and farm boys prove to be natural combatants and war an excellent tonic for personal growth. Where Francis Ford Coppola was making thoughtful, critical films like *The Rain People* (1969) and *The Conversation* (1974) and war operas like *Apocalypse Now!* (1979), Lucas left behind the complex societal problems pictured in his *THX 1138* (1971), and signed on with a vengeance to the postwar American myth of the Great Generation and just-cause wars. If America's experience in Vietnam had briefly turned the cultural tide against war, Fuller's *The Big Red One* marked the resurgence of belief that combat produces true masculinity. The film also coincided with Ronald Reagan's arrival in office and the renewal of the Cold War as presented on screen by the *Rambo* (1982–2008) and *Missing in Action* (1984–1988) franchises, *Firefox* (1982) and *Top Gun* (1986). Fuller's *Big Red One* reminded audiences about the importance of primacy, which continued to be associated with heroic deeds and a refusal to quit. By the time the Second World War was finished, the Big Red One's patch meant more than just a plain badge: it was a sign of willingness to persist and die, if necessary, in staggering numbers. The troops didn't hesitate to provide their own caustic version of the Division's nickname, calling it "The Bloody One" and "The Big Dead One," a somewhat different perspective than the military's.

While other patches are similarly plain, some, like the Second Army's insignia, border on the kind of visual play we will see in overtly modernist designs. The powerful, blocky 2 comes from a typeface called a slab serif, where the serifs are often as thick as the characters' arms or stems (many serifs are only small ticks at the letters' ends). In slab serifs, the ends boldly anchor each character in the font. Once more the colours are the familiar cavalry guidon's red over white, placed on a dark green ground that intensifies both.

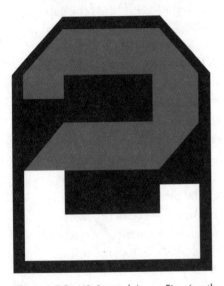

One consistency between this and other early patches is the unusual hexagonal tag shape that we saw above in the Fifth Army's badge. In this case the hexagon neatly fits the 2, suggesting that with the goal of standardization in mind, the shape might have been unsuccessfully adapted

Figure 7.9: US Second Army: Figuring the groundwork.

to the Fifth Army's patch. This particular slab serif, familiar in the last few decades as a version of Player or Campus, has become associated with college athletics, as the typeface names suggest. From the 1960s onward, typefaces like Superstar, Princetown (presumably deliberately misspelled so as to avoid a law suit from the school itself), Allstar, and Collegiate became more than large, clear letterforms marking athletic jerseys intended to be read at a distance, and instead serve as a generic sign for college life. What was once largely functional became a style.

This early version is distinguished by its unusual crossbar: in many typefaces the downstroke from the 2's upper to lower bowl is a diagonal that drops from the character's middle right to bottom left side. In this case the form is resolutely square, more so even than famous early modernist slab serifs like Rockwell and Stymie. This typeface's blocky industrial look matches the intriguing visuals that occur at the character's centre. Because the colour split lines up with the horizontal crossbar, the character appears to pop back and forth in space. It looks as though the character has been folded in half, as if we're looking at two different faces, one coloured red and the other white. Perhaps if the top were unfolded (where the red and white meet) we'd see it had a white back, or if the bottom opened out we'd see red on the character's other side. Which is the foremost part of the number—the upper or lower half? Longer light waves (warm colours) are supposed to advance and appear nearer in the human eye, which would make the red dominant. But the stark white against the dark green ground is visually arresting as well. The appearance of a fold raises the figure above mere functionality and suggests the kind of perceptual game that is one signature of graphic modernism.

5. THE NEW. Some of the simplest patches hold the most complex surprises: one such is the First Army's large black A, part of some unidentified sans serif grotesque font set on an inverted white-over-red-guidon-coloured ground. The A, boxed in by a narrowing almost coffin-like trapezoid, suggests a new design sensibility. Instead of picking any large grotesque face's A, a letter typically formed by leaning one slanting arm against another to create a point, the military chose this singular form.

Figure 7.10: US First Army: Block letters.

The A appears in a number of variations for other services. In each case the A's counter (any letter's enclosed space), is modified to indicate the military specialty. A counter filled with red means the artillery, yellow for the cavalry, gold for the quartermaster; in some cases another geometric shape is added between the A's legs (a red, white, and blue roundel for the Air Service). I can find no particular origin for this character, no typeface or font from which it might have been taken. More likely someone drew the letter and then the unusual boxy shape around it. In some ways the form seems to owe more to the late nineteenth than early twentieth century. The character's broad shape is reminiscent of decorative fonts that appeared on hand-lettered posters, particularly those art nouveau fonts based on Charles Rennie MacIntosh's lettering, or on similar high-waisted fonts like Gustav Schroeder's Eccentric (1881). Other graphical cousins point to the Wiener Werkstätte's typography. The wide, unusual top bar borrows more from something floral and organic like designer O. Weisert's famous 1904 Arnold Böcklin than from a typical grotesque sans serif like Erbar (about 1922) and Rudolf Koch's Kabel (roughly 1927). Nothing of the decorative remains. The form is relentlessly spare, stripped of all adornment, barely recognizable as the letter A when rendered on fabric.

It is much closer in sensibility to the font used on the 1910 packaging and advertising for Kaffee HAG's caffeine-free coffee, where we see the A's familiar near-solid block.[36] The letter's flat top may be recognizable from the nineteenth century, but the character's final form owes more to the Dutch modern school known as De Stijl ("The Style"), whose star designer Theo van Doesburg's 1919 nameless near-cubist typeface was based on a square divided into twenty-five smaller squares.[37] The First Army's insignia can be seen as a perfect piece of modernism. It rationalizes and destroys art nouveau's romance while maintaining the striking visual quality of a letter that almost isn't one at all, its odd container emphasizing its density and force.

Compared to British heraldry the insignia might seem tediously quotidian, but its starkness looks ahead to much American and German modernist interwar design. Steven Heller concludes that graphics like these are "simple, timeless and readily identify the organization."[38] What appears to be design can, however, be accident. Hitler's infamous brown shirts came about because the material was cheap and abundant. There was nothing special about the material—not at first. Its use by anti-Semitic, racist, homophobic fascists was what made the colour terrible. Perhaps the First Army's A is the product of yet another of many utilitarian design decisions made out of necessity. Heller argues that since "Modernism" (he doesn't specify the type, country or time period for his modernism) found its ideals in the purity of basic geometric forms like the square, the First Army's A could be close to perfection.[39]

Similarly unusual and revealing a variety of influences is the Seventh Army's famous pyramid. The original patch was unadorned, but subsequent variations made the graphic more discursive in form and philosophy. Like most patches for the US Army, the number inheres in the design. Here the seven steps on either side of the triangle give the Army's number. The patch soon became known to the troops as "Seven Steps to Hell," an unofficial subtitle that was added to the sleeve immediately below

Figure 7.11: Seventh Army without later variations: Heralding military sacredness.

the triangle. The words appeared on an embroidered strip that ran the width of the patch's base, and in either gold, or gold and red, read "Seven Steps to Hell," with the final two words rendered in red. The seven-step pyramid is drawn in gold over blue: both the gold design and overall insignia shape spell A for Army. Other Armies, particularly the Fourth and Eighth, include a number (the Fourth is a four-leaf clover, with each leaf taking an A shape; the Eighth has a series of triangular A forms that fit together to make up the insignia's octagonal, somewhat propeller-like pattern of alternating red and white).

The badge's red, gold, and blue signify, as is true for early armoured units, the combination of three ground forces: infantry (blue), cavalry (yellow or gold), and artillery (red). The overall patch was later nicknamed the "Pyramid of Power." Although the badge appears to have been influenced by Native American designs, the steps took on clear Christian meaning when the patch gained its "Hell" subtitle. A second alteration came in 1957 when the Army was reorganized. A small, whimsical, blue cloud outlined in silver and reading "7th Heaven" appeared floating above the triangle's right shoulder. The second modification was officially acknowledged and wound up tacitly legitimizing the first. Soldiers wore them both. In a way the patch became its own achievement, although not one recognized by any British heraldry officials. It contains a war credo, an explanation of the religious cosmogony of the war world bounded by heaven and hell, where combat presumably pushes the enemy down to hell and raises the believer up the battlefield steps to salvation. The final design is cluttered but unique. The overall form may be unwieldy, blocky, as are so many of the interwar or early Second World War patches, but it passes the vexillogical test that once seen, it will be remembered. All the elements, colours, shapes, numbers, have their own meanings—the patch compresses much information into a small, pure geometric space.

Taking its cues from the deceptively simple geometries found in Asian design, the 69th Infantry's patch works with interlocked red and blue figures (the 29th Infantry's badge is the yin-yang symbol that, curiously, does away with the two small centre dots of opposite shades that make it an expression of harmony). The central silver line not only separates the 6 from the 9, but also becomes the patch's outer binding. The result is a sinuous silver strip flowing through and around the design: it is a clever combination of numbers, infantry colours, and interlocking reversible forms. Figure–ground relationships that rely on the brain's difficulty grasping intricate tessellated forms allow the viewer to perceive the 6 and 9 together or alternately as each jumps off its ground and highlights the other. Are we looking at a red 6 on a blue ground, or a blue 9 on a red ground, or an equal interlocking of the two? If we focus on the silver dividing line we may lose sight of the whole. Colour theory says we will see the longer-wavelength colour red first, then the shorter blue, but our eyes may jump to the silver "S" at the form's centre. The patch is geometrically clean and has the kind of elegance common to contemporary figure–ground logos like Apple's Macintosh profile-frontal smiling faces, the FedEx word mark with its embedded forward arrow occupying the negative space between the "E" and "x," and the

Figure 7.12: 69th Infantry Division: Three ways of seeing.

Figure 7.13: 71st Infantry: Futurist angles.

Formula 1 logo that suddenly reveals a white "1" on its black ground to the viewer.

The 69th's badge is a new graphic statement, thoroughly different from any nineteenth-century sentiment, firmly set in a world of compact, spare designs that keep the eye in motion. The graphic solution could have been a plain sans serif 69 on a basic ground. Instead the outcome is arresting, unique, perceptually puzzling and intriguing, shunning decoration in favour of linear forms that demand our attention.

Another new form is the 71st Infantry Division's forward leaning patch known as "the Red Circle" because of its border.

The graphic is all motion, pushing rightward and up. The "1" cannot be contained by the border, and we see only part of the 7's angle—neither character has a baseline. The negative space between the two numbers makes another 7, another chevron that moves the eye outward, while the white bar inside the blue lines causes the colours to vibrate excitedly. We meet the insignia already engaged, always advancing, seeing it as if through a telescope lens. The clarity and attractiveness of the design are enhanced by its instability. The arrow, as in the FedEx logo, is a useful modernist shorthand for speed and movement, a trick made notable by the Wrigley's Doublemint chewing gum logo with its two-headed red arrow, indicating twice the value in one package. The 71st's ball logo will be quoted decades later by Union Oil of California (Unocal), and repeated in the 1932 "76" brand of gasoline (originally named for The Spirit of '76, and earlier based on Phillip's famous "66" logo that dates from 1928) which evolved into a stark white-outlined blue 76 wrapped around a bright attention-getting orange ball.[40]

Of the insignia that have become famous largely because of the battlefield accomplishments, few are as well known as the first Airborne Division, the 82nd Infantry. Created during the First World War, the 82nd wouldn't be physically airborne until 1942. The back-to-back double A originally stood for "All American" since the Division was composed of units drawn from across the lower forty-eight states. The so-called Airborne "tab" (the blue arch subtending the

Figure 7.14: 82nd Infantry: Wings before flight.

red shield) was added during the Second World War, and the Division was mocked by the other then-Airborne 101st Infantry (the "Screaming Eagles") as being "Almost Airborne."

As with so many of the patches, the colours quote the American flag, but have the pleasing simplicity of a roundel inside a square. The unusual "A" form looks ahead to Herbert Lubalin's famous 1970 retro-gothic font Avant Garde (originally the word mark for a magazine of the same name, then a few years later a wildly popular typeface), known for its signature characters that lean in different directions. The 82nd's A, like the First Army's, initially seems to have much in common with the previous century, its rounded arms leaning over from art nouveau organic forms seen on poster designs that bridged the nineteenth and twentieth centuries. The striking back-to-back As proved fortuitous when the Division became airborne, since the letters formed stylized wings. The eye struggles to close the bottom of the open circle and complete the design symmetry—if the As' lower arms connected at the bottom, the circle would nearly be quartered. As with the swastika, *Prägnanz* keeps the image in motion as the eye persists in following the unconnected lines in order to resolve the graphical phrase. A short time contemplat-

ing the form causes the letters to shift, to become a set of related abstract shapes. The very lightness of the letters' strokes makes the design that much more effective. This is no blocky, crude letterform but instead an elegant logo in motion, something that is stable at its core only because one half rests on the other, a fitting logo for a Division that brought together the country's diverse population. It is another quintessential piece

Figure 7.15: 89th Infantry Division: Your vision depends on you.

of modernist design that puts function first, but finds much play and pleasure in the form. The added tab gives the whole the sense of an inverted shield, a welcome change from the attempt (as with the 76th Infantry's confused shield and rake) to ape older heraldic forms.

Graphically similar to the fusion of organic art nouveau forms and geometric modernist solutions of the 82nd Division is the insignia for the 89th Infantry, another unit formed during the First World War that went on to see much Second World War service.

The roundel, with its familiar flag colours, is known as "the rolling W." The patch may strike viewers differently: some will see the white forms as connected "V's" that form a "W," or even a Bishop's miter; others may focus on the blue ground, seeing in it a fragment of a cathedral, stained-glass window, or piece of architecture. Because the Division was initially formed by soldiers drawn from the Midwest (Kansas, Missouri, Colorado), contemporary interpreters argue that there are both a capital "W" for "West" and, when rolled 180 degrees, "M" for "Middle." More meaning was attached later when the military realized that the Divisions' first three commanders' names all began with W (Major Generals William Wright, Leonard Wood, and Frank Winn).[41] Herald Barry Stein further advances the somewhat strained interpretation that the W could also be the Greek upper-case sigma resting on its side (sigma is used in math to indicate summation, which Stein interprets as completion; were Stein to pursue the mathematical interpretation he would be forced to add that sigma is also used in statistics to indicate the standard deviation—the norm—presumably not the effect a designer was after). We can't know if any of these meanings were intended. The patch's strength comes from the fact that viewers can cause it to mean a number of things. Usage, not design, dictates interpretation. The sign's graphic power is clear. It is an intriguing use of basic geometric forms that become more complex because of their interrelationship. The badge is easily repeated but is fresh. The fact that the sign supports multiple possible significations underlines its popularity: it can be remade, without becoming too outlandish, to mean more than what was probably first intended, creating an interpretative community around it.

Few patches are as recognizable as the 101st Airborne's Screaming Eagle (the unit's official name), both of which are rooted in the nineteenth century. While the 82nd Infantry's reflected double A broke new graphic ground, the 101st's insignia seems very familiar. Birds of prey are historically a popular device for badges, flags and insignia, appearing at various times on the heraldry of the Roman Empire, the Habsburg monarchy, Serbia, Poland, Austria, Russia, and Germany. The United States' version, with its striking white on black, gold beak and red tongue, makes a strong colour combination that avoids the typical red, white, and blue.

The insignia comes with a full charge of meaning, most of which is apocryphal or overtly mythological. According to two sources, one of which is the United States Army, the eagle motif is taken from an actual eagle named Old Abe. Thanks again to Native Americans (in this case a Chippewa, that is, an Ojibwe) Chief

Figure 7.16: 101st Infantry: A story to scream over.

Ahgamahwegezhig (Chief Sky) trapped two eaglets. One (Old Abe) was bought by a Union militia captain early in the Civil War and carried into battle tethered to a perch. C Company of the 8th Wisconsin Volunteer Infantry Regiment became the "Eagle Regiment" on adopting Old Abe as a mascot.[42] Old Abe became a national symbol when, in 1921, the bird's head in profile became the source for the 101st Infantry's patch.

While the United States Army proposes this as known history, heraldist and insignia manufacturer Barry Stein prefaces the whole tale with the caveat emptor "the story goes . . . ."[43] The black shield, relatively rare in itself, is presumed to refer to the Iron Brigade, a collection of infantry divisions that adopted Old Abe as their mascot. The insignia gathered power during the Second World War when the 101st participated in famous battles: until its relief by Patton the Unit held Bastogne during the Battle of the Bulge. The whole semi-mythological narrative of a chief who hands down a bird of rare spirit and iconic power (a Confederate general seeing Old Abe on his perch in battle was said to have declared "that bird must be captured or killed at all hazards, I would rather get that eagle than capture a whole brigade or a dozen battle flags"), a bird dragged into some thirty-six battles until the war was over, is the kind of rich, entirely unreliable history that supports the creation of memorable logos.[44]

What's important about the Screaming Eagles' patch is the story, not the design. It is the narrative that gives the patch such signifying weight. The chain of fables, from eaglet to cranky Civil War general to battlefield mascot that works as a good luck charm, is as bankrupt as those surrounding the 76th and its "Onaway" battle cry. When all are brought together they produce a useful lustre to shine up any story needing framing or reframing. Commentary on narrative power comes in a typically charming way from Damon Runyon's nameless narrator when he is hustled for money at the racetrack. Determined not to have "the bite" put on him by Hot

Horse Herbie, the narrator refuses Herbie's racing tip. "'Now,' says Herbie, 'wait a minute. A story goes with it,' he says." The narrator immediately changes his mind: "Well, of course, this is a different matter entirely. I am such a guy as will always listen to a tip on a horse if a story goes with it. In fact, I will not give you a nickel for a tip without a story, but it must be a first-class story."[45] Runyon's cleverness in capturing the particular New York grifter locutions is outdone by his understanding of the way oral cultures operate and the joy people take in telling and hearing stories they know very well have little, if any, relationship to fact.

As well known as the 101st's Screaming Eagle is the 1st Cavalry's horse head. The 1st Cavalry's patch was burned into the popular consciousness during the Vietnam war when the unit became the first mass mobile helicopter assault force. The shield, with the diagonal stripe known in heraldry as a "bend" (in this case

a "bend dexter") and what is intended to be a thoroughbred horses' head, dates from 1922.[46]

There is an intriguing quality to this patch that is neither completely antique nor fully modern. It has the direct impact of some of the first shields dating back hundreds of years in British heraldry. For centuries the horse was the exemplar of mobile power and status. Having the resources to train and use a horse for combat meant the rider was literally above the unmounted around him. The

Figure 7.17: 1st Cavalry: Stalled between times.

1st Cavalry's patch came to be more about technological mastery when it was adopted for helicopter units in Vietnam. The Vietnamese had never seen helicopters, and they envied the US military that possessed them. Here was the new mounted force, announcing itself with a sign at once historical and threatening.

One of the newer patches has been considered by soldiers to be a bizarre addition to the heraldic order. But consistency has made the patch, ugly as it may be, into a familiar icon. The infamous Tropic Lightning patch, used by the 25th Infantry in the Pacific Islands and then in Vietnam, is an overt piece of modernism. It is unlike anything that preceded it, clearly an attempt to break new design ground.

Known by the troops as the electric strawberry, the Tropic Lightning design might have looked reasonable on paper, but when rendered in fabric, crumpled and distorted by wear, the results could be particularly unsightly. The Division got its nickname from its quick movements from island to island in the Pacific war. The yellow lightning bolt framed by what was supposed to read as a red taro leaf was overly bright and without any graphic charm. In Vietnam tank commander Dwight Birdwell's eyes, "it was the ugliest damn patch in the combat zone and was mocked .... I had thoughts of staying in the army and didn't want to be sentenced

Figure 7.18: 25th Infantry Division: Design short circuits.

to wearing that unheroic blob on my right shoulder as my combat patch for the rest of my military career."[47] It's an indication of how important the patches are that Birdwell considers joining another unit because of the insignia. Despite his extreme distaste for the patch, however, he signs on with the 25th. He may hate the electric strawberry but the patch is an unforgettable reminder of the Division's history, its longevity and stability in world of chaos that is armed combat. Heller notes that "an unchanged insignia lends to its legitimacy, just as the attributes it portrays are regarded as timeless; no fashion trends, political winds, or personal taste should be allowed to override established work."[48] As bad as the brand sign is, abandoning it may be worse; better to stick with something ugly and recognizable than to begin again and have to manufacture a new history.

It may be difficult to imagine, awash as we are now on vast seas of information, how little American soldiers, military non-combatants, and civilians during the Second World War, knew of United States military heraldry. Communication about the military's patches was nonexistent. The public mostly didn't know and hadn't seen the colours. The solution to the problem of spreading the news is proleptic of what happened with this part of the propaganda war overall: it was relegated to the private sector. Unlike the Nazi sign system, which was unavoidable wherever Nazis or their images travelled by newsreel or photograph, the United States' military system was invisible. Not so with the swastika, a graphic that worked almost as well in black and white reproduction as it did in full colour. Ignorance of the unit patches meant the United States had failed in part to lay groundwork on which the Nazis could rely: German civilians were daily implicated in the military.

Surely it's a good thing that, when comparing communication in a democracy to that inside an authoritarian dictatorship, we find democracy's system is less efficient, less successful. On the other hand, the United States had a war to fight, and the Second World

War was to that moment its greatest expenditure. I return to this slightly later on, but recall that by 1945 the government had undergone six major bond drives to keep the war going. The seventh bond drive's target was an astonishing $14 billion dollars, or what James Bradley, son of one of the Mount Suribachi flag-raising survivors, was to characterize as "a mountain of money that must have seemed as formidable, in its own way, as Suribachi."[49] The amount represented roughly $100 for every human then alive in the United States, at a time when, as Bradley notes, a family of four lived well on $1,700 a year. What raised the money, finally, was a perfectly organized propaganda tour with three of Suribachi's living heroes, who travelled on a carefully planned bond drive that "combined the old-fashioned elements of vaudeville, the county fair, the Fourth of July Parade."[50] To imagine that Americans gave without persuasion is to ignore the reality of "an effort by the government to communicate face-to-face with as many of its citizens as possible, and to make its case for voluntary sacrifices," which Bradley intriguingly considers to be "a gargantuan feat of popular democracy."[51]

Information about the war isn't enough to convince people to sacrifice for it. Information needs to be transformed into a convincing narrative that will compel pledges and donations. This particular fundraiser was driven by photographer Joe Rosenthal's remarkable images, famously made and remade as the day on Iwo Jima wore on, of the five Marines and one Navy corpsman raising first one flag, then a larger one. That the flag raisers are misidentified, that the act of raising the flag was too good a photo opportunity to miss, that it had to be repeated until it produced the best shot, that the photograph unusually won the Pulitzer Prize the same year, all are apparently just part of a democratic communication process. In the end, it was a show that people paid to enter and in which they could participate. What's important is that for James Bradley, who researched the specifics of the seventh bond drive in which his father was a key player, people joined freely, as opposed to what he calls the simple confiscation of money carried out by fascist regimes. Part of the great success of the United States propaganda campaign was that having been shown precisely how it worked as he wrote about it in the 1990s, Bradley is still convinced no coercion was involved.

Where the Nazis understood about educating the public and deeply implicating them in the war, the United States military engaged in similar manoeuvres in different ways. Understanding that the public needed to see and have a feel for its military, to be able to read the code book the military used to identify itself, Gilbert Grosvenor at the National Geographic took matters into the hands of private enterprise. Even as America joined the Second World War, there were no guides to the services' patches, let alone graphic standards for them. It was long-time editor of the *National Geographic* magazine Gilbert Grosvenor who took on the job of reporting to the public what the military's signs meant. In a famous June 1943 *Geographic* issue Grosvenor printed dozens of badges in colour. Until that time only command, the soldiers, and the people working in concert with the army understood the military's codes. Even inside the military it could be a closed book—soldiers and civilians might know about one unit, but not all of them together because it had all grown haphazardly. The *Geographic* had already been at work supporting the war, "marked by the same patriotic fervor as in World War I. Once again it published detailed maps, placed one major war-related article in every issue, and established a semiofficial status for its activities through its participation in the war effort."[52] After the *Geographic* was successfully popularized by Grosvenor, it took on the reputation of an arm's-length scientific, anthropological tool that reported objectively about the planet's natural and human worlds. Its presentation of facts was, however, deeply political.

To step out of the chronology for a moment, the *Geographic's* coverage of the Vietnam War was as instructive about the war as it was about the magazine. The magazine's ambivalence about how to present Vietnam can be contrasted to its thorough coverage of the two world wars. Reportage on Vietnam was minimal, rarely discussed politics, and took refuge from moral problems by telling stories about specific men and their local issues. The magazine studiously avoided an overt stance on the war, preferring to support the troops without evaluating the ethics of pursuing an undeclared colonial war that was increasingly genocidal. As American forces routinely carpet-bombed not only Vietnam but also other countries, like Laos and Cambodia, caught in the crossfire, destroying hamlets and histories thousands of years old, the *Geographic* fell silent. Despite publishing some astonishing pictures from the war, the magazine refused to come out against it. Even after the war's end the *Geographic*, with its deep archives of famous photographs, with one notable exception from 2002, didn't publish coffee table books about the war as did other art publishers like Abrams or Thames & Hudson. Where other media saturated the audience, inside the magazine's famous yellow rectangular border the war seemed to be only a sad event unworthy of attention.

During the world wars the magazine's implicit politics supporting America's mission in the world, the continued rolling out of global manifest destiny and execution of Frederick Jackson Turner's frontier thesis, were never in doubt. Cultural scholar and Vietnam veteran Philip Beidler cautions that "remembering in wartime became a function of propaganda as official policy at every level of operation."[53] The less that needed to be said overtly, the fewer instructions given to the press, the more the government and military could claim there had been no interference with it. The best influence on information was the one self-imposed by the press. Grosvenor's mission was, as his magazine stated so often, an educational one first before all: "Anyone possessing a copy of this issue of the *National Geographic Magazine* will be able to answer whatever questions may arise concerning the meaning of any form of military and naval insignia, except those of the new women's organizations."[54] The ambiguity about the questions that "may arise" suggests a public deeply in the dark about the way its military was organized, how it operated and behaved. Even then, those at home, millions of whom were women, were crossed off as an afterthought. Grosvenor not only produced a code book explaining America and its military to each other, but more: "Not even the services themselves have printed [the insignia] in color."[55] The enormity of such a statement may not strike home until we compare the United States' and Nazi's graphical policies, about which more shortly.

The *Geographic*'s cultural standing is inordinately strong, claiming to have been "Exploring and Protecting the Planet Since 1888," as if the *National Geographic* and *National Geographic Society* are covert governmental organizations speaking for the United States' better angels.[56] The very fact that the *Geographic*'s politics are apparently invisible makes the magazine's hitting power all the more fearsome: here is a source of perceived objective news that speaks for the nation's benefit (and much depends on the definition of the word "nation"). As Lutz and Collins point out, the *Geographic* is a comfort, not truth, provider: "It strategically occupies the spaces between science and pleasure, truth and beauty; it presents an idealized and exotic world relatively free of pain or class conflict, a world stumbling or marching on the path to modernity."[57] The *Geographic* is an engine of normalization: whatever passes through the magazine or any of the society's many media outlets emerges as safe, worthwhile, reliable news to be spread. Here is hope for a better future made possible by science, the fruit of the Enlightenment, free market capitalism, democracy.

Unless the reader has set positions on issues, the organization will appear objective and unbiased because it takes no particular stand.

The *Geographic*'s publication of contemporary military heraldry was not only overtly pro-American, pro-war, and pro-military, it also naturalized the idea that the military engaged in all of its activities for the public good. The full strength of the magazine's shoulder was applied to the wheel. A woman is shown putting on an enamelled blue star pin ("She Wears a Star for a Man at War"); two generals (one British, one American) smilingly look at the insignia for the Flying Tigers; a white French naval petty officer holds a happy white boy in his arms while a white American sergeant clasps the child's hand and "Makes Friends in French Morocco" (no native Moroccans appear in the image: it is entirely concerned with the meeting of the two Allied Caucasian forces that represent war-making powers).[58] Each subject in the photograph is part of the narrative that the war is about a world shared by allies and friends who "respond more forcefully and more happily to beauty, poetry, and romance, all of which insignia convey, than to cold fact."[59] While the task appears to be pedagogical, it is at base ideological and coercive.

American military heraldry has since become more diverse, more recognizably corporate, and on some fronts, deliberately arcane. The contemporary military reflects the worldviews of its youngest recruits, born in the late 1990s and early twenty-first century, who are capable of being simultaneously patriotic true believers and deeply ironic about a globalized economy that shut down industry, broke towns and cities nationwide, replaced living wages with minimum-wage service jobs, and dispersed the family whose members searched vainly for steady work. For these soldiers the post-Second World War promise of employment and stable home places has long grown cold. What was rebellious during the Vietnam years becomes amusingly banal. About to go on patrol,

Colby Buzzell, famous for writing one of the first unvarnished Iraq war blogs, tells about pinning a peace badge, like the one worn by Corporal Joker in Gustav Hasford's *The Short-Timers* and Stanley Kubrick's *Full Metal Jacket*, onto his flak jacket. Where Joker is dangerously close to being militarily disciplined, Buzzell is greeted sardonically by his squad leader with the line, "Is that some kind of sick joke?"—the same question Joker faces in the film. Buzzell soon finds that everyone in his unit "started spitting lines out of *Full Metal Jacket*" at him on seeing the pin.[60] There's nothing upsetting about wearing a peace symbol and being on patrol because the cultural context has undergone the same kind of massive shift it did during the First World War.

The current heraldic scene is best documented by journalist Trevor Paglen, whose books about black projects and their associated insignia, are a record of how military and popular culture interact. Travelling near various Air Force bases, Paglen observed rare or unknown patches worn by Pentagon employees engaged in black work, leading him to document what he could. Among the many typical patches with ghosts, panthers, wizards, or skulls, is a sort of brown-black patch that has, blind-embroidered around an apparently empty circle, the words "If I tell you, I have to kill you."[61] What's striking about this patch is how it both announces and conceals itself. The patch would be nearly invisible, particularly on a dark uniform or coverall. The signification is both all and nothing—the sphere that so often stands for the globe in Air Force patches, and the empty figure, a zero. It is so dark it can't be read from a distance, but the knowledge that something is there excites the viewer's curiosity. Paglen interprets the paradoxically secret patches to represent the desire to "tell the world that one is part of something larger than oneself," but also to unite with others who are members of a secret society.[62] The patches generally share a tendency to boast about mystery and threaten the interested. If you're not an initiate, you don't get to know anything more than that you're in the dark. One of Paglen's interlocutors notes caustically about the patches, whose graphics have much in common with the design vocabularies of motorcycle clubs and heavy metal rock: "I've seen that sort of thing a lot . . . . Those are gang colors."[63] Such patches declare the work done by their wearers to be essential but taboo—the patches are the antithesis of heraldry's original purpose.

As Eugene Zieber wrote in 1895, "No error is more common than the idea that heraldry is a completed science, and that crests, devices, and coat-armor are only to be found in the musty pages of old records. Heraldry is an exact, living, and progressive *art science*."[64] Zeiber was particularly right about the way America pursued its armorial future: it is anything but moribund. The newly signifying patches, however, do follow some basic rules. Lightning bolts usually mean data control or gathering; dragons and wizards have their meanings, too. The signs have shifted but still have meaning. Paglen understands this and knows that "if you could begin to learn its grammar, you could get a glimpse into the secret world itself."[65] As fast as humans encode information, others work to break open those secrets, represented by Beifuss and Bellini's excellent 2013 *Branding Terror*, which does its best to catalogue insurgent and "terrorist" organizations across the globe. In stark comparison, the Nazi heraldic system could not have been more different. There the focus was on clarity and full explanation to all concerned how the heraldry supported and was integral to the Reich. In today's business terms, the swastika was apparently about absolute transparency.

CHAPTER 8

Planet Swastika

The Nazi Brand in Action

STEVEN HELLER CONSIDERS A FAMILIAR, UNHAPPY, conclusion that "the graphics of the Nazi party have been referred to as the most effective identity system in history. The swastika was integrated into hundreds of official logos, emblems, and insignia and inspired countless unofficial versions."[1] In the design world, as elsewhere, the problem of the swastika cannot be diminished or ignored. As Heller's study's subtitle ("Symbol Beyond Redemption?") implies, perhaps the sign is forever poisoned. Like other icons from the twentieth century that cannot be dissociated from their histories (the atom bomb's mushroom cloud, six men raising the American flag on Mount Suribachi, a silhouette or photograph of the Bell UH-1E Iroquois "Huey" helicopter), these images are so loaded that only the disappearance of their contexts will free them for resignification. Heller argues that the swastika cannot be emptied of its previous meanings because it is "not just any vessel. Nor is it like the marks for Coca-Cola, IBM, Apple, CBS, or other venerable corporate logos that front a company or represent a brand that ultimately rises and falls on popular acceptance."[2]

These comments open the way for a discussion of how much, as Robert Herzstein's famous study suggests, propaganda and visual branding was *The War That Hitler Won* (1978). Parallel to the previous section, I look here at the creation and persistence of the Nazi brand's world. In a long study of German graphic design from Weimar through Nazi Germany, Jeremy Aynsley suggests that "rather than regarding political propaganda and commercial graphic practice as antagonistic and mutually exclusive fields, it is more useful to think of official propaganda as learning from and adapting strategies of marketing. A clear instance of this is the way the swastika emblem took on the character of a brand identity."[3] Like all signs, the swastika is burdened by its history, but it's a mistake to make assumptions about just how long is needed to bleach out the sign's associations. Heller's subtitle "Beyond Redemption?" contains a comforting promise, like the familiar wishful declaration "never again" spoken in regard to the Shoah. "Beyond Redemption" is synonymous with "never"—it's a long time, as Heller's final question mark indicates. Similarly "never again" has proved to be more a statement of desire than reality: genocides continue unabated. Heller's title also suggests the swastika itself has sinned. If the swastika is a sinner, does it follow that other signs representing oppression and death to others are equally sinning?

In the course of my research I never came across arguments that the flags of the United States, Canada, or Great Britain be remade, yet all countries have engaged in colonial behaviour, have at one time pursued policies of extermination, slavery, or both. Entrenched signs that once meant and still may mean declarations of power over others can become battlefields of cultural contest, as the American South's renewed crisis over the Confederate flag has demonstrated. Display of that flag by troops fighting in Vietnam caused ongoing struggles between African American and white soldiers, particularly at the end of the 1960s.[4] Some cultural signs may be natural to one group and anathema to another. How many North Americans remark on a Christian cross or ichthus each time they see it? Of those, how many are themselves devout, follow a different religion, or have had bad experiences associated with the signs? How many are hailed by the sign, for good or ill? Outside the culture Christian signs may draw more negative attention. Thousands of years of meaning fill the images. For the cross to be unloaded, all memory (personal, oral, written, photographic, filmic, architectural) of the associated history must perish. A Celtic knot may have very specific associations for descendants of particular groups, but most North American viewers may look (if they do at all) at such signs, make general assumptions about a part of the world and its culture, and move on. Signs that once were calls to arms or memorials of grave injuries done to families or whole peoples may now be understood as decorative. Each sign has multiple audiences that fall on continua between followers, supporters, believers; those injured or oppressed by the sign's agents; and those entirely ignorant of it. For the swastika to fade, become of historical note only, the whole of the fascist program, complete with its death machinery, would have to wither.

The volatility of signs that many consider to be taboo, representative of the worst humans can do, can't be underestimated. It's a fantasy to believe that signs can be made so toxic that they won't be reused. American cavalry lieutenant Piers Platt is deployed to Iraq with his tank battalion where he commands an M1-Abrams main battle tank that has stencilled on its barrel the phrase "*Gott mit Uns*" ("God with us"), a saying embossed on Wehrmacht belt buckles in the Second World War. The usage goes as far back as 1701 when it was adopted by the Prussian military. Most of the United States' main battle tanks bear similarly stencilled names or phrases. A chance interview between the tankers and a German news crew (it turns out to be a group of representatives from a model-making company seeking good images of the Abrams tank in order to make an accurate mould for a toy), brings the Americans and Germans to an embarrassed halt when they jointly confronted the barrel inscription. However the embarrassment doesn't last as "one of the Germans, leaning forward ... whispered conspiratorially, 'Das ist Waffen SS!?'" to which the sergeant in charge answers "'Ja, genau.' Exactly." Realizing how deep are the ironies they confront, all the men "burst into laughter."[5] It's deeper than they know: the Waffen SS motto was *"Meine Ehre heißt Treue"* ("My Honour is Loyalty"). The men from a specialty war toy company producing historically accurate reproductions of materiel are wrong, as are the self-professed war buff Americans.[6]

A mere sixty years finds the children of once bitter enemies united on another battlefield, joined in forbidden awe of a fabled combat force responsible for a vast array of the Second World War's atrocities. We could take their combined ignorance of the real motto as a promising development: another twenty, forty, sixty years and the signs might have little or no meaning. But all understand and enjoy the cool irony of one force adopting another's dedication to slaughter. How long before Nazi emblems can be understood as just more pieces of cultural flotsam to be appropriated for someone's personal expression? How long before a brand tries to capitalize on that desire?

Look no further than the British clothing line BOY London, which in 2014 put the *Parteiadler*, Hitler's famous streamlined eagle clutching the roundel and swastika in its talons, on T-shirts. The brand removed the swastika but otherwise left the logo untouched (the eagle holds the logo's capital "O"). BOY London similarly used a modified version of the SS uniform and cap's *Totenkopf* badge. A spokesperson declared that "the brand is in no way connected to Nazism or the idea of anyone being discriminated against for their creed, colour or religious beliefs ... [the logo] was inspired by the eagle of the Roman Empire as a sign of decadence and strength. Its aim is to empower people rather than oppress."[7] The brand refused to budge from its position—the logo not only appears on shirts, but has been printed on them in an even larger, oversize format. Such a public fight is pure tonic for sales, keeps the brand in the public eye, and guarantees at least temporary survival. The argument that BOY London draws its inspiration from the punk music movement of the late 1970s, when breaking taboos meant engaging in the most overt forms of rebellion, carries the viewer only so far.

Many teen buyers simply don't know about images' heritage. I can imagine a reader shaking their head at this statement—out of shock, disbelief, perhaps in denial. After twenty-five years of teaching courses about war at different universities, I've come to believe that we all suffer from blank spaces in our memories. Consider Steven Okazaki's excellent 2007 documentary film *White Light/Black Rain*, which starts by interviewing Japanese teens and people in their early twenties living in Hiroshima. All who are asked what happened on the day's anniversary (August 6) are ignorant of the bombing. The brand's creators operate from experience that shows them rebellion can be marketed and purchased. In 2012 one of the brand's captains argued that only the strong could really wear the clothing: "BOY lends itself to so many different styles and subcultures .... Ultimately, it's all about *how* you wear it as an individual. You have to have the confidence; otherwise you won't pull it off. I think in a lot of ways, people are still intimidated by the brand today, the same as they were when it first came out."[8] Small surprise the brand mangers have no anxiety about using whatever signs they please; if everything means what the designer desires, then the historical record is immaterial, the signs are there to be emptied and refilled by the producer and consumer. Having confidence means facing down someone in the street who recognizes and is offended by the sign, telling them that history is finished, that the *Parteiadler* now identifies the wearer as a proud supporter of some particular politics. Those politics might well deserve exposure, public attention, and alteration of public thought. Does that legitimize use of the eagle? Can anything be made to mean anything?

There are limits. It's worth noting that while the BOY brand managers make aggressive interpretative claims, they also stopped short of putting the swastika itself on the clothes, and when challenged publicly resorted to a more distant historical example about the Roman Empire, presumably something about which no one would get upset (in terms of design there's no doubt this particular eagle came from Hitler's revised *Partei* sign). A wearer who bought the shirt in ignorance can now parrot the brand's line about the Romans (itself sophomoric) and end the complaint. The shirts continue to be sold, and the brand has adopted the *Parteiadler* into its logo. The time will come when some brand will be the first—then the gate will truly stand open—to declare the swastika as a signifier with an unwritten signified that can mean whatever one chooses (except of course for its support of the brand, which is guaranteed). All of this is an index that signs can rapidly lose both their historical and contextual power, in this case even before the generation of Second World War survivors dies out.

When considering the longevity of the Nazi brand, note brand evangelist Marc Gobé's conclusion that corporate brand identity "was designed to last forever and look appropriate in any context as a true reflection of the conservative values of the time."[9] Whether one favours an optimistic (the swastika will be remembered for what it symbolized and be banned in public unless shown in historical context), pessimistic (any sign, no matter its provenance, that makes money or expands a market will ultimately be used to do so), or pragmatic view (people cannot be expected to remember history forever, events that once caused wars will be forgotten or become abstract), the sign's potency must be reckoned with. Like most memorable brands, the swastika is a transcendent entity that represents a cluster of potential meanings over which the user has some power, although not to the extent that BOY London claims, I would argue. Like most logos and other arbitrary signs (the Nike swoosh) that have been so burned into the public retina, the swastika holds a "phantasmagoric ability to conjure up the image of a frozen time, a time beyond, before or outside the quotidian."[10] The logo points its membership to another, better world, a dream place where things exist the way the audience desires they should. There is either a return to a pre-lapsarian state, or transmission to a post-apocalyptic time where revelations have purified the world, and human existence with it. Wherever and whenever it is, it's better there.

For these existential reasons, Heller argues, Hitler sought to cloud just who created the swastika. Hitler sought "to detach the swastika from its occult history [and] ensure its reincarnation as a political symbol" over which he had complete control and in which new universe the *Hakenkreuz* was "his exclusive invention."[11] Heller designates Hitler as the Nazis' "director and image manipulator," who established the "rightness of the form," but stops short of calling him a brand manager. Yet it was under Hitler that the swastika became the instrument to enact "a *Gleichschaltung* [co-ordination] of all-party imagery."[12] Here the differences between the American and Nazi approaches to heraldry are the most staggering. The Nazis treated their sign system like the crucial coercive information program it was. They worked to standardize corporate expression, to create and enforce the employment of reusable templates that could be explained to a newcomer, could be handed not only to other artists and designers across the Reich, but to clothiers, metal workers, architects, and mark makers charged with reproducing the logo. Some of the first legislation the Nazis passed once they gained power governed brand protection, forming "a tidal wave of new laws, both blueprints for Nazi symbols and prohibitions against the abuse of them."[13] The wave began with the 1933 Law for Protection of National Symbols, supported and enforced by Goebbels's propaganda ministry, which issued Franz J. Huber's *Propagandisten-Fibel* (*Propagandist's Primer*). Huber's handbook directed members of the *Gau* (one of many administrative districts organized by the NSDAP) in the correct usage of the Nazi brand (including displays, decorations, appropriate music, and venues for meetings). Huber also understood the threat to the new sign system posed by foolish sentimentalism, warning that kitsch is "possible in every area of art, particularly in the visual arts. Even so-called national *Kitsch* is covered by the previously mentioned Law for the Protection of National Symbols. Any examples of *Kitsch* that the local group propaganda leader observes should be reported to the *Gau* propaganda office."[14]

Just as corporations establish house styles and publish design manuals governing the approved use and placement of the brand's marks, so too did the Nazis order the creation of a guide to the Reich's signification system. That book, known as the *Organisationsbuch der NSDAP* (Organizational Handbook of the NSDAP), became the chief task of Dr. Robert Ley, chief of the German Labour Front (the *Deutsche Arbeitsfront* or DAF).[15] Finally appearing in 1936, a thick, full colour, silver-embossed, cloth-bound doorstop clocking in at over 500 pages, the book is set entirely in the unreadable but suitably Nordic black letter Fraktur.[16] Ley claimed that his book (sometimes mocked as "Ley's fairy tales" since it had taken so long to produce that it seemed divorced from reality) would "answer all questions" about how uniforms, ranks, and insignia should appear.[17] [18] The

Organisationsbuch is a piece of managerial efficiency, standard-izing political expression through the party and across a rapidly expanding Reich. There would be no unofficial adoption of a wildcat badge to identify a whole army.

To see and handle the book is to feel the weight of a moment of pure gorgeous war in full toxic flood with its repulsive language of genetic laws and genocide. What makes a potential fiancé and marriage acceptable is diagrammed using a series of "good" white circles and various kinds of circles of undesirability (the interiors are dotted, lined vertically or horizontally, or are solid black, much as heraldic crests were before the advent of color reproduction).[19] These shields signifying pure or poisoned genetic membership (the language is full of words about sickness) are queasily similar to those early heraldic family crests.

The book is much smaller than it appears on screen, where it expands to fill whatever space the interface application permits. At 15 × 23 cm, it can easily be held in one hand and used as a reference text. It's the size of a compact dictionary. The concentration of wretchedness in such a small volume is a reminder that there is no replacement for coming in contact with the original artifact, never so clear to me as when I first stepped into a train car used for the deportations. The smallness of the car made claustrophobia explode in my chest: this was not the massive rolling stock of the late twentieth century but a car designed to be pulled by rela-tively underpowered steam engines. That meant there had to be thousands of them, tens of thousands more trips on small cars in short trains than had ever occurred to me, even having read the numbers, to carry the millions of the Reich's targets. Here, finally, was the book I'd been studying only as a digital scan.

I have no idea which Nazi first opened this particular copy, and whether they flipped through it or turned its pages method-ically. How many hands had this volume passed through before it was saved—and how did that occur? Was it taken by an Allied soldier as a souvenir, or preserved in an attic somewhere until it sold to a book dealer? This was, after all, the 1940 edition, published to replace the 1937 edition the organization had been working with until now. While prose paragraphs are composed of nearly indecipherable Fraktur, acres of it, made harder to read by the type's gray appearance on yellowed, partly transparent low-cotton-rag-content paper (one can see the splinters of wood pulp in the pages), the bound-in signatures of color plates remain as bright and clear as if the book were new. Likely the text pages were more readable, if not legible, in 1940 when the combination of acids in the paper and oxidization hadn't yet begun to burn the pulp.

The paper on which the full color flags, uniforms, weapons, and military hierarchical signs appears is not, as it often was with quality books published before the late twentieth century's advances in printing technology, a high-gloss "plate" finish, but instead a high-cotton rag fresh white paper that makes the colors snap forward sharply. The book's production values are demonstrated by the crispness of the image edges, the exaction of color registration and the precision of detail. The ½ mm × 2 mm red stripe that drives exactly through the centre of a swastika in a miniscule lozenge on the left front pocket of girl's Hiter Youth uniform (plate 60) and the complex text on a pennant (plate 38) are a measure of the care some anonymous press operators put into reproducing the images (were they obsessed fanatics, too, or perhaps terrified of turning in bad presswork, knowing the books' destinations—the hands of Hitler and the Party elite?).

The pennant, to be flown at the front of a staff car, bears the compressed all-capitalized phrase "NAT.SOZ. DEUTSCHEARBEITERPARTEI" (a partial abridgement of "Nationalsozialistische Deutsche Arbeiterpartei"). Despite being printed in 6 point type, in white on red with a black outline, the text is distinct and readable. (Technically the white text is not printed as much as it is "dropped out" of the red, meaning the red plate is missing the space taken up by the text: when the red prints, it will leave behind it a red area with the white text "reversed out of it," as it was sometimes called.) The contrast between the overwhelmingly illegible Fraktur on relatively poor paper and the high quality of the color plates could not be more striking, underlined by the fact that the book falls open to the plates: they are its stars. Here is a vivid illustration of the struggle in the party between the *Volkisch* forces that insisted on Fraktur, and the moderns who won the struggle for the image with the sharp, well-made plates not only of the standards, medals, and party pins, but also the fashionably displayed (we use the term "fashion plate" for a reason) uniforms not just for the SS and SA (including an SA man holding a javelin, dressed in his sports gear, complete with SA-branded athletic shirt with the aggressive logo in baby blue), but also for the young women's Hitler Youth. Each uniform is modeled by smiling blond and brunette men and women. No volume could be more sumptuously reassuring that the party and its military were not only beautifully organized but, when it came right down to it, also beautiful. Even if the current generation was full of people with the typical inheritance of wartime poverty (bad teeth, general poor health, physical and mental disorders, as with people everywhere), this was the book for the future.

The colour (a serious expense at the time) recording the back, front, and side views of belt buckles, caps, and assorted impedimenta from garrison and field, reinforced the book as a style manual. This was how to display various emblems, insignia, badges, and flashes on each piece of clothing, in case you couldn't visualize it yourself. Heller concludes, "It is not exactly clear how much Dr. Ley ... was personally involved .... But it was his office that determined the standards of stationery, enamel signs, flags and pennants, awards and badges, party uniforms and all things involving the swastika and ancillary symbols. So someone in Dr. Ley's office knew what he was doing."[20] When we compare the *Organisationsbuch* and the similar work of Ley's *Deutsche Arbeitsfront* with the United States' official interwar military design, the overwhelming force of German *Gemeinschaft*, what today would be typified as "identification with the brand promise," is palpable.[21]

Americans had to wait until the middle of the war for Gilbert Grosvenor's *National Geographic* to produce a partial guide to the military's signification; nearly ten years before, the NSDAP had put in place extensive rules about how and where to wield their brand. Patches weren't being sewn by tailors in foreign countries where troops were stationed; pieces were milled at home to the Reich's exacting specifications. In brand specialists Riesenbeck and Perrey's view, the only successful brand is a "lived" one, which requires identifying with and taking pride in the group's communal work. Crucial to such work is the "*brand book*, a document that is shared widely across the organization, that defines the core brand identity and provides a common language for consistent brand execution."[22]

Predictably the Nazi's brand book has a great deal to say about the proper use of the brand's cutting edge, the black scissors of the swastika. The Reich's design achievement is impressive in part because it stayed unified even as it grew. It's as if the swastika had encoded in its DNA the whole of the party's graphic plans. The early, presumably handmade, brassards worn by the first Nazis in the 1920s could be put on or taken off quickly and easily, were removable signs that would stand out on drab clothing common to ex-military and the unemployed surviving in a depressed economy. In the emotionally heated language of the *Organisationsbuch*, the swastika roundel was "the first symbol of National Socialist solidarity": it identified the early true believers, the ones "who fought actively for the Führer against the mockery and persecution and bloody terror which they encountered whenever they wore this symbol. With this sign they won the fight for Germany."[23] The result, particularly after the party seized power and closed down all but Nazi political processes, was to encourage those eligible but reluctant to join, to evoke in non-Nazis an intense desire to belong, to inspire in them the wish to "equal the self-sacrifice, the readiness for battle and the attitude of those first National Socialists."[24] This particular *Organisationsbuch* author (it might have been Ley, but the book was likely the work of many hands) writes with the fervour of an original party member and survivor of various intraparty battles, or the zealotry of the recently converted. The offer of membership to a select Aryan audience is based on complete submission to a single signifying system.

How successful that recruitment was is an ongoing debate. One of the more extreme positions regarding the penetration of Nazi ideology through the German public and into its private world is occupied by Daniel Goldhagen in his 1996 *Hitler's Willing Executioners*, considered by many as too extreme a denunciation of a whole nation. A more conservative but compelling account of the common person's complicity in criminal acts ordered by the state is given by Christopher Browning's *Ordinary Men* (1992), which methodically examines the behaviour of non-Nazi police battalions engaged in daily atrocities on the Eastern front. Browning's text supports the conclusion that the vast majority of regular soldiers who were not party members and did not belong to elite units (the SA, SD, or SS) chose to participate in atrocities, despite being given overt permission to stand down from such actions without suffering punishment or ostracism. After the war, ironically, the book itself became part of the mythic structure the Nazis laboured so hard to create. First editions (it was revised multiple times) now command prices in excess of $500 USD.

The swastika was the opening act of a performance of power. Historian Ian Kershaw considers that "deep into the dictatorship itself Hitler's own ideological obsessions had more of a symbolic than concrete meaning for even most Nazi supporters," where one of Hitler's key tasks was acting as the visible sign for a world-view, and so he "transformed himself into a function, the *function of Führer*."[25] The creation of what scholar Roger Griffin calls a "plait of a mythicized past ... intense modernization ... [and] systematic purge of everything ... detrimental to the process of national regeneration" preceded the Reich's atrocities. The Reich was a work in motion, and as with Ley's perpetually unfinished *Organisationsbuch*, there was ongoing revision and extension of the brand. The Nazis embraced new technologies as pragmatically as they jettisoned the old that no longer served (Fraktur was out, Futura was in). Newness was an accepted part of the Reich, even as it worked to anchor itself in some legendary past with its rituals of blood and honour.[26] The Nazis took what they needed from other cultures, from rationalism as much as from "pseudoscientists, folklorists, and occultists who believed that [the swastika] was a sacred totem of Aryan or Indo-European culture."[27]

To meet a fully dressed SS soldier was to confront a combination of the sudden present and the deep past. The silver *Totenkopf* badge centred alone on the black headgear meant the full force of the grotesque, almost medieval (it actually dated to the mid-eighteenth century), somewhat flattened skull missing its lower mandible was juxtaposed with the stark contemporary streamlined uniforms and visored caps. A few inches away on the right collar tab were the pure modernist SS "runes," adapted from the Armanen "sig rune" (sometimes "*Siegrune*" or victory rune), usually woven in aluminum or silver wire. Here was more instant history expressed in modernist terms.[28] The adaptation of the sig rune was the work of Bonn graphic designer Walter Heck, who worked in a studio focused on military designs. Heck paired two sig runes, turned and adjusted them, creating the twin lightning strokes. The bolts commanded their own key on Nazi typewriters, usually above the "3" on the keyboard's top row. The simplicity and power of the twin-rune design is equal to the swastika.

The SS logo belonged to the same design world as the renewed swastika and took on an intangible power that transcended the sig letterform (compare the relative failure of the *Sturmabteilung's* "SA" logo, which was overly complex, crowded, and hard to decipher). The SS lines seemed to have been abruptly jarred to the right, as if caused to stagger by speed and movement. Although they officially stood for "*Schutzstaffel*" ("Protection Squadron"), when given a quarter turn on the uniform tabs they became abstract, unusual patterns. They were no longer simply letters, but a new sign that meant either membership and inclusion or exclusion and death. There were fussy additions to the uniform, including the "distinctive cuffband bearing Hitler's signature, and white leather dress belts" permitted to the *Liebstandarte* for parade, but the most important signifying work was performed in daily life, not on the parade ground.[29] Most of all, the runes required no colour to be powerful. Rendered white on black, they were unmistakable, unbeatable. Even without the special "SS" key on the typewriter, the runes could be (and still are) communicated by similar character pairs: "88" or "HH" are immediately understood by white supremacists as standing for twin lightning bolts and "Heil Hitler" respectively. "88" is particularly useful. Since H is the Latin alphabet's eighth letter, writing "88" simultaneously indicates the SS and Hitler salute. If you don't know this flag, you won't see it. The quality of the instant classic is underlined by the fact that many of the key design motifs pioneered by the Nazis were adopted by the post-war militaries of East Germany and the Soviet Union.[30]

Paul Fussell, exquisitely attuned to the Reich's inadvertent black humour (usually produced by its attempts at Teutonic high seriousness), notes that Germany, already "a nation besotted with the wearing of military and paramilitary uniforms of all kinds," soon became a nation in full uniform. The Nazis extended their regalia to include virtually every occupation, including miners, postal workers, bus and tram conductors, even a "senior loco-motive driver got to display on his left thigh a sword in a fancy scabbard with sword knot."[31] School children of all ages and sexes were similarly recruited by wardrobe. When divisions of the Waffen SS disappointed Hitler, he ordered their woven cuffband identifiers torn off, which Fussell gets immediately: "he punished their uniforms, which by that time had acquired all but mystical significance."[32]

Glancing into the *Buch* itself is instructive. The following example was printed in colour in the first and subsequent editions of Ley's *Organisationsbuch*. This image represents half a page from a number of pages concerned with the Hitler Youth and the Girl's Youth League (*Jungmädelbund*).

The piping, an aiguillette or *Führerschnüre* (literally "leader cord") used to identify rank was often worn strung between the left shoulder tab and breast pocket button, sometimes from a central shirt button to the left pocket. Apart from the ridiculously elabor-ate ranks (there are nine) from the lowest *Kameradschaftsführer* to the most exalted *Stabsführer*, two things are implicit in the cords. The first is that the Nazis knew that to ensure ideal behaviour, it was necessary to have prizes to award. Orders or instructions given by older to younger children might be hard to enforce, but establishing a clear system of rewards meant that children would learn the many lessons of hierarchy, not least of which is that in order to gain the group's approval, one may agree to participate in events one otherwise might disdain. Indicators of endorsement, whether from the local troop or beyond to the village, town, county, or *Gau*, can be read in a second by understanding the aiguillette colour codes. The higher the colour, the more trusted and admired the group's member. The second job achieved by the aiguillettes was that the youth would, having become nat-uralized to a tiered system of incentives, unquestioningly carry it into adulthood in some further directly military, paramilitary,

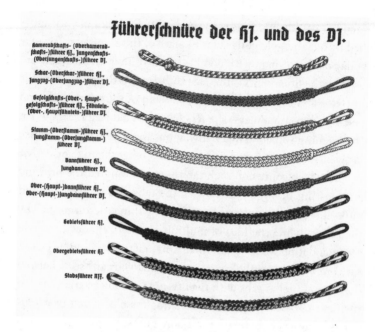

Figure 8.1: Hitler Youth Leader cords (*Führerschnüre*) from Ley's 1940 *Organisationsbuch*: Rewarding colours (plate 62)

or hierarchical organization. The cords trained their bearers into a way of understanding, acquiescence, progression, and success, much as does any rank of merit badges. As it happened, the conversion from paramilitary to military came a great deal sooner than expected when the Hitler Youth had to be mobilized to stand beside the *Volksstürm* and defend Berlin late in the war.

The many ranks allow for advancement even when the tasks might seem relatively meaningless (cleaning things, running errands, generally being of service). Inconsequential chores that demonstrate trust can be later converted into the passing of information about adult citizens, or if necessary, parents. The bestowing of approbation—"likes" in our present culture—habituates the user to agreeability. Once adulthood arrived, the Hitler Youth member could shift fluidly to the NSDAP's hierarchy as signi-fied by red and gold collar tabs in place of the aiguillette (similar collar tab identifiers with combinations of pips and leaves were used by the SS and SA). The NSDAP divided the political ranks in two: each of the two groups consisted of fourteen levels and one overall commander—the *Reichsleiter*. What that meant when approaching someone in a hallway was that one had one chance in twenty-nine of identifying a political officer's rank correctly.

The deep confusion such tabs caused prompted the printing and posting of large guides with the tabs and their associated ranks illustrated in colour. As with many things accomplished by the Nazis, while the idea of multiple tiers and chances for state commendation was good in theory, in practice it could be chaos, sure proof of the vexillological maxim that you can't see what you don't know: collar tabs with twenty-nine different variations can turn even good design into a meaningless blur. Such problems persist wherever there are too many ranks. Contemporary US Marine Maximilian Uriarte records in one of his early comic strips the meeting between a hapless Marine Corps boot (trainee) and an approaching non-commissioned officer of undetermined but apparently high rank. Desperately trying to read the sleeve patch in time to give the correct salutation, the panicked soldier mentally clicks through a list of possibilities ("Gunny, Master Sergeant, First Sergeant, Master Guns, Sergeant Major"). Just as he victoriously concludes "Master Sergeant," the NCO passes him with the deadpan note: "Too late, Fuck-knuckles." [33]

North American audiences may or may not have come in contact with an original Nazi flag, banner, pin, medal, SS or SA uniform. Separating the thousands of documentary and fictional representations (films, photographs, TV shows, toy soldiers and other war memorabilia, books about the Second World War) from the number of times one has come face to face with an original (in a museum, the rarer war museum, special collection, state archive, private gallery, or auction house) can be instructive about how distant the war's reality has become. The gap between the original and the artifact has, for many, been filled by the popular. Part of the problem with originals is their function as a fascist honeytrap.

While some buildings and monuments were destroyed by the Allies and Russians when they overran and occupied Germany, others, like the death camps, the Atlantic Wall, and even Hitler's "Wolf's Lair" (now in Poland), have been allowed to survive as evidence of Nazi methods. The problem with such structures, as with Hitler's birthplace, is that they can become sacred destinations for fascists and neo-Nazis. There's no killing fascism any more than there is eliminating the swastika. There might be diversions from the official visual system in the major cities, at least before they were bombed flat and the famous art they'd housed was dispatched to various caves, tunnels, or mines around the country. Urban citizens had access to art galleries exhibiting Reich-approved art, Nazi posters, and films all pushing the war. But in rural areas it was more likely that one would see either Nazi kitsch, or official expressions of the Reich's power in the armbands, party pins, flags, banners, even gardens.

That lesson was driven home with the accidental discovery in 1992 of a grove of golden larches planted in an evergreen forest in Zernikow, a region of Uckermark, Germany. All was well during spring and summer, but in the fall the larches, as suggested by their name, turn a bright yellow while the surrounding trees remain green. The consensus is that sometime in 1938 either a Hitler Youth group or some particularly ardent Nazi foresters planted 140 larches in a swastika pattern that covered nearly an acre and was visible only by air during autumn. The discovery of the larch swastika (it took an additional three years for them to be cut down, and even then the job wasn't done properly until 2000) brought out other stories across Germany of trees planted in various Nazi patterns, including the swastika. Outside the urban world, the swastika remained the strongest visual bond uniting the people.

I offer the larches not only as an example of the swastika's persistence, and the persistent toxicity of its fascist connotations, but to point to the way the sign escaped its official jail. While the Reich worked to control its brand, and to eliminate the kitsch that blurred its modernist clarity, ultimately the sign was impossible to police completely. While such failure might have aggravated Goebbels and propaganda purists, it ultimately strengthened the sign and gave it a life that has extended beyond 1945, growing in power and reach. Wherever there are fascist groups one will find modernist variations on the swastika, some quite sharp (South Africa's Afrikaner Resistance Movement's flag, Hungary's Arrow Cross Party's flag, Greece's Golden Dawn party, with its striking angular coil of black and white on red), others much duller (the historic *Parti Populaire Francais*' logo, the New British Union party's fatigued powder-blue lighting bolt on a red ground). The best designs date from the war and are drawn from SS division patches (the Afrikaner and Hungarian flashes were originally SS badges), themselves often taken from runes that were put through the same modernist stylization process as the swastika.

I pause here because there is such a great deal of careful documentation not only of the uniforms, but the whole of the Nazi, particularly SS, regalia. Some currently available books are meticulous, detailed accounts of the Reich's sumptuary practices, lovingly photographed and produced, which go into lapidary specifics about SS and SA uniforms, weapons, and decorations. These are large expensive books slathered with hundreds of colour plates solely concerning often niche artifacts like the Reich's cloth military headgear, belt buckles used by the Wehrmacht, or four volumes alone on daggers. The details show more than just sweat-stained original garments of particular provenance, such as who wore them and when, but also the kind of stitch work and materials, both cloth and metal, that compose the uniforms and their construction, inside and out, and with the weapons and buttons, front and back. Books like these, filled with obsessive detail, bespeak zealous amateur historians who will have complete sets on the shelf, who can accurately answer inordinately specific questions in online fora, and who can and will correct all but the most dedicated military historian about where and when the variations in colour, fabric, and cut appeared. Most of all, books like this are an index of people looking for and saving up to buy originals.

The hunger for Nazi artifacts seems perhaps as existentially threatening as the relentless staying power of neo-fascism. Even the most desultory research into the *Organisationsbuch* reveals the ongoing fetishization of original Nazi memorabilia by Americans and other members of the Allied forces. Just as Henry Ford was once busy filling a museum with souvenirs from a way of life he was destroying, many children and grandchildren of the war generation are fascinated by remnants of Nazi material culture. There is a curious quality about the desire to own, not just see, originals.

One such is British multimillionaire collector Kevin Wheatcroft, whose obsession with the Nazis and their artifacts began at age five and has become the most significant practice of his life. Wheatcroft's collection is "widely regarded as the world's largest accumulation of German military vehicles and Nazi memorabilia."[34] Such obsessions invariably lead the investigator to ponder the attraction these objects command, how fragments of a catastrophe that swallowed up tens of millions of lives can be appealing. The process of amassing Nazi memorabilia is, like many things having to do with completist collectors, a study in a compulsive behaviour. The transfixion before Nazi materials suggests the strength of the forbidden, the power of the particular sign system, the mystery of a genocidal cult. Collectors will defend themselves by arguing that history compels them, they desire to preserve an awful past for pedagogical reasons ("never again"), they believe in the importance of understanding how close the world came to destruction—it's a public service. Typically hidden is the admiration, adoration, and emulation of the Reich's ideals. While a collector like Kevin Wheatcroft can afford to buy originals, most cannot. Many souvenir hunters publish guides to Nazi artifacts like the ones I've mentioned. One of the key uses such books have is their pedagogical use instructing buyers in how to detect fakes.

One of Philip K. Dick's astonishing early insights into the world of simulacra was his understanding of the importance of the duplicate. Dick proposed that fakes entirely undermined the existence of the real, and that once a culture had accepted a fake, it would cease to exist in any meaningful way. The beginning of *The Man in the High Castle* (1962) centres on an antiques dealer who, knowing the supply of genuine war artifacts is running out, ensures that beautifully made "authentic" fakes (instant classics) will keep the market supplied. Every collector knows the pool of originals is finite, so the search for the authentic is that much more competitive. As the craze for war souvenirs grows, the collecting public tacitly accepts that copies will soon outnumber the originals: it's part of a desperate existential game to be able to distinguish between a perfectly made historically accurate fake and an object that once played a part in lived existence. In our world, hobby Nazism is widespread—the global trade in originals is thought to be worth some $40 million USD annually.[35]

Consider one merchandising site that offers, among others, carefully accurate reproductions of Hitler's own Nazi standard. Their ad copy reads in part: "Once again we move forward coming close with each day to being able to offer the complete 'DEUTSCHLAND ERWACHE' STANDARD for the first time since the fall of the Reich at a price everyone can afford, and yet have one of the most sot [sic] after and Rarest [sic] of items which will totally enhance any display for your museum or war room that will totally set you far apart from the restless crowd of collectors!"[36] The language speaks to multiple anxieties: the collector wants something original (despite the fact that it's a replica), striking, that identifies one as a member of the cognoscenti (you are not just another restless boor), that won't break one's limited collector budget. More importantly is the world implied by "war room," a private (probably male) place in the house reserved for treasures, antiques, rare volumes, maybe even elaborate tabletop *Kriegsspiele* with armies of accurately painted soldiers frozen in the midst of famous battles. To that room you would add the full-size facsimile political standard, pole, top (gold painted Nazi eagle), and box that encloses the *Liebestandarte der Adolf Hitler*: $1,250 USD.

The above consideration not only of the swastika but of the uniforms looks ahead to Chapter 10, where I connect the reading of the Nazi sign system and the larger propaganda campaign to the brand's continuation. The swastika's good health has led me to feel that its iconic usage is clear enough in our minds, and that generally it doesn't need more exposure, particularly since political movements that we once could reassure ourselves were fringe organizations now represent themselves in democratically elected parliaments, state and federal council chambers. If one wishes to see the swastika and its relatives in use, one need only look at daily images from across the web. Such ideas don't spread by themselves: they need persistent, staunch work to be communicated. That labour, accomplished by propaganda, no matter whether it occurs in a democracy or fascist regime, exists to take control of every ion of the message, a process on which the next discussion focuses.

CHAPTER 9

THE UNITED STATES OF ADVERTISING

Propaganda in America

THE DIFFICULTIES IN WRITING ABOUT WHAT IS AND IS not propaganda are so great that media scholars often refuse to attempt a definition at all—but one needs somewhere to begin. The most basic definitions remind readers that the notion of propaganda was originally religious, Christian, papal. The modern sense of propaganda derives from the constitution of an office by seventeenth-century Pope Gregory XV, whose 1622 direction to form the *Sacra Congregatio de Propaganda Fide* (Congregation for the Propagation of the Faith, now intriguingly reworded to omit "propagation" and read "The Congregation for the Evangelization of Peoples") was part of the worldwide mission to spread Catholicism and the Catholic church's struggle against the Protestant Reformation.[1] There was nothing sinister about the word "propaganda" initially, since it was a directive about communicating ideas. In the contemporary era one problem can be distinguishing between education, advertising, and propaganda. One group's education may be another's propaganda. The general differentiation between propaganda and advertising is usually that the former works to "affect belief or inculcate attitudes ... in ways that circumvent or suppress ... rational reflective judgment,"[2] where the latter, according to Merriam-Webster, involves the announcement, publication, and promotion of ideas' or objects' beneficial qualities.[3]

In some definitions advertising sounds a good deal more scientific and rational than propaganda which, since Joseph Goebbels got his hands into mass media, has only had dire meanings. The idea that an audience will internalize the values espoused in propaganda, will believe that it arrived at these thoughts independently is, for Pratkanis and Aronson, the key separator between propaganda and advertising. The "dexterous use of images, slogans and symbols that play on our prejudices and emotions ... with the ultimate goal of having the recipient ... accept this position as if it were his or her own," is supposed to be particular to propaganda.[4] Yet if advertising functions as its adherents wish, the mass of buyers would believe that they are not influenced in choosing what to buy, that consumption is a natural way of living, and that people's choices about what they buy are declarations of their freedoms, expressions of their individuality. They are who they are specifically and uniquely because of the consumer path they've chosen. Both advertising and propaganda wish to render themselves invisible, normalize their claims, and convince users that they are free agents in charge of their own beliefs. The biggest distinction between the two is that advertising is supposed to culminate in the purchase of a particular product, and propaganda to aid or injure a cause or a person (or accomplish both simultaneously, helping a cause by harming a person or group).

Definitions of advertising and propaganda may be useful in the media environment of mid-twentieth-century America; they have become less useful in the early twenty-first century when buying ideas, products, and worldviews seem inseparable and where the concept of injury has become more complex. Viral, lifestyle, and brand marketing long ago demolished the idea that buying is the final step in an ad campaign. As the information environment becomes murkier, the clearer it becomes that the definitions are invidious. Media watchers are often puzzled about exactly where the differences exist between the "propagation of the faith" and convincing a mass to buy, and to buy buying as a way of life.

I use the term "propaganda" to refer to a practice that may initially appear to be part of education, advertising, or communication, but at some point in its career begins to abuse, reject, or destroy rules aimed at keeping information relatively clean. Over the last hundred years in North America, consumer advocacy and protection has risen with the aim of giving consumers useful information about the products and services being advertised. Outright lying, shading of the truth, abuse of statistics, bending and sifting of information, all of which result in a knowingly false view of a product, are now supposed to be illegal. When it comes to education and advertising, we expect to be able to hold the source up to high standards of what author Neal Stephenson calls "informational hygiene," that is, information that has been verified by disinterested third parties and has, to the best of our current knowledge, been produced and reproduced accurately, and is if possible free of rumour, desire, and ideology.[5]

Propaganda is communication that is coercive, that preaches, exhorts, extols, or commands. Many would argue that both education and advertising do these things. But where education seeks clean information, propaganda knowingly uses lies, half-truths, and argumentative fallacies as necessary: no tactic is ruled out.

Propaganda will reveal itself through irrational claims, ad hominem attacks, character assassinations, claims of guilt by affiliation or association, slippery slope chains of reasoning. Propaganda will support one group or alliance over all others. It may promise a better world by creating hatred toward, or calling for the expulsion or extermination of, a part or whole of a group or groups of people. It will make emotional, unfounded charges against whole populations that result in harm to or the death of others. Advertising and propaganda employ the same "dexterous use of images, slogans and symbols that play on our prejudices"; the first presumably stops when we buy, the second when we take local or global action against the target. Propaganda is marked by signifiers like "other," "savage," "terrorist." Who is meant by these terms will change over time, but the results are the same. Those so labelled will be refused treatment accorded citizens—members of the groups at the structure's centre. The expunged will have little or no access to "civilized" values like "justice," "mercy," and "leniency." Propaganda creates, manipulates, and ultimately works to destroy groups that the culture may for long periods have tolerated, integrated, defended, even prized. During the whole process propaganda will inform the collective of what is right and declare that it is only telling hard truths, telling it, in the vernacular, "like it is."

Up to this point it would seem reasonably easy to distinguish advertising from propaganda. The closeness between the two forms of persuasion tightens if we take an example from more recent discussions about "ethically sourcing" materials and labour. I've spoken before about corporate behaviour in other countries. For the moment let's imagine a corporation mounts an advertising campaign aimed at consumers buying certain pieces of clothing or technology. Both advertiser and corporation know that the conditions under which workers operate are dangerous, inhumane, potentially fatal; these facts are suppressed or denied by both actors. The ad campaign causes people to buy the products and along the way inadvertently support toxic labour conditions. The aim is selling, which means the medium is advertising. But people get injured or killed on a regular basis in the production of the items. Because the destruction of other human beings is a byproduct, not the desired outcome, we can say the process is still advertising. Have the ads, now knowingly lying about the human costs of production, moved over into propaganda's territory?

What about advertising for goods that are either themselves unethical (ivory, body parts from endangered species) or are produced at great cost to the local population (conflict diamonds; garments, toys, or technology made by children)? How much known injury and death is it legitimate to charge against the product's cost? What about ads for products (water in plastic bottles, batteries containing mercury) that are known to be harmful but pass consumer inspection under current laws? In the longer term an ad campaign for water delivered in plastic bottles will cause serious worldwide health hazards that will be unequally borne by the planet's countries. If the end result is the harm to a whole people, that would suggest we're looking at propaganda, not advertising. Necessarily the advertiser will say such damage is an unpleasant aspect of life, but the intention is clear—to sell, not kill. Try another case: an advertising campaign for diamonds. Surely nobody means harm when they buy a diamond. If we know ahead of time that collateral damage will be suffered along the way, that's a shame, but it isn't the point.

We could try to distinguish between advertising and propaganda by focusing more closely on intention: is the corporation's desire to cause us to buy a product, or to privilege and damage a people (even if the group hasn't been specified—workers in another country, children in a sweatshop)? Supporting a brand, buying the "images, slogans and symbols" that make for a successful company, can be seen as giving tacit permission for the destruction of those far enough outside our group that they aren't real to us. Humans may be suffering, but when haven't they, people tend to ask. What about ad programs that encourage us to believe that having products (oil, water) is our right, that they are integral to a lifestyle we believe we've earned? When advertisers, corporate managers, and participating consumers are all aware of the harm done to individuals through corporate neglect, abuse, or desire to cut costs, then all are involved in the knowing commission of violence against others. It is indirect hurt. Buying propaganda means direct participation in harm to others, but that is not the only product we desire when we accede to propaganda. We are in search of something better, the true commodity. I offer these questions in order to illustrate just how much advertising and propaganda can and do overlap: propaganda and advertising may start differently, but may share the same outcome.

The struggle to identify advertising as an open, neutral force is crucial to the ongoing permission advertising needs to operate largely unchecked in Western democracies.[6] Advertising must be differentiated from propaganda because the first signals a trustworthy, rational free market, and the second a repressive regime with a controlled economy. One example of the anxiety propaganda triggers in the West is the recent coverage of a story that under the guise of public service announcements, famous Chinese movie stars like Jackie Chan, Li Bingbing, and Donnie Yen are shilling for President Xi Jinping's "Chinese Dream." Before a Chinese viewer sees a film they must sit through a three-minute speech from one of thirty-two stars.[7] The story is mildly amusing (Chinese filmgoers mostly found the announcements irritating and had no patience for them, many came in late so as to avoid the pieces altogether), but was covered in depth by *Time Magazine*, *The New York Times*, *The Hollywood Reporter*, the BBC, and others. In North America, banks, as well as car, soda, and technology corporations have advertised in cinemas for decades. The movie industry uses time with its captive audience to screen as many as eight two-minute ads (trailers) for upcoming releases before a film.[8] In 2013, ad revenue in Canadian theatres made Cineplex $26 million CDN, and in the United States was worth over half a billion dollars.[9] Twenty minutes of pre-film ads are understood by North Americans to be part of the film-going experience: the majority of viewers don't mind them.[10] The only attention such a practice has received in the last few years is when Canada's Scotiabank launched its tough-talking animated 3D computer graphic army character "Colonel Kernel," who sells popcorn. An article in *Marketing Magazine* quotes one of Scotiabank's advertising VPs who enthuses, "The storytelling of what's going on with the popcorn, the theatre of the mind, suggests we could tell wonderful stories in the future .... It could become a very important part of our overall Scene [a reward points program] storytelling."[11] It may come as a surprise to learn that popcorn holds a place on the mind's stage. The important thing is that the first story caught and kept the attention of the international press, while the second was read only by people in the trade press. The first is anathema in free-market democracies and the second is an accepted fact of consumer life, the price one pays for buying.

In the middle of the twentieth century, French sociologist and theologian Jacques Ellul warned scholars about the wilful blindness they practiced when it came to propaganda: "American sociologists scientifically try to play down the effectiveness of propaganda because they cannot accept the idea that the individual—that cornerstone of democracy—can be so fragile, and because they retain their ultimate trust in man."[12] Advertising and propaganda, theorized Ellul, are so close that they each accomplish the other's job. Ellul distinguishes between two classic forms of propaganda: agitation propaganda (usually known as "agitprop," a term coined in the interwar Soviet Union); and integration propaganda. It is the second that requires the most care because it is the subtlest and works to pull people into the system by convincing them that they are in full control of it. The people most at risk are those who are persuaded they aren't its targets. The West likes to believe that one cannot successfully propagandize a "free" people because they have too much access to information, are too educated about doubt (a serious roadblock to narrative control), and have the full support of a free press and courts, that last of which is independent from a potentially oppressive government. I've examined the blurred lines between advertising and propaganda; what happens when propaganda takes the form of patriotism?

One recent case of patriotism becoming propaganda is Clint Eastwood's 2014 film *American Sniper*, based on SEAL sniper Chris Kyle's book of the same name. Having earned over half a billion dollars worldwide since its release (with another $80 million in DVD and Blu-ray domestic sales), the story was embraced by the American public which, until that time, had largely avoided films about the American wars in Iraq and Afghanistan.[13] Of over fifty films about the two wars, some with high production budgets, marquee directors, and actors attached to them (films like the Bourne franchise director Paul Greengrass's Matt Damon vehicle *The Green Zone* [2010], and Paul Haggis's *In the Valley of Elah* [2007], starring Tommy Lee Jones and Charlize Theron), only a very few turned a profit. Most didn't recover production costs, and in some cases produced disastrous studio write-downs, as occurred with Brian De Palma's much hated film *Redacted*, a filmic retelling of an actual rape war crime perpetrated on a fourteen-year-old-girl and her family by American soldiers in Samarra.[14] De Palma's film was so disliked in North America that despite a loud publicity campaign it cleared only $65,000 domestically; foreign markets proved to be more receptive, and were where the film earned the bulk of its $780,000 profit (likely not enough to cover advertising, let alone production, costs).

De Palma has toured this territory before with his more popular 1989 film, *Casualties of War*, about the notorious rape of a Vietnamese civilian by American soldiers. Although it drew the ire of many viewers at the time, the film was lauded for its uncompromising look at rape as a war crime. European support for *Redacted* is indexed by its winning the Venice Film Festival's Silver Lion. Stateside, a "Boycott Redacted" website was set up to kill the film's domestic release; it was unsuccessful, but the site's authors needn't have worried. While the two texts had vastly different contexts (one war that nearly broke America as opposed to one that the public largely supported or ignored), what differentiates the films is that in the first, Michael J. Fox plays a Quaker, a clean-cut American hero against Sean Penn's thoroughly repulsive chief perpetrator. In *Redacted* there are perpetrators, victims, and no heroes. *Redacted* might have been funded because of the strong critical and financial success of *Casualties of War*. Even De Palma, a grizzled Hollywood outsider and contrarian, sounds shocked when he recounts, "What I didn't think is that nobody would want to see *Redacted*. Even the good reviews said, 'Well, this is very difficult to watch.' So that was surprising—that they just don't want to see any movies about Iraq."[15] Even bad press and scandal couldn't make the film marketable in the United States. There actually are times when any press is bad press.

The most successful films about the two wars are either uncomplicated soldier hero films or genre texts like *Source Code* (2011) or *Battle: Los Angeles* (2011), both of which owe more to science fiction and video games than to typical Hollywood war films. The massive and persistent audience rejection of a wide variety of films about Iraq and Afghanistan has been discussed by a number of writers: what stands out is the enormous box office gap between *American Sniper*, *Lone Survivor* (2013), and every other film about the wars. [16] Even Tina Fey's sympathetic action-comedy *Whiskey Tango Foxtrot* (2016) couldn't earn back its budget.[17] *American Sniper* is the film the American public has chosen to represent the wars in Iraq and Afghanistan to itself. The much touted *Hurt Locker* (2009) or *Zero Dark Thirty* (2012) didn't have the draw of *Lone Survivor*, let alone *American Sniper* (*The Hurt Locker* and *Zero Dark Thirty* earned $49 million and $132 million respectively worldwide).

American Sniper is almost entirely ahistorical. The soldiers act in a political vacuum where they do not ask for and are not offered reasons for killing on foreign soil. Chris Kyle is portrayed as a good ol' Texas boy who is taught by his father to shoot and kill animals. He and his brother tour the Texas rodeo circuit enjoying a happy macho existence until one night in 1998 when Kyle sees a TV news story showing the Nairobi, Kenya, and Dar es Salaam, Tanzania, embassy bombings, to which he responds, mouth agape: "Look what they did to us." Without investigating why the embassies were bombed or what the United States was doing in East Africa (the film offers no explanations), Kyle joins the Navy SEALs, is activated and sent to war as a sniper after 9/11. While Kyle's bestselling autobiography offers a reasonable position explaining his politics, the film eliminates that discussion entirely. There are no insights into Kyle's thoughts. Like the narrator of Creedence Clearwater Revival's "Fortunate Son," Kyle is just a plain American boy—unlike CCR's narrator, he's eager to go to war. Unlike innumerable war films that begin with the titles "Based on true events" or "Based on a true story," *American Sniper* makes no claims to truth. It begins by showing the worst thing the audience can imagine: Kyle shooting first a child, then his mother, engaged in attacking a Marine unit. If the story starts here, the film seems to say, how can there be any redemption?

Although shadowed by 9/11, it's unclear exactly when Kyle is in Iraq—that Kyle fights in Iraq, which had nothing to do with 9/11, goes without comment. The film then focuses on a fanatic Muslim and Olympic-level sniper known only as "Mustafa." Kyle and Mustafa spend the balance of the film engaged in what is known as a sniper duel—an entire subgenre of war films exists about snipers and the duels between them. Some recent examples include Tom Berenger's 1993 film *Sniper* and its franchise, Jude Law and Ed Harris's star vehicle about Stalingrad, *The Enemy at the Gates* (2001), and Mark Wahlberg's 2007 *Shooter*. In every case particularly talented snipers are pitted against each other. These are narratives about top predators; only one of them can survive. Both snipers are independent, resourceful, efficient, gifted at killing over nearly inconceivable distances. Usually the bad guy reveals himself to be cunning and ruthless, but also a sadist, child-killer, or both. The story's climax is almost invariably a long-distance shootout where the hero miraculously fires right down the other's rifle barrel, at once blinding and killing the enemy, symbolically smashing the gun's reticle, its artificial eye. Over the given distances, such shots are purely fictional. *American Sniper* includes the spotter, a crucial job in a sniping operation, but shows Kyle's spotter as a crude, useless team member: it's all up to Kyle. Other films often omit the spotter entirely to underline the hero's solitary nature.

American Sniper follows this narrative exactly, putting the bronco-busting, patriotic Texan Chris Kyle up against Mustafa, a Syrian (that is, not even a local, but a hired gun). Kyle performs four tours in Iraq until he finally takes an apparently impossible long shot and kills Mustafa. The Iraqis are uniformly referred to as "savages" by Kyle and his commanders. The film begins with Kyle's killing of a child because it shows his dedication, the terrible but necessary things soldiers must do in war, and because later he will nearly be unable to repeat the act. It is one of Eastwood's few attempts to subvert the obvious white and black hats narrative. The movie is divided between two storylines: one about Kyle's wife, left alone to raise the children; the other about Kyle's battle of nerves with Mustafa. The moment Mustafa is dead, Kyle, using the rare but in this film's case, ubiquitous satellite phone (it permits an ongoing plot device), calls his wife and announces that he's ready to come home and commit himself to the family. The two-hour thriller about seemingly perfectly matched enemies was taken from a single paragraph in the book.[18] In the original, although Kyle has an exchange with Mustafa, he rotates home and never sees him again—some other soldier kills the man.

The sniper duel has a familiar pattern to it: no matter how egregious the killing gets (children, women), the snipers always know they're killing the guilty. Kyle sees everything, knows, even when he has to kill the supposed innocent, that his shots are justified. The only person who sees and knows more than Kyle is Eastwood himself. There is to be no doubt, says the film, that the people Kyle kills deserve to die. The lack of grey areas in the film's war is underscored by one SEAL, hungry for revenge, who declaims "Lex Talionis!"— and the hunt is on. "Lex Talionis" is the Latin shorthand for Old Testament, eye-for-an-eye justice: this *is* your grandfather's war, if your grandfather fought in the Second World War. What's even more ironic about the invocation of a rule that is at the basis for just war theory (*jus ad bellum*, Latin for "right to war," generally refers to the idea that a war is justified if one party or nation deliberately attacks another: in just war theory it is legitimate to counterattack), is that Kyle and his SEAL team fight in Iraq, not Afghanistan. Iraq didn't attack the United States, nor did it have chemical, biological, or nuclear weapons, as the United States leadership and command knew. There was no just cause for the invasion and occupation of Iraq, no excuse to invoke Lex Talionis.[19] The sniper is more than just a soldier, a boot, a grunt, a walking gun. He is, like Sergeant James in *The Hurt Locker*, a super-soldier, a specialist, a dedicated, perfect killer who, in this case, comes to be known as "The Legend." These soldiers are the epitome of the contemporary military: technically skilled and in full mastery of the battlefield. They don't get it wrong, they don't slip, and they don't lose.

As in many war films, women, particularly mothers, are not made out to be attractive. Kyle's wife, Taya, comes across as a common scold, a shrew who relentlessly nags her husband that he's away at war too much and is missing crucial years of his family's development. While portrayed sympathetically when the film focuses on her and her difficulties at home, Taya doesn't value Kyle's work sufficiently. It's clear to the audience (who sees what she cannot) that she lives in blissful ignorance about the war—if only she knew what we know. She relentlessly pushes Kyle to leave the war and he persistently returns to pursue Mustafa, the specter haunting Iraq. Later saying he wishes he'd killed more in order to save his own men, Kyle begins taking wounded men suffering PTSD from the VA hospitals to train them in target shooting. The connections between guns and gender aren't subtle: "Got my balls back," says one grievously wounded paraplegic wheelchair-bound amputee after hitting a target. Shooting and killing are essential to masculinity; raising children and being a nag are women's work. It's no mistake that the day Kyle's wife praises him for finally returning to her emotionally is also the day he is killed. If you surrender, especially to your wife, you will die. At least Kyle isn't killed by one of the "savage" Iraqis who so disgust him—it takes an American soldier to kill The Legend. The film ends with documentary footage of Kyle's actual memorial service at the Dallas Cowboys' stadium and his subsequent burial with full Navy honours. Here is the truth claim Eastwood has forgone at the film's beginning. If you were in any doubt that the events you just witnessed were real, remember that an actual human being died so you could see this movie.

Reducing a long series of difficult war experiences to two simple parallel narratives about Kyle and his opposite enemy sniper, and Kyle's struggles with his shrewish wife, the film evades the politics of the war entirely, justifying Kyle's over 150 killings. He's only doing his job, which is to perform sniper overwatch for lesser soldiers on the ground. The cause, justness, legality, and issues at work in the war are accepted at face value. The only note of doubt comes when Kyle meets his brother, also now a soldier, in Iraq. A shaken, haggard figure obviously suffering from his experiences in country, the brother has no belief left in Iraq, the mission, or America's politics, telling Chris bluntly: "Fuck this place." An uncomprehending Chris can only goggle at his shell-shocked brother. At this point the audience recognizes that the father's message about the human race must be true: there are only three kinds of people in the world—sheep, predators, and sheepdogs. The brother is a weakling, a failed sheepdog who is really a sheep. Only Chris, living by Lex Talionis, is the sheepdog that can protect the flock from predators like Mustafa. The film refuses to move beyond the father's homespun simplicity: there are no shades of grey when a person is always one thing. One cannot be a sheep in some situations, a predator or sheepdog in others. The idea that Mustafa, the predator, might be a sheepdog for a different group of people isn't worth consideration.

The film's ending, elegiac and reverent in its treatment of Kyle as a saviour about whom it is hinted that he is too good for terrestrial life, reinforces that the true winner is the SEAL with the most service pins pounded onto his coffin lid; the SEAL tradition at funerals is that those directly affected by the dead soldier hammer their own gold SEAL insignia into the teammate's coffin lid. The hard-earned, beloved unit insignia pin known as the "SEAL Trident" or more commonly "The Budweiser" (the name comes from the BUD/S initialism for "Basic Underwater Demolition/SEAL" course) is crucial to the ritual. We've seen SEAL burials earlier where a paltry few SEALs add their pins to the coffin: only Kyle has row on countless row of badges on his coffin.[20] As with Ross Katz's much less known but equally heartfelt treatment of a soldier's death, *Taking Chance* (2009), the film portrays dead US soldiers as sacred individuals who are spontaneously recognized by the local and national communities as Old Testament protective sacrifices who bloody themselves so that the rest of us sheep may safely graze.[21]

American Sniper is superb propaganda. It looks like a plain truth without claiming to be the truth—it never promises to be anything but a story, until we see Kyle's coffin. The gritty quality Eastwood gives the film makes it feel believable. It speaks in simple actions and emotions, declaring its intentions upfront—after all, in how many films does an American begin by killing a child and its mother and still emerge not only as the good guy, but as a national hero? The film has no apparent politics and takes no political positions, left or right. Everything is normal, except for the regular American who, we discover, is exceptional when pressed by circumstance. By implication everyone could be Chris Kyle if they chose to be. Historical context is unimportant. An undeclared illegal international war with neither *Jus ad bellum* or *Jus in bello* is converted to a comfortable grudge match between their best and ours, planing down the world's rough complexities to a few nineteenth-century or Old Testament proverbs about good and evil, protectors and predators. At the end America stands, bloody but unbowed, the exemplar of moral and physical power. Chris Kyle is a common man who stands up for his country because it is his country and discovers that there are really only two kinds of people in the world: Americans and savages. The ritual at the film's end is one familiar from a different country and war: the country is refreshed and its cause renewed when the flag is dipped in blood.

American Sniper viewers may agree that the film makes them proud to be American, but would likely dispute that the film was political. Such viewers are identified by Jacques Ellul as people who would argue, "of course we shall not be victims of propaganda because we are capable of distinguishing truth from falsehood."[22] Ellul is most concerned about this viewer because he or she "is extremely susceptible to propaganda, because when propaganda does tell the 'truth,' he is then convinced that it is no longer propaganda; moreover, his self-confidence makes him all the more vulnerable to attacks of which he is unaware."[23] North American audiences who believed *American Sniper* had shown them the Iraq war's hard truths unleashed thousands of tweets as they left theatres. Some of the most famous comments tweeted in the first week of the film's release represented how an apparently apolitical text could immediately generate political expression. While some praised the film, others used the film to confirm standing prejudices: "Nice to see a movie where the Arabs are portrayed for who they are—vermin scum intent on destroying us. #Deblasio #AmericanSniper," and "American sniper [sic] made me appreciate soilders [sic] 100x more and hate Muslims 1000000x more"; or indicate their desires: "now I really want to kill some fucking ragheads."[24] Some made a direct connection between the two, as did Hunter Jeffries (@HunterJ_25) with his tweet, "If you don't come out of American Sniper wanting to cap towel-heads than [sic] you're not an American. #Merica"[25]

The tweets demonstrate the power of a text that sanctions racial and religious hatred even as it upholds the notion of national character. A true American hero knows how to act and calls it like he sees it. If the enemy are unworthy "savages," who would know better than our straight-talking advocate? These Twitter users were already prejudiced against Muslims, but now want to act on their hatred. Rage at the out-group becomes a high fever of nationalism: to be an American patriot is to support the film, hate the other, and join with fellow true believers who accept that *Amor patriae nostra lex*—Love of country is our law. Ellul traces the path propaganda cuts: "Propaganda offers him an object of hatred .... And the hatred it offers him is not shameful, evil hatred that he must hide, but a legitimate hatred, which he can justly feel" so that the enemy's death transforms "crime into a praiseworthy act."[26] Propaganda may also be the closest contact a citizen has with the war. How many ferocious racist Twitter users left screenings of *American Sniper*, joined the military, and wound up serving in Iraq or Afghanistan?

One of propaganda's strongest attributes, apart from rendering itself invisible, is to make its messages appear to be plain common sense. While Goebbels's 1943 "Total War" speech is a striking example of agitation propaganda, it is less effective than the steady ongoing communal reassertion that hating another group is normal and just, and that in order to protect a way of life one will have to forfeit it temporarily. Basic necessities like food, fuel, clothing, shelter, and medicine may have to be sacrificed in order to guarantee their return. Democracy, too, may have to be put in abeyance while the war is on for that same democracy. Protecting a way of life will be elevated to a moral cause from which only cowards retreat. The citizen's capitulation to the state in surrendering personal rights guaranteed by foundational doctrine (a charter or constitution) requires a good deal of reassurance from propaganda. War scholar Philip Beidler points out that gradually widening propaganda means it may be the most authentic experience of war the citizen has: in the Second World War "the wartime information and entertainment industry became so integral to American attitudes and understandings at home and abroad that by the time of victory in 1945, short of actual combat or direct involvement of a family member, it could be said that such productions came to constitute for most Americans the primary dimension of their experience of the war."[27] The overall goal would be that all cultural expressions support each other, that official statements, corporate media productions, popular and folkloric utterances and even discussions within a family reinforce the same message.

Agitation propaganda like war posters can also function like integration propaganda. Both world wars have been extensively examined in their reflections and representations by Allied and enemy propaganda posters. American posters from both wars are galleries of gorgeous war. Partly for that reason I deal with only one example here: the art has been discussed extensively. Intriguingly the critical propaganda poster texts often become valorizations first of the art and design, which are certainly remarkable examples of modernist graphic success, but soon slide over into approving of the wars and militaries that fought them. Unblinking scholarship has, however, been done not only by Sam Keen in his 1991 *Faces of the Enemy* and Walton Rawls in his *Wake Up, America!* (2001), but also by Monte Beauchamp and John Petrie, creators of a little-seen set of 1992 trading cards, *War Cry! Propaganda Poster Art of WWII.*

Of the hundreds of images, some particular few have been burned into the public imagination: James Montgomery Flagg's older but still virile Uncle Sam pointing at the viewer; an image of a gas-guzzling phantom Hitler riding in a partially empty car; a muscle-flexing Rosie the Riveter declaring "We can do it!"—all have become memes to be repurposed for whatever the advertiser or buyer wishes. In the late 1990s Rosie gained a tattoo and advertised for Tampax, a surreal *volte-face* in which propaganda became advertising. The most recent enraged and engaging commentary on war propaganda posters came from cartoon and comic book writer and previous Airborne Ranger Micah Ian Wright, whose dismay at the American attacks on Afghanistan and Iraq post-9/11 brought about his remixing of the canonical war posters, collected in his 2003 *You Back the Attack, We'll Bomb Who We Want!* and subsequent volumes. Because this territory is deep, requires a great deal of context, and has been covered at length already, I feel it is best hinted at. The following analysis of the famous " … because somebody talked!" poster is a suggestion of how intricate the issues can be.

While many war posters are calls to arms, to work, to conserve resources, some of the most famous are softer in appearance. The Office of War Information (OWI), the United States' official propaganda arm created in 1942, initially had its greatest successes with sweeter rather than more savage appeals to the public.[28] Foremost would be the poster of a sad-eyed cocker spaniel looking out at the viewer across a sailor's neckerchief, framed by a gold-star service flag given to families that had lost a soldier in the war. The partial tagline " … because somebody talked!" not only exhorts the viewer to silence, but casts a shadow on possible villains. The sailor might have been lost because the war was going badly, because the ship fell victim to a U-boat attack, or any of another hundred reasons. Were there really people giving away information, or was the poster's main point to draw together the in-group, to unite the homeland by encouraging paranoia against all others? The OWI learned that pictures of dead soldiers were the least popular on posters. Here the body is a ghostly presence: the skilled rendering, strong composition, and sentimental image of the dog is all soft power that divides the audience into those who adore the poster and what it stands for, and the fearsome internal, invisible enemy who plots home's downfall.

The poster was an enormous success—requests for reprints, which reached into the millions, outstripped all others.[29] *American Sniper* and the cocker spaniel both appear to be honest statements about loss, emotional pleas for sympathy from those who simply wished to do good and were betrayed not by governments but by their fellow citizens. As Winkler notes, the mission of the OWI was not just to illustrate how bad the enemy was, but how good was quotidian American existence, how much it required protection: the "OWI constantly sought to generate an appreciation for the American way of life. It issued stories on everything from ballet to baseball. It showed Americans fighting boll weevils, planting victory gardens, and going to church."[30]

Advertising and propaganda worked as a unified force, selling products and a war economy with them. Media outlets, from radio to print, existed not just to dispense information, but to join in the creation of national character, a flexible definition of what it meant to be a patriot. For T. J. Jackson Lears "national advertising was the quintessential institution of the developing image empire. Through the mass circulation of visual aids to fantasy, it promoted perpetual, unfulfillable longings, and focused those longings on commodities,"[31] which, for Susman, produced "a set of significant symbols to give more Americans a sense of belonging and role."[32] Advertising made promises about the future that could only be fulfilled by following the script jointly produced by corporations and government. The aims of the OWI and the ad industry were the same: to win, and in winning, create a nation that physically, industrially, militarily brought about a particular world of economic values and morals.

OWI director Elmer David framed the "basic message" of American forces and nation this way: "that we are coming, that we are going to win, and that in the long run everybody will be better off because we won."[33] Brand evangelist Simon Anholt, credited by some "as the instigator of the scientific discussion on place brands and place branding,"[34] suggests that Americans have since learned to let soft power do the bulk of the work in changing minds: "One reason why culture is so effective at [breaking borders] is that consumers aren't so suspicious of it as they are of commercial messages. Even if it's popular culture, it's still art, or at least entertainment, so people relax their vigilance and don't look for hidden agendas. Until recently, Hollywood movies could get away with some fairly explicit celebrations of American values, and foreign audiences just sat back and enjoyed the show."[35] Whether or not one agrees with Anholt's assessment, his comments about culture line up with the OWI's pursuit of its early propaganda campaigns. As the war worsened, the OWI had to change tactics. Managing images in order to generate a shared fantasy world to which the harried wartime citizen could retreat became more crucial in the United States and Germany as the war slogged on. But while images can be consumed, they can't be eaten, can't endlessly replace the physical world, something countries facing wartime staple shortages learned about propaganda. In both countries "it was equally recognized that propaganda by itself cannot win any struggle for allegiances—hence the need in many instances to back it up with force or coercion."[36]

Despite its stated wish not to use propaganda, the OWI was designed to tell the war story the United States needed to hear. Even though they admitted to bending information, those working at the OWI "insisted vigorously that they were honest and forthright in what they did."[37] Being direct and deeply believing in one's work aren't the same as telling the truth. While the OWI agreed that it was a propaganda office, it's unclear how much that statement would help the audience, particularly since the office "acknowledged that they made selective use of the truth and shaped it to their own ends."[38] The problem for any viewer who cannot see the whole picture is that it becomes impossible to decipher what pieces have been altered or are missing altogether. As soon as the door is open to information control, determining the degree to which it has been left open, what data has been refused entry and why, is impossible. There's no such thing as partial propaganda for the audience. The viewer can practice maintaining perpetual skepticism about the source, question every statement and conclusion, but after a long enough time the ongoing guessing game becomes exhausting. Few will have the resources or inclination to dissect the bigger picture and by deduction puzzle out what's been changed. Even if one had access to some mythic complete data stack, few would have sufficient ability to sift it for the crucial as opposed to the inconsequential.

Brand proponent Simon Anholt gives warm, if slightly embarrassed, support to the OWI, claiming that, "whatever the news, the OWI gave a truthful story, but perhaps not what we would call a straight story."[39] Such a sentiment must blush: how is "not ... a straight story" also not a lie? If we're sympathetic to the teller, we might call it a "half-truth," something that isn't as bankrupt as a lie, that lies by omission, or is unimportant. But in no propaganda-heavy environment can "not ... a straight story" be used as a synonym for "truth." Anholt's acceptance of manipulation lines up with his profession of image maker: if one is going to make a brand sell globally, it will have to be welcomed by many diverse populations. Somewhere in there a gap or gaps will open between what the brand promises and what it actually delivers. It can't actually be all things to all people. The picture will be sweetened or sharpened; the viewer will be lured in by various appeals. In order to persuade audiences to leave one brand for another, something different, better, and closer to an ideal has to be offered. Whatever is missing is what the new brand will provide. Wartime propaganda's coercion is aimed more at convincing people to surrender what they already have, to work as hard or harder than before and get less in return. Only so many appeals to indefinable abstracts like country or national identity will be answered before people start to wonder what they'll get in exchange. It's a bitter pill to swallow that multiple sacrifices net one a lesser version of what one had all along. The propaganda war on America by Americans wasn't to prevent Americans from opting for a German, Italian, or Japanese brand, but to keep Americans signed on to supporting the cause for the war's duration.

George Roeder, image and propaganda scholar, notes that "despite this comparative openness of American information policy, the story told in this book is mainly one of control. Because of growing public immunity to overt propaganda, civilian and military leaders realized that often they could have their greatest impact on public attitudes by withholding information."[40] Initially the result was a sanitization of photographs, posters showing corpses, and war films in general (soldiers famously booed John Wayne when he appeared before veterans of Iwo Jima and Okinawa, while another soldier professed his irritation on seeing gratuitous fictions like "Humphrey Bogart whipping a whole German armored-car column single-handedly").[41] Explicit photos of the bloody American dead only appeared in 1944 and 1945 when the public had ceased responding to bond drives. Finally the OWI unleashed its photographic arsenal, despite its concern that the public's emotions would burn out, leaving them inured to graphic violence.[42] The OWI's desire to avoid propaganda both in the United States and overseas ultimately failed, leading to "the least successful American propaganda agency until mid-war reforms changed its doctrine and ideological complexion."[43] The shift from sanitized to graphic images fits agitation propaganda's general trajectory, which is from quiet to loud, less to more, mild to extreme. The process continues until the subjects no longer respond.

In regard to Nazi propaganda David Welch notes that "often, propaganda is concerned with reinforcing existing trends and beliefs, to sharpen and focus them," rather than solely being aimed at changing "attitudes and ideas."[44] Some might wish to restrict Welch's comments to the Nazis' endeavours alone, but the tools are the tools wherever they are used. The difference between Anholt's "not ... a straight story" and the word "lie" depends a great deal on the audience. A civilian might be entertained and heartened by a film about war heroes, where the soldier is annoyed. For Jacques Ellul there is no easy difference between propaganda as used by different nations. Rejecting the notion that propaganda can be employed for good purposes, Ellul asks, "why always fall into the error of seeing in propaganda nothing but a device to *change* opinions?", reminding the reader that "propaganda is also a means of *reinforcing* opinions, of transforming them into action. The reader himself offers his throat to the knife of the propaganda he chooses."[45] Change and continuity, reinforcement, reassurance—propaganda will be exercised for all these jobs, most invisibly or in ways the society accepts as legitimate.

To live in a democracy is to confront the paradoxical claim that speech, information, and ideas are—largely—free. It is the caveat to which we must attend. As Stanley Fish notes about expression, "when the pinch comes (and sooner or later it will always come) and the institution (be it church, state or university) is confronted by behaviour subversive of its core rationale, it will respond by declaring 'of course we mean not tolerate ————, that we extirpate.'"[46] Boundaries around speech exist in the best of times; they may not be as visible as they are during wartime when expression becomes more hotly contested, when definitions of patriotism and justice narrow, when fear makes censorship and repression seem reasonable. Sooner or later the citizen will knock against these barriers and discover the difference between what is professed and practiced. To live in a democracy is to believe that the people chooses, even while acknowledging strong corporate and governmental forces for persuasion exist, that billions of dollars are channelled into coercive speech in order to promulgate a particular way of life. Semi-public socializing mechanisms like families, schools, and religions will take up the same instruments of persuasion in order to create new citizen believers.

Despite the visible daily power being exercised, the inescapable flood of corporate messages about how to behave, citizens in democracies hold to the idea that they are free to choose, and at worst free to opt out entirely. When confronting the tools designed to create mass behaviour, consensus on central issues and ways of living, and agreement about what is and is not divergent from the norm, the citizen who wishes to assuage the angst about living in a contradiction can take up a number of positions. The person can claim that persuasive tools like advertising inform and educate us about the market but don't in themselves create values—the citizen does that; that advertising and propaganda may work on those less well educated about and alert to their freedoms, but such forces don't affect the individual, who knowingly creates their own ideas and promulgates them (the person is a leader, not a follower); that advertising and information management works to better the system, to help people choose what's best, to show people how to improve their lives; that advertising and propaganda are daily examples of the free market in motion, producing a sort of commercial Darwinian selection that eliminates the weak and leaves behind the fittest consumables.

Advertising in a democracy can be trusted, goes the argument, because it serves the people in the market. You cannot hurt, damage, or kill the consumer if you wish to stay in business. You can show the citizen examples of coercion or damage. The gap between the Takata Corporation's workers warning its executive about car airbag problems (2004) and the subsequent cover-up by and bankruptcy of Takata after the recall of seventy million airbags was twelve years and sixteen American deaths. In early 2017 the United States Justice Department formally charged Ford, Honda, Nissan, and Toyota with knowingly installing Takata's faulty airbags in their cars, participating in the cover up that, Justice alleges, dated to 1999. Such a story could cause the citizen to panic. One way to resolve the fear is to point to openly repressive global regimes and take comfort in the fact that things are infinitely worse there.[47] After all, someone is sure to say about the airbag problem, only sixteen people in the United States died because of the bags before the system sorted itself out, which seems reasonable if you aren't one of those sixteen or part of their families. What's intriguing about the Takata case is the idea that there was some magic number that would trigger an investigation and fix: did actuarial scientists determine that the collective could afford to handle fifteen deaths, but that at sixteen, the cost overruns would be too high? Or was it more banal and that at sixteen deaths the exposure for the big carmakers and Takata had just become too great, had drawn too much attention? There is also a persistent optimism that coercion in democracies will ultimately fail because one cannot sell the impossible. Enough people must want the product (whether it is information, a physical item, a service) or nobody would buy it: it isn't some fad pushed on an unwitting populace but something people have deliberately chosen on their own.

Simon Anholt, engaged in advertising, branding, and writing educational books about persuasive practices, declares that democracy's citizens needn't worry about information being turned to malicious uses because "in the end, it's not the law or the morality of politicians that protects citizens from propaganda, but the fact that they probably couldn't do it if they tried, especially to a well-educated population in a modern democracy."[48] At root is the same belief that drives the characters, particularly Kyle's father, in *American Sniper*: you can't cheat an honest person because they know intuitively there's no such thing as a short cut or a fast buck. The righteous will be protected by their modest desires, inherent nobility, and trust in the social contract. It's instructive that the three top-performing Hollywood war films about Iraq or Afghanistan, *American Sniper*, *Lone Survivor*, and *The Hurt Locker*, all have white heterosexual family men as heroes. None of the soldiers has gone to fight in order to secure a green card, and while the implication is that they are blue collar or working class, they have not grown up in racial ghettos. They are the great generation and Clint Eastwood's inheritors. Anholt's belief that you can't successfully propagandize the elite (it isn't clear what his definition of "well educated" is, but his readership is likely to have at least a college education), is informed by his own position as one of those very men invested in convincing people that they, not information handlers with their persuasive techniques, are in charge. To suggest otherwise would seem cynical.

CHAPTER 10

Paraded to Death

Nazi Propaganda

GUY HAMILTON'S 1969 *BATTLE OF BRITAIN* TELLS ITS STORY by juxtaposition. A calm island nation of young, beautiful people and crusty but honest older people is suddenly and traumatically attacked, with barely the resources to fend off the assault. The narrative works the way most David and Goliath stories do, particularly common in the American Western tradition of the underdog sheriff or the boxing-ring counter-puncher. All goes badly for the heroes, and just when it appears there might be a break in the beatings, they worsen. Characters we like die bloody, agonizing deaths. Then more of them die. The Americans refuse to come. We know, and are desperate for, the moment when the underdog gets up from the floor. He's all clarity, calmness, and justice in his eyes, and not only defeats but destroys the opponent. There is no cheering when this occurs because the hammer of retribution is so final. Nobody needs to tell the hero or us, the audience, who has won. Hamilton's film works by initially alternating between the British leadership, grimly drinking tea in the face of certain elimination, and happy Nazis standing around medieval castles, watching as the skies are darkened by endless waves of Luftwaffe bombers passing overhead. The British side of the story is so bleak, sodden, and brown (brown uniforms, brown London in the rain, tight-lipped expressions of gloom), where the Nazis are all smiles, sunlight, Göring's operatic uniforms, and imminent victory that it's a relief to leave the losers behind and shift over to the Nazis, even if they are, well, Nazis.

The film's strategy is enormously effective. The British have nothing, and from nothing slowly drag out a victory, and not just some sullen partial victory but a true drubbing. All of this is evident from the film's use of color, wardrobe, scenery, and props. It could almost be a silent film, so clear is the sign system about what winning means, and how resplendence, the external, that which is for show, cannot overcome a steady internal will. It's important to remember, though, that looking good is half the battle, or in this case half the film.

If the American propaganda system was, like the country's heraldic effort, weak, particularly when compared to the Nazi juggernaut, the overall effectiveness of the Nazi's graphic plan across media as diverse as clothing, banners, film, and badges causes designer Steven Heller to conclude that Hitler's "identity system" is in fact "the most ingeniously consistent graphic program ever devised. That he succeeded ... is attributable to his complete mastery of the design and propaganda processes."[1] Hitler held full control of the design, production, distribution, and display of the brand; he also governed the brand's context. There was no visual or ideological noise, nothing to compete with the worldview's pure signal. Each piece of design also acted as propaganda, each performed a job for the Reich, each, having been stripped down to its essential function, was part of the overall machine. All around them was the brand—those not yet included were presented with innumerable ways to consume and be consumed by it, in keeping with Welch's note that "propaganda is as much about confirming as about converting public opinion."[2] Propaganda wasn't incidental to Hitler and Goebbels' understanding of the war: it was indispensable to it. Capturing an audience was only the beginning of the job. Successful propaganda would mean instructing the community in its new Nazi behaviour and winning the war. Historian Ian Kershaw points out the "extraordinarily ambitious" Nazi propaganda goals burdened the machine with "the reconstruction of a value system."[3] A decisive propaganda victory gave its creators, they believed, an unfettered hand in pursuing political and military goals "without worrying about the moods and opinions of the nation."[4] That proved false after Goebbels scored a huge propaganda victory with his February 1943 *Sportpalast* "Total War" speech (*"Nun, Volk steh auf, und Sturm, brich los"*). The speech burned off some of the cloud that was the massive loss at Stalingrad, but the war soon reasserted itself. No propaganda success was so powerful it could overcome the Reich's imminent collapse.

At the same time, the definition of success has to be examined. If propaganda functions perfectly and creates a vibrant inner world for the subject to inhabit, then the reality of external events is secondary and can be denied. That world outside exists because the impact it has is undeniable, but it is also perceived as a mistake. Magda Goebbels and others like her, with the determination to plan and then murder her six children, were examples of complete propaganda victories. Historian Richard Evans points to the "vast wave of suicides without precedent in modern history," where thousands of deaths accompanied the Reich's end.[5] Reprisals by the advancing Soviet army against German civilians for atrocities committed on the Eastern Front were an added incentive for suicide. Choosing suicide before submission to any other than the propagandized worldview is a demonstration of an information victory. In many religious economies opting for death in martyrdom over life through recantation is the mark of a true believer (or zealot, depending on your point of view). Magda Goebbels was arguably both. Even before Goebbels killed her children and herself, Hitler understood that she had stepped through into his world, awarding her his own golden Party Badge for being the "First Mother of the Reich." When one world ceases to be sustainable, in this case brought about by the physical reality of the war's end, the individual retreats into the unimpeachable ideal that comes with death. Propaganda has ceased to be packets of information and has become everything. As appalling as Magda Goebbels's acts were, they signal, as with other Germans who murdered their families and then committed suicide, that the new worldview had so enveloped the audience as to force out any other ways of seeing. One world remains: if the individual cannot have it, then existence literally ceases. Magda Goebbels's behaviour may produce a level of disgust in the reader such that we hit a wall: belief derived from propaganda is one thing, but belief strong enough cause the murder of six children is insanity. But propaganda's tools don't vary that much: to sign on to and repeat Patrick Henry's 1775 "Give me liberty or give me death!" is to read from the same script.[6] Some may claim these are very different, that Magda Goebbels's actions are those of a brainwashed victim while Patrick Henry's speech represents the sovereign being's declamation about exercising choice. Our understanding of these different events likely has to do with the extent to which we believe in the individual's supremacy and inviolability.

For scholar Roger Griffin, brainwashing isn't a helpful term: propaganda can be taken as "'brainwashing' on one level, it *also authentically* expresses a quintessentially primordial human drive to resolve the unprecedented sociopolitical and *nomic* crisis through which European history was passing after the First World War."[7] Beliefs that in one group's eyes are visibly false and manipulative are no less real to their followers, nor is it more or less correct to believe one way as opposed to another. At some point in the discussion one side will make appeals to what is "natural" or inherent in "human nature," referring to some form of moral or legal authority found in religious guides, books of social conduct, or definitions of legality. Propaganda's results are that much more dramatic when people are not only convinced by it, but repeatedly argue that the morally proper actions they take are entirely of their own choosing. Magda Goebbels's actions may strike us as abhorrent, as will thousands of other attacks on the innocent, but the ideas that drove her to choose filicide and suicide made as much sense to her as our beliefs, complete with evasions, denials, contradictions, do to us.[8] Propaganda went beyond the sound and light shows organized by Goebbels, Speer, and Hitler. The overall spectacle of the Reich was composed of many expressions, some of which I look at here, beginning with the idea of the concept of the whole as a unified piece of design, and the subsets I've glanced at before: uniforms as heraldry, graphic and industrial design.

The Reich's propaganda effort can be visualized as a parade. At its best the parade is a genuine public show to the public by the public; it is a routed through public and private spaces, the shared ideas and strengths of a people. It is the visible negotiation of power between the citizenry and state. The parade takes time to pass—one part of it isn't enough to demonstrate the collective's power and breadth. Seeing and hearing one part of the parade isn't sufficient for the citizen to be convinced that the right people are both included and excluded. Acts, music, speeches will need to be repeated. Looking back over the procession, it may or may not be possible for the individual to locate the precise moment their thinking shifted. In historian Frederic Spotts's view of the Nazi's aesthetic machine, Hitler was at times like a composer, at others a painter who deployed "Storm Troopers and other party units in their black, brown or red-brown uniforms, he blended and contrasted colour," and "arranged regimented blocks of human beings in geometric formations as though he were an architect."[9] The people who aren't invited, just as much as those who are, perform crucial roles in the ongoing show. The persecution, degradation, and slaughter of the dispossessed are just as central to the whole expression.

In such a regime it becomes increasingly difficult to draw a line between the overall design and the collective because the government is founded on "'aestheticized' politics, featuring, for example, the marshalling of masses in geometrical formations … uniforms, insignia and ranking symbols and the integration of individuals in secular rituals of acclamation and submission."[10] There are few, if any, public expressions of Nazism that are not both spectacle (including very real deaths and atrocities) and propaganda for the regime. Each act of power is a demonstration of the aesthetics of force, speed, and efficiency. Even the losses can be beaten into useful mythic forms of Norse tragedy illustrated by epic Wagnerian scenes that explain catastrophes like Stalingrad, the collapse of the German lines in the Battle of the Bulge, or the firebombings of Dresden and Hamburg. As historian Jill Stephenson points out, "virtually every public statement or project became an act of propaganda," which meant that "every office of the party and state [became] a propaganda agency."[11] The ongoing attachment to spectacle was demonstrated by Hitler's fascination with Speer's maquette for *Welthauptstadt Germania*, particularly in the Reich's last days when the *Volkssturm* had been killed off and the Hitler bunker was about to be overrun. Perhaps the "real" Reich was a Platonic creation, an aesthetic form that existed outside the world of appearances. Vanishing into tragedy and suicide "contained its own solace for many Germans and especially for their leaders. Victory was elusive, but in the celebration of heroic death an individual might transcend himself and become part of what Adolf Hitler called 'national immortality.'"[12]

The rituals of reassurance and reinforcement accompanying the salute and swastika included the uniforms themselves, both for the Brownshirts ("*Braunhemden*," *Sturmabteilung*, or SA) and the black-jacketed SS (*Schutzstaffel*). What for the SA had once been determined by cheapness and affordability became, over time, an integral part of the brand. A massive excess of dark khaki material used by the Weimar's army for its tropic uniforms, then obtained cheaply and in quantity by the Nazis in the mid 1920s, became the marker of the whole.[13] As Steve Luckert at the Holocaust Memorial Museum says about the uniform, "even looking at some of these uniforms ... fills a lot of people with dread and terror."[14] The uniforms that preceded the famous SS black leather coats were made, but not designed, by the now upmarket clothier Hugo Boss (among others), then a small company with barely enough income to remain solvent. Boss joined the party in 1931 partly because he believed in the cause, but mostly to save his nearly bankrupt firm. Later on he accepted 180 slave labourers from Poland and France into his factory. Boss manufactured the infamous uniforms but did not, it has taken sixty-five years to rediscover, produce the designs.

The historical study commissioned by Hugo Boss AG eventually established that Boss had been a manufacturer not instigator, although the company certainly used slave labour.[15] In 1997, when the story first broke, the press and public connected the haute couturier's present designs with fashions devised for the SS. One of Boss's sons, Siegfried, said bluntly in 1997, "Of course my father belonged to the Nazi party .... But back then, who didn't? The whole industry worked for the Nazi army."[16] As Roman Köster, the historian hired by Hugo Boss AG notes, "the frequent focus on Hugo Boss is likely due to the fact that observers 'project' today's company back into the days of the Third Reich. In reality

[it] ... was not a fashion company at all. Rather it was a manu-facturing plant."[17] About the publicity fracas that overwhelmed Boss AG in the late 1990s, spin expert at Hill & Knowlton Frank Mankiewicz correctly predicted that little harm would follow: "They're [Boss] going to lose some business," he commented, "but they'll probably gain some notoriety."[18] By 2012, when a *Sunday Times* business reporter wrote about the status of Boss AG post market crash, the issue had become a mere subheading: "The brand is back—and that awkward Nazi link addressed."[19] Köster's note that a twenty-first-century public will tend to map the present day Hugo Boss AG onto the interwar company points up the main issue: the uniforms were powerful, stylish, more than functional—they were high fashion items straight out of mod-ernism. We identified the uniforms as items that the present-day Boss AG might produce: the brown shirts and black SS uniforms had a magnetism of their own, so it wasn't a big step to assume Boss was responsible for the Nazis' sartorial finery.

For many, it would make no difference who designed the clothing, only that Boss AG was complicit in helping the Reich. For my purpose, the uniform designer is important. Was the SS uniform, like the colour of the SA shirt, an accident, or was this a calculated piece of design that clicked into the overall propaganda array? In the end it turned out that the uniforms were specifically designed for the SS, a collaborative effort between SS officer Karl Bietsch and graphic designer Walter Heck.[20] Pictures of SS offi-cers reviewing new uniforms properly displayed on tailor's dum-mies indicated just how seriously the Reich took the whole pro-cess. We can compare that depiction with Paul Fussell's comment about the way American soldiers wore their uniforms, which he describes as "*sloppery*," and quotes Victor Klemperer's first sight-ing of American troops who didn't appear to be "soldiers in the Prussian sense at all. They do not wear uniforms but overalls."[21]

Uniform historian Brian Davis argues that "the German Army's uniforms and equipment during the National Socialist period were much in advance of other contemporary nations both in design and manufacture," concluding that they "were well designed with inbuilt smartness and practicality" that continued to be evident in post-war uniforms of various militaries (both East and West Germany as well as the Soviet Union).[22] Of the things that survived the war, uniform design was one of the most visible.[23] The dozens of varied uniform tabs, designs, and colours integral to Nazi insignia "included some striking and very attractive designs, many of which have reappeared in the insignia of the *Bundeswehr* of West Germany and the National *Volksarmee* of East Germany."[24] The practice of weaving cuff titles and decorations with aluminum thread made the uniforms that much more unusual. The weaving was precise, driven by a Jacquard process that used early punch cards to program the looms. In hobby circles the garments are referred to as "BeVo" pieces because they were manufactured by the *Beteiligung Vorsteher* (the Vorsteher Partnership), a clothing manufacturer. Using aluminum, a light, shiny, pliable metal that wouldn't tarnish, was in every aspect smart design.

While the uniform, based in part on the Black Hussars' history, was crucial to the newly formed army, it was also another way to indicate the circles of power in which one travelled. Those who joined early and survived the murderous intraparty battles could become political leaders. They had earned their own uniforms because, according to the *Organisationsbuch*, there was to be "a clear distinction between the type of person who is a Political Leader of the NSDAP and the civil politicians of former Parties and States," the latter being "a Preacher and a Soldier at one and the same time."[25] It was a long haul, in the eyes of uniform historian David Littlejohn, from the nascent distinguishing signs of the *Kampfbinde*, the swastika-marked brassard carried furtively and worn with risk, to the installation of these once-rejected people as the leaders of leaders.[26] For Paul Fussell the "wholly black uniform of the German SS was a triumph of originality .... For the SS, blackness could be associated with a whole rich folklore of intimidation and useful wickedness."[27] The uniforms' signifying power vastly outplayed the literal drabness of American and Russian gear. In Fussell's view this was the chance for the Germans to "dress up" for their starring twentieth century role (win or lose, they still got to wear uniforms, about which Fussell twits them for being "a nation besotted with the wearing of military and paramilitary uniforms of all kinds").[28]

Few things escaped the brand, which was evident at every level of the uniform. In the 2009 *Hitler Dans Mon Salon*, an unusual collection of photographs curated by *Charlie Hebdo* cartoonist Riss (pen name for Laurent Sourisseau), Riss brought together photographs he purchased from various sellers on eBay, people who had opened to the public family photo albums depicting Nazis young and old relaxing at home, as the title suggests, and on picnics, at the shore, generally having a good time.[29] These informal shots taken from what one article calls "*des tranches de vie*," include pictures of men in black bathing suits complete with the SS twin runes in a white circle placed directly over the penis. One picture shows friends at the seaside, a man in a white undershirt complete with encircled black SS logo on the centre torso.[30] The shirt's design looks ahead some thirty or more years to a time when brands and ads would become selling points. While the SS bathing suit might seem more like something dreamed up by Mel Brooks or Monty Python than Hitler, it remains a useful index of the depth of belief expected from the elite corps.

Of the rare design misfires, one was the gorget worn by soldiers as diverse as bandleaders and police officers. Hung around the neck on a silver chain, the steel semicircle was stamped with the unit's identification. In most pictures of soldiers on the move the unfortunate collar bounces around clumsily, a failed reference to breastplates from history. A delighted Fussell points out gleefully that the other troopers found the gorget laughable and snidely referred to any who wore it as "*Kettenhunde*" (chained dogs).[31] When the Nazi signification machinery failed, it did so extravagantly.

Susan Sontag wrestled with the fact that the SS uniform became a fetish of increasing power after the war. She concluded that the uniform's continued attraction lay in the fact that it was an "ideal incarnation of Fascism's overt assertion of the righteousness of violence, the right to have total power over others and to treat them as absolutely inferior."[32] The uniform was all that was taboo: it was the antithesis of the heterosexual, familial, conformist promise of post-war American life, a destroying blackness that meant death to all but the wearer. It was a sign of pure negation, a shouted refusal to whatever was considered normal. At some point in the 1960s, as the Vietnam war threatened and finally cracked open consensus about America's place on the planet, the black uniform, in concert with black leather, masks, collars, chains, whips, and restraints of all kinds, began to be useful to the world of bondage and domination.

For a period in the 1970s sadomasochism and Nazism seemed coterminous (not that such an equivalence was accurate then or now), a mainstream perception reinforced by art house films of the European new wave like Visconti's *The Damned* (1969) and Cavani's *The Night Porter* (1974), spawning an American subgenre of schlock soft-core sex and death films of which *Ilsa, She Wolf of the SS* (1975) for a long time remained the apotheosis. In the twenty-first century there has been a return to Nazi exploitation films, if there can be such a thing, which have combined Nazis and zombies, producing outright or spoof horror films like *Outpost* (2007), the Norwegian *Dead Snow* (2009), and the Finnish *Iron Sky* franchise (2012–2017) about Nazis on the moon. The shortest route to upsetting the established order was to deface its valued signs and wear or inscribe the worst markers from the past. Swastikas, SS runes and uniforms, inverted pentagrams, all signalled violent rejection of Main Street. Nazi signs continue to be indexes of psychological, ideological sickness and taboo breaking.

The black uniform with its high-peaked cap reinforced by wire, woven aluminum or silver braid, black leather coat, and hobnailed jackboots, are part of the visual, tactile machinery that converted not just the parade grounds with their massed troops, but the streets, shops, houses, and culture overall. One of the best recent treatments of the uniform's power can be found in Wolfgang Murnberger's 2011 film *Mein Bester Feind* (*My Best Enemy*). The film relies on and visually orbits an SS uniform worn at different times by a Nazi and his once good friend, a German Jew and laager inmate. The uniform subtly transforms whoever wears it into a person of unquestioned and unquestionable authority. While the text is not magic realist, the uniform embodies an existence of its own, wearing the characters rather than the reverse. Murnberger films the clothing such that its material qualities can be felt. It is always shown in perfect, depthless blackness. For Jeffrey Herf, "the reactionary modernist tradition reached its end point in the SS," which by 1944 had become the avant-garde of the Reich, both as a fighting force numbering nearly a million soldiers and as the locus of new weapons research. Herf suggests that, luckily for the planet, the reactionary modernist attachment to its parochial roots made chemistry and engineering, even rocketry, acceptable areas of study, but that these modernists considered the high energy physics required for development of atomic weapons to be insufficiently Aryan.[33]

The larger dressing of the world, outside the uniforms and the endlessly rotating *Hakenkreuz*, occurred on the German industrial stage where the Nazis engaged with modernity. Herf notes, "now that technology had become part of the *Volksgemeinschaft*, it had assumed clear and beautiful forms."[34] For scholars Roger Griffin and Jeffrey Herf, modernity and modernism were hard to separate when it came to industrial design. For Peter Fritzsche newness was integral to National Socialism, where "renovation was a state of mind, a process rather than a destination."[35] Nowhere was this clearer than in the NSDAP's building projects, from the outsize architectural and industrial works to the minute details of industrial design. Mark Antliff points out that Nazi cultural instincts were curious, illuminating: "the Nazi regime—like its Italian counterpart and fascist movements in France—looked to both a mythic past and a technological future in a manner that seems highly contradictory."[36] Even after the 1933 shuttering of the Bauhaus, Mies van der Rohe continued submitting work to the Reich, causing Griffin to ponder the ways in which "the image of the Reichsminister for Propaganda and Enlightenment, Joseph Goebbels, encouraging Mies van der Rohe to tender for prestigious regime projects encourages us to 'revisit' the whole subject of Nazism's famed jihad against modernism."[37]

Some of the Bauhaus's ideals and designs had been employed "openly in the interests of the National Socialist system."[38] The Bauhaus's closure has been understood by historians as a sign that modernism was finished in the Reich, but in Antliff's view, the symbolic quality of the Bauhaus's end "has obscured the relation of Nazi industrial design to that developed under the Weimar Republic and the degree to which the Nazi regime actively embraced modernity."[39] Mies stayed and went on designing buildings and furniture, submitting Reichsbank plans at Goebbels's urging, only leaving Germany in 1938 when he became convinced that, between them, Hitler and Albert Speer had closed off all avenues to modernist architecture. Mies who had, with the German Pavilion at the 1929 Barcelona Exposition, shown what the world could expect from pure Bauhaus architecture that refused all decoration and made visible the workings of the structure, continued to be an accepted voice in the Reich.

The Nazis' ongoing passion for a future of high technology pushed the building of the *Autobahnen*.[40] The roads, like the radio networks, were first to unite Germany and then the larger Reich. Even as it built roads the state planned green spaces in both rural and urban settings, which, as Griffin notes, were "symptoms of a concerted effort to establish a new harmony in the relationship of technological modernity to the forces of 'nature' and 'life',' " all of which were "were decades ahead of their time."[41] The roads were also another spectacle: "No mere superhighway, the autobahn told the world that dictatorship was more effective than democracy and that Nazi Germany had reconciled technology and aesthetics, machinery and nature, the past and the future."[42] Hitler's dream of roads could only come to fruition when the people had the freedom to get away from the dangerous influences of the dark urban environment and be renewed by nature. Here was another way in which the most recent form of modernity could release people from an older version of it, or as Christopher Hurndall notes, "what the construction of the railways meant to the nineteenth century, the building of the autobahn meant to the twentieth."[43]

Having read Henry Ford's autobiography while imprisoned in Landsberg, Hitler later began to think about and sketch unusual organic designs for a small car that could double as a military vehicle.[44] Finally he gave the job to the Porsche motor works with instructions to produce a small car as dedicated to (and affordable by) the people as had been Ford's Model T. The car was to be extremely fuel efficient, an ongoing problem for a regime struggling with oil supply problems, and able to take a crew of three, one of whom would carry a machine gun—the ammunition would occupy the fourth space. The car's civilian configuration allowed for carrying three adults and one child.[45] In either case the car's design followed from its function: resolving practical goals would produce the most natural, economical, and aesthetic solutions. The perfection of forms (simple geometric shapes) would eliminate the need for ornament. Good design would be self-evident: at the magic point where affordability, engine power, fuel-efficient shape, and best interior space organization overlapped there would exist a pure vehicle. Few pieces of industrial design are more successful or are better expressions of modernist design than the *Volkswagen*.

In Hitler's vision the car's name was intimately tied to its function: it was to be for the people, what Hitler called "the broad masses," to "give them joy and happiness."[46] "Joy" (*Freude*) the significant word here, was the heart of the *Kraft durch Freude* (KdF, "Strength Through Joy") state leisure program that oversaw the Volkswagen's production. Joy through technology was familiar to those buying into Ford's dreams of freedom through car ownership. American and German city-bound families would escape to nature in their cars. The inherent contradiction of using machines to rediscover the natural world fascinated American modernists like Sheeler, Hopper, Driggs, and Joseph Stella. In Germany, it was Nazi poster designer Ludwig Hohlwein who best captured the exhilaration of machine living. His 1939 poster with the headline "Your Own KdF Car" shows a laughing Aryan couple, the vision of health with tans and perfect white teeth, the woman standing in the passenger seat waving delightedly through the sunroof. Behind a background of green forest and fields are snow-capped mountains. The ad displays the Reich's colours: the vivid red of the woman's sweater is set off by her bright white shirt and headband, the clothing is SA uniform brown, and the black car grounds everything. The Reich's pride in modernity returns the original Aryan couple to a delirious prelapsarian state.

Contemporary car designer and creator of the VW Concept One car that became the 1998 reissue of the Beetle, J. Mays, says about cars that "people need an escape and an experience that is different from their day-to-day lives. I often use that analogy with our car designers: we're not creating great automobiles, we're trying to create great experiences."[47] "J," as he is casually known, retired in 2013 having left a distinctly late-modernist (dubbed "retrofuturist") imprint on car design at Audi and Ford. Mays's retrofuturism was the synthesis of respect for past design as well as determination to move into the future (he names contemporary designers with similar late-modern or postmodern sensibilities such as Philippe Starck, Frank Gehry, and Helmut Jahn as influences). Mays also speaks about beauty, and implicitly, the joy in going "far beyond simply trying to create a beautiful product," where the item transcends the physical and carries one "into all the psychological aspects of what a person does with their life."[48] Both Hitler and Mays understand that form follows function, but that the whole work far surpasses the pieces, leading to a new world for the consumer, culture, and nation. At some intuitive level Hitler understood how modernity could have a signal impact on a Germany he was intent on simultaneously anchoring in the past and forcing into the future. Seeing cameras designed to be used at home, he responded immediately: "'Every German family must have one. Every aspect of the nation's growth would be captured,'" he commanded, knowing that documenting the new nation would give him the images he needed to continue creating his new mythology.[49]

As before, the logo, another piece of genius, captured everything. A flawless combination of wordmark, hallmark, icon, the famous VW was created at some point in 1937 by Porsche engineer Francis Reimspiess, working on his own time. Porsche rewarded Reimspiess with a 100-mark bonus, and the logo has been in use ever since.[50] The VW logo and swastika belong to the same clever design world. The figure–ground game played by the V and W, where the almost invisible slice through the middle of the W's mid-bar produces the V, captivates the eye that alternates between seeing the V, the W, and the two letters together. The ongoing visual switching makes the logo as active and mesmerizing as the turning swastika. The vehicle ("Wagon") literally carries the people ("Volk"). The subtle elision in the centre of what would have been a classic nineteenth-century W letterform visually separates not only this logo but the whole technological project of the car from its antecedents. Porsche branded the car as a new object, a gift to the people. Unlike other cars that required specialized knowledge and care from their owners, the Beetle was designed for hard wear in battle and rough handling by amateur mechanics. Although the Reich's end meant the car never performed as intended, there's a deep irony to the fact that it came to represent American youth's rejection of Detroit iron consumerism in the 1960s and 1970s. Hitler's dream was appreciated by students, hippies, and cultural exiles for its hardiness, stinginess with gas, and more than anything, determinedly functional capability. Despite its original politics, the car proved to be exactly as promised. It was a rebel.

At the moment it is impossible for Volkswagen and other corporate entities that weren't disbanded in post-war Germany or Japan to fully live down their histories. Volkswagen's corporate historian Manfred Grieger was dismissed in 2016 after reporting that the company had used a great deal more concentration camp slave labour than had been previously reported.[51] Grieger's massive account, *The Volkswagen Works and Its Workers During the Third Reich*, caused Volkswagen AG to decide that transparency was one thing, but full confessions were something else. The legacy of Grieger's dismissal and the protest it occasioned by seventy-five German academic historians brought about further interest in Volkswagen's dismal record of behaviour in Brazil from 1965–1984 when the country suffered a military dictatorship. Volkswagen has been accused of collaborating with the regime that ran the country, blacklisting workers and other possible crimes. A different historian, Christopher Kopper of Bielefeld University, was commissioned in November 2016 to study and report on Volkswagen's interaction with the Brazilian dictatorship. Whether Volkswagen will accept the report or terminate Kopper's contract and disavow the report has yet to be seen.[52] The public accounting is not quite finished, it seems.

Historian Peter Fritzsche notes that what accompanied the Reich's move into power was "the unmistakable victory of the technocrats in the late 1930s [that] underscored the spirit of renovation that prized improvisation, application, and practicality in difficult situations."[53] Technocracy is diagnostic of modernity, bringing with it various means of production that chain workers and technocrats alike to impossible, ever-increasing expansion. Hitler's focus on industrial design produced "examples of how the dictator combined aesthetics, technology, social engineering and a political vision."[54] The Reich adopted modernity whether the *Völkisch* forces liked it or not, and with it necessarily came new ways of doing things. One example of industrial design forced on the Nazis by desperation and speed was the creation of the Atlantic Wall. Even after the Bauhaus had been expunged, its design sense survived. The Atlantic bunker complexes remain prime texts where form followed function: these were machines intended to survive saturation or area bombing. The cast concrete structures meant "there are no more intervals, joints—everything is compact; the uninterrupted pouring avoids to the utmost the repairs that would weaken the general cohesion of the work."[55] In concrete Virilio sees the effects of compression: these are vast heavy shells built to withstand the final acts of total war. The wall was an astonishing preview of what the post-war urban environment would look like, whether built in the Soviet bloc or appearing as North American brutalism.[56] All these pieces are expressions of what Jeffrey Herf calls "reactionary modernism," or for Roger Griffin, "alternative modernism." This different modernism was rooted in the fact that the Nazis "were not rejecting modernity, but using the built environment to lay the cultural foundations" for a new vision that, while it was in many places bursting with kitsch, was dedicated to newness, high speed transport, communication, design, war, and genocide.[57]

CHAPTER 11

KILLER CARTOONS

Disney's Graphic Violence

HERE IS ONE LAST PICTURE, ACTUALLY, A STRING OF them. There might seem to be a pause between the last discussion of design, the enormous reach of it in Nazi Germany, and popular films. I have worked to connect modernist design at work in the two militaries with the extension of that project to corporate identity and their brands. What we've seen in the history of American heraldry is a series of failures. The government's unwillingness to turn the military into a propaganda tool (which didn't obviate the need for the desperate bond drives and new income taxes that funded the war) ultimately created the need for private enterprise to step into the propaganda war. Recall the role played by the innocuous *National Geographic*, a stalwart, apparently neutral, scientific, trustworthy educational tool that was volunteered by its parent, Gilbert Grosvenor, to show America how robust and well prepared its military really was. But this time it was the overall design of the patches that had to be taken over. There had to be a master, a guide who knew design, understood America, and could frame the war in firm but friendly terms. That person and corporate force turned out to be Walt Disney.

Of the hundreds of unit insignia and early brands I looked at, one group of patches came from an unexpected source: the Disney Studio. In what follows unless I specifically refer to Walt Disney, I use the terms "Disney," "the Studio," and "Disney Studio" interchangeably to refer to the collective of artists, whether writers, animators, cartoonists, musicians, or inventors, who worked at Disney over the years. Before dealing with Disney's wartime design work for the United States government, I want to place the Studio in the context of the preceding chapters. The story of the extent to which Disney embraced modernism, propaganda, and branding begins with the Studio's establishment in the animation world.

Much of modernism turns on fracturing the familiar. In Walt Disney's case he wanted to recapture the best of animation that had been lost and push this relatively new art into undiscovered territory (film-based animation, as opposed to animation machines like the phenakistoscope or zoetrope, typically dates to J. Stuart Blackton's 1906 "Humorous Phases of Funny Faces"). Animation pioneers like Émile Cohl, Winsor McCay, Pat Sullivan, and Otto Messmer skilfully explored the medium. They were forced to learn as much about cameras and vision as about how to make movement convincing. Early animated films occupied both high and low registers. Cohl and McCay's films, while popular, took risks at the boundaries of form and content, creating stream of consciousness, "incoherent," and dream texts.[1] McCay and Messmer each investigated in depth the relationship between animator and animated creation. A good deal of pre-Mickey Mouse (1928) animation was reflexively astute about creativity and art.

Late in his life McCay addressed a gathering of his fellow cartoonists and animators, telling them that "animation should be an art. That is how I conceived of it. But as I see what you fellows have done with it, is making it into a trade. Not an art, but a trade. *Bad luck!*"[2] The lessons of the past weren't lost on Disney, who, by pressing his small studio and particularly relying on Ub Iwerks's technical wizardry, drove forward to create the Academy Award-winning short *The Old Mill* (1938). The Studio won all of the Academy short film awards in the 1930s, making for an uninterrupted eight wins. What animators admired about *The Old Mill* was the emotion the artists elicited from audiences that responded enthusiastically to the film despite the complete absence of human characters or substitutes like Mickey or Goofy. Two of Disney's most famous animators, Frank Thomas and Ollie Johnston, wrote that when they first saw *The Old Mill*, "our eyes popped out when we saw all of *The Old Mill*'s magnificent innovations—things we had not even dreamed of and did not understand."[3] The short was also a showpiece for one of Iwerks's lasting works of engineering genius, the multiplane camera, which gave animated films the illusion of depth of field for the next fifty years until the arrival of advanced computer graphics.[4] Between the technical and artistic advances discovered by artists at Disney, animation became a serious cultural force for audiences of all ages (early animation was aimed at adults). Animals that once were fabular representations of human types (the fox, the pig) became more lifelike than they ever had been, clearing the way for believable humans to appear. The groundbreaking work done on the first feature-length animated film, *Snow White* (1937), would reach the height of its early realistic mode in *Bambi* (1941). That animation was a new art form is clear, one driven and made possible by advancing modernity: no animation studio could survive rapid production schedules without Fordized labour. Whether or not the work was modernist is something else.

To what extent was the art created by the pre-war Disney Studio modernist in form or content? What kind of social effects did Disney, as an auteur, have on his culture? Disney's Silly Symphonies, short films on individual subjects, arguably had as much or more impact as the feature films, but those features packed considerable punch. The key films then and now remain solidly dedicated to upholding, even rendering sacred, the values of typically white (more recently African American or Hawaiian) heterosexual American middle-class life. One of the planet's most boastful democracies has taken to its republican heart films laud-ing monarchy and primogeniture. From *Snow White* (1937) and *Cinderella* (1950) to *The Lion King* (1994) and *Frozen* (2013), happy endings are usually signalled by the successful establishment (often by astute politically arranged marriages) of a patriarchal royalty that assures itself of a productive royal bloodline. In the case of *Frozen*, that the rulers are women moves some of the pieces around on the board, but the game largely remains the same.

The popular can also be modernist, and wildly financially successful mainstream texts may be as much about challenge and alteration as they are about maintaining the norm. Such texts will be marked by quintessentially modernist impulses: the presence of textual reflection such as the *mise-en-abyme*; complex interactions between form and content; disruption of linear narrative; focus on working class societal concerns (work conditions, various kinds of social justice).[5] Historian Warren Susman puts it succinctly: "while political historians generally see the [interwar] period as the age of Franklin D. Roosevelt, cultural historians are more likely to call it the age of Mickey Mouse."[6] Focusing on what's happening on the ground means seeing and coming to terms with different views of events. Interwar modernism is, I have been suggesting, a great deal more varied than and cannot be limited to the small constellation of authors orbiting 1922 and its now-canonical texts—Woolf's *Jacob's Room*, Joyce's *Ulysses*,

Eliot's *The Waste Land*. Inaccessibility doesn't necessarily make a text modernist, and accessibility doesn't rob a text of subtexts, subtleties, and contradictory intentions on the part of its various authors and interpreters. Certainly the popular may operate as an enormous reassurance engine, as Philip Beidler suggests: "one of the hallmarks of the World War II classic would be its capacity to found much of its enduring appeal as a popular-culture genre in resistance to such change—or, to be more direct, in its audience-pleasing tendency to reproduce the presentational look and feel of wartime and immediate post-war genres."[7]

Cultural objects may contain contradictions and inconsistencies that make them more flexible and longer lived than we once thought. When Snow White panics in the forest and emerges into a clearing to sing a song about being afraid, it makes sense that a 1937 Depression-struck audience would resonate with her fear and be reassured by her near blank verse (it's one iambic foot short in each line) as she confesses to assembled woodland creatures:

> … I'm awfully sorry
> I didn't mean to frighten you,
> But you don't know what I've been through.
> And all because I was afraid,
> I'm so ashamed of the fuss I made.
> What do you do when things go wrong?
> Oh! You sing a song.

An audience beset by real fears of survival was ripe to experience the princess's terror in the dark woods, and could breathe (or perhaps cry quietly) in relief when she emerges into a sunny clearing to find the world is not, as she felt, against her. Connected to nature, she is helped by the creatures around her—what she thought were predatory alligators become logs again and the birds begin to speak. Launching into a number with what was to become, over the course of the canonical Disney texts, a familiar choir of woodland creatures infatuated with princesses, Snow White instructs her subjects to face tough times "With a Smile and a Song." That was the story as delivered by the people behind Mickey Mouse. At the upper reaches was the kindly patriarch Franklin Roosevelt saying the same things, reminding people that they had "nothing to fear but fear itself."

That working people identified with mythic royalty is also complicated. The early princesses are either in hiding (Cinderella) or on the run from an evil queen. Snow White shows her domestic skills as soon as she lands in the dwarves' cottage, cleaning, cooking, and forcing them to wash. She sets to work, proving that even princesses know how to be democratic scullery maids and are not above getting their hands dirty. Cinderella feels no remorse over her lost social position, suggesting that the best monarchs live among the commoners. There is no criticism of monarchy in the Disney texts—it's a legitimate dream any republican can have. There are always pretenders, Machiavels, and corrupt rulers, but that is inherent in character, not the system of royalty itself. The Disney princess industry maps the castle onto the middle-class home, shows kind, wise, unilateral rule as the best form of governance. Monarchy is natural because the common people are naturally kings and queens in the making, and empire necessarily follows monarchy because people love their fair, just, wise (and beautiful) leaders. Every princess and prince, queens and kings in their own suburban castles, can also seek out their proud heritage and learn to bear arms—that is, hang the family achievement over the hearth.

The idea that the whole system is itself corrupt precisely because of the way it structures class, power, and law is never investigated. The Disney Studio's depiction of the princess or prince as a natural ruler brings America's monarchic fantasies to life, and even the films that seem to be set in an Edenic early America are stuffed with heraldic trappings (*Cinderella*, *Sleeping Beauty*). What began as reassurance to a scared populace then became a brand, "Disney Princess" (distinct from "Disney Fairies"), now worth an estimated $1 billion annually.[8] Snow White and Cinderella begin as losers in the social order but their indomitable spirits and can-do mentalities make them into successes who are rewarded for being gracious, upright, and by definition, attractive. Snow White is at home with the lesser blue-collar workers, the seven miners so beautifully animated by Shamus Culhane, as, singing, they cross a log to return home at sunset. The workers seem insignificant, even "deformed," when compared to the heroes because their labour is foundational. They are the small, submissive, loyal people who know their place, anchor empires, and love their royalty as gifts from the heavens. As Disney enshrined the royalty that America still worships (solely in fantasy, of course), Germany had signed on to Hitler's *Führerprinzip*.

Disney's understanding of nature is that it smiles on the good folk and is an enemy to the bad. There is no such thing as malicious nature—thorns, swamps, dark places appear only around evil characters or deeds. While the dwarfs, staunch working-class heroes who step aside when Snow White's prince finally arrives, are not royalty, they *are* entrepreneurs, owner-operators of their mine and labour. Their work ethic is classically liberal: if you put your labour into something, you make it yours, and it in turn makes you naturally wealthy, as they explain in their first song that it "ain't no trick to get rich quick/if you dig, dig, dig with a shovel or a pick." It is the workers who preserve and elevate Snow White and are responsible for the wicked Queen's off-screen death. Shamus Culhane remembers observing on the film's opening night how Snow White's apparent death stilled the audience, reflecting that this was "the first time grief had been so dramatically depicted in an animated cartoon."[9]

The Disney Studio's films soon came to be equated with deep sentimentalism, a sanitized, often saccharine worldview that shut out the surreal, irreverent, bawdy laughs that Tex Avery and his artistic followers at Warner Bros. would get from characters like Screwy Squirrel, Droopy, the Big Bad Wolf, Red Hot Riding Hood (in her various incarnations), and later Bugs Bunny, Daffy Duck, and the Coyote–Roadrunner duels. While Disney's Mickey diligently went off to work, Warner Bros.'s cartoons paired Ralph Wolf and Sam Sheepdog, two luckless clock-punchers whose jobs as predator and protector had been converted by the animators' satirizing of the conformist 1950s into men in grey flannel suits. The Mouse might bring a smile, but the repeated sucker-punching of the Wolf and crushing of Wile E. Coyote was hilariously, brutally recognizable to every organization man in the technostructure. Disney films were relentlessly optimistic, demonstrating that even the darkest of times and the villains who produced them could be overcome by honesty, hard work, true love, and music. While there are periods of rebellion against such messages, the public has never turned its back on the Studio. The problem for people at war was that, when Disney rendered a story, it would be grounded in the same kind of representation as films showing Humphrey Bogart single-handedly killing a column of German soldiers.[10] In Paul Fussell's mind, the attack on truth and "optimistic publicity and euphemism had rendered [soldiers'] experience so falsely that it would never be readily communicable. They knew that in its representation to the laity what was happening to them was systematically sanitized and Norman Rockwellized, not to mention Disneyfied."[11]

Propaganda is successful when it convinces the audience that it is the last word: no other information or discussions are needed once effective propaganda has spoken. A propaganda success should leave the audience satisfied that the data it has received is complete and that any details or interpretation remaining are for conspiracy theorists on the lunatic fringe. Some texts inadvertently work to cap off discussions on their own. Oliver Stone's

1986 *Platoon* operated this way in the national discussion about the Vietnam War. Although Hollywood refused to fund Stone's film (it was financed by a British production company), once it was screened and went on to win four Academy Awards, the argument about Vietnam was largely over. Even when Stanley Kubrick's *Full Metal Jacket* appeared a year later, the Academy of Motion Picture Arts and Sciences signalled it was finished with the topic, giving only the screenplay a nomination that it then failed to win. I'm not arguing that Stone's film is propaganda, although it does, as do Stone's other putatively historical texts (*Salvador* [1986], *Born on the Fourth of July* [1989], *Heaven & Earth* [1993], *JFK* [1991], *Nixon* [1995], *W.* [2008]), make free with facts and timelines, offering a synoptic view of Oliver Stone's America. In the struggle over filmic versions of Vietnam that Hollywood and the American public deemed acceptable, after dozens of excellent fictional and documentary texts, smaller films (Post's *Go Tell the Spartans* [1978], Ashby's *Coming Home* [1978]), and operatic ones (*The Deer Hunter* [1978], *Apocalypse Now!* [1979]), the American public seized on *Platoon* as the best summative tale of America's intentions during the war. *Platoon's* rave reviews from critics and veterans alike allowed the culture to step beyond the famous, if critically and politically divisive texts, like *Full Metal Jacket* and *Hamburger Hill* (1987). Just as canonical texts can have the final word, so too propaganda can stop discussion. Reopening the debate comes with attendant pain, something for which none may have any stomach.

A recent example of an exhausted issue, one crucial to the American imaginary, comes from the ongoing story of the flag-raising on Mount Suribachi by six Marines. Although for decades the Marines stated that John Bradley, father of author James Bradley's (*Flags of Our Fathers*), was in Joe Rosenthal's famous image, in 2016 the United States Marine Corps agreed that they'd misidentified Bradley for Harold Schultz. Marine General Robert

Neller commented brusquely, "to Marines it's not about the individuals and never has been."[12] John Bradley *did* participate in raising the flag the first two times, but not in the third, now-canonical, image. Even if James Bradley's book title refers directly to the event, there was a certain point at which the specifics ceased being important. As Bradley said later, "my father raised a flag on Iwo Jima .... The Marines told him way after the fact, 'Here's a picture of you raising the flag.' He had a memory of him raising a flag, and the two events came together."[13] Despite the power and importance of the photograph and its greater-than-life-size statue replica in Arlington, this detail became a footnote to the event's history. The record was corrected, Schultz's name was instated in place of Bradley's, and the discussion ended, even though the facts had been wrong for decades and Schultz and his family had gone unrecognized.

There will be a struggle over deciding what events should be remembered, how they should be interpreted. Sooner or later one version will emerge and, pushing aside the others, be accepted as (accurately or not) representative of a felt reality, a sense that this was how things were. How many parallel or differing versions of the same events the audience will tolerate depends on the affair's severity. If an audience is going to entertain more discussion about a painful topic, there had better be a good reason for digging up grief. One fascinating failed attempt to represent a horrific event was the Smithsonian Institution's National Air and Space Museum's 1994 exhibition of the B-29 heavy bomber *Enola Gay*, whose crew dropped an atomic bomb on Hiroshima. The exhibit, which started as a well-intended, wide-ranging educational display about the events leading up to and following the August 1945 bombing, was ultimately reduced to a single exhibit with no commentary.[14] The discussion was so fraught that the different stakeholders ultimately silenced each other: the result was a complete lack of speech on the subject.

Just as Ford was busy opening his museum of the recent past, Disney was developing the highest, newest, most expensive technology to push complex sentimentality. The Studio's geographic context was the recently erupted city of Los Angeles, as much the creation of oil wealth as of the image factory for which it was already becoming famous. Organized around the car rather than the streetcar or bus, fuelled by high speed roads and a commuter lifestyle, the grip of modernity led to "Modernist impulses [that] flowered everywhere in Disney's world of fantasy, which constantly blurred the line between imagination and reality to produce a wondrous universe where animals spoke, plants and trees acted consciously, and inanimate objects felt emotion."[15] Using the pieces of fantasy worlds that had once belonged to the oral and then written tradition of cautionary tales told to children to educate them about the dangers of straying from the path and risking the dangers of life's dark woods, Disney refashioned the American imagination.

The Studio understood exactly what it was doing in remediating cultural texts, beginning many early features by opening and closing a book, invariably a leather-bound *objet* with hand-tooled bindings, studded with gems, lettered by some nameless secular or religious scribe (all the books seemed sacred), illuminated in gold and other vivid colours. Most of the audience would have never seen such a thing—expensive, rare, beautifully made and handed down from antiquity. The Studio put such a volume in the audience's lap so it could at least be seen, if not handled. Here was the real past, the true story, the best of all the versions. Grounding itself in a book with the physical weight and authority of a Bible one might see on a church lectern, Disney proceeded to push out all other versions of the narrative. Fables of dark woods and light heroes were now glowing objects on a screen, stories recast in the American idiom that were entirely fresh and relevant.

Just as the Nazis developed their alternate or reactionary modernism, so too did the Disney Studio create it's own version: a much softer, accessible, attractive form of the new. Disney historian Steven Watts calls it "sentimental modernism," which "had several key characteristics. First, it blended the real and the unreal, naturalism and fantasy, and manipulated each in an attempt to illuminate the other. Second, it secured nonlinear, irrational, quasi-abstract modernist explorations comfortably on the cultural map by utilizing certain tropes from the Victorian past—an exaggerated sentimentality, clearly defined moralism, disarming cuteness—as familiar artistic signposts."[16] Presenting the new in a way that made it familiar and reassuring was essential to Disney's method for handling change. Disney clouded modernity's dangers with a sweet combination of decoration and dazzle, just as animation itself prolonged the myth that it was a magic art form inexplicable except to a very few initiates.[17] While one animation pioneer, American cartoonist Winsor McCay, used animation to explore dark, often terrifying, fantasies (as well as his animated "documentary" of the *Lusitania's* sinking), others like Emile Cohl and George Meliés flew audiences into strange dreamscapes or planets, all the while creating enchantment. The new could be surreal and provocative, but that didn't mean the worldview needed to be bitter or indigestible.

In America there was a marked difference in tone between animation produced in New York City from that produced in Hollywood, the two major US animation centres. American animation began in New York and gravitated to Hollywood only after Disney's success. The audiences were different, too. New York audiences reflected the city's ethnic and multicultural world; Los Angeles' viewers would be some of the first suburban commuter audiences anywhere. Early animation created by the Fleischer brothers (most famously Koko the Clown and Betty Boop cartoons at the Inkwell Studios) was replete with jazz and references to the urban African-American population and its diverse culture. In his study of regionalism in animation, Mark Langer points out that the "New York [animation] studios were less likely to use the fable convention of animal or child characters. Instead, New York animation tended to present adult characters with adult concerns, including employment, sex, and death."[18] As the best animators were lured to Hollywood by Disney, animation informed by New York's dense history, successive waves of overlapping immigration, and Harlem's influence, died. In the new west, about to undergo massive industrial changes because of the Second World War, the spaces were open and sunny, the cities low-rise, new and clean. Frederick Jackson Turner's frontier myth was fresh here. Disney and his animators took up polo and other outdoor sports typically available only to the wealthy in New York, and became model train enthusiasts (these trains were large enough to carry a number of adult riders—Walt Disney's fascination with them looked ahead to the theme parks).[19] For Langer, "by the mid-1930s, modernity in American animation became synonymous with the West Coast style—a style that was assumed to be the inscription of Walt Disney."[20]

Most early Disney cartoons were either flights of imagination (like the seventy-five Silly Symphonies the studio produced between 1929 and 1939, about which animation historian John Grant notes, "it is hard for us to realize fully the colossal impact that the early Mickey Mouse short and Silly Symphonies had on the public: Walt Disney, the world seems to have thought, was creating magic [as, in a way, he was]") or were retellings of classic fables like "The Tortoise and the Hare."[21] Many were odes to the pastoral world ("Flowers and Trees" [1932], "Water Babies" [1935], "Wynken, Blynken, and Nod" [1938]); very few showed cities, and those that did tended to characterize them as places where everything was false ("The Country Cousin" [1936]). Ensconced in its new home in the west, animation not only rejected the worlds of the urban and the adult, but sanitized and reformed life's difficulties, infantilizing all subjects. Mothers (often absent) are urgent in the Studio's texts: motherhood is presented as a sacred thing in the films where Disney was personally involved.

The politics of Disney's pastoral left some of the animators agog. Jack Kinney, a talented animator famous for his work on a series of funny Goofy short films skewering the idle rich's pastimes, recalls being assigned to the new film, *Bambi* (1942), drenched in a mixture of pastoralism and Christian sentimentalism. A Christian allegory about the birth of the New Prince (the characters refer to the Prince with a quite audible initial capital letter) shows an Edenic forest that "Man" comes close to destroying, first by slaughtering Bambi's mother, then by carelessly letting fire get out of control. At his and his peers' second meeting about *Bambi*, Kinney recounts Perce Pearce, then running the meeting, rendering the opening lines in the film that occur in a scene "somewhat like a depiction of the Nativity" (the line "Bambi … Bambi … my little Bambi" is spoken by Bambi's mother) as "Bam … beeeee … (long pause) … Bammmm … beee … my … litt … tullll … Baammm … beeeeeeeeee," upon which, having ended "his emotional rendition, Perce blew his nose and gently dabbed at his eyes." Kinney was so aghast at the pretension of it all he demanded of his boss, Ben Sharpsteen, "For crissake get me off that goddamn *Bambi*, onto shorts, anything," which is how he "got back to normal again."[22] Like many talented animators, Kinney soon left Disney.

New York cartoons embraced sexuality, poverty, drunkenness, rage, race, and fighting. Betty Boop was always comfortable as movie star and pin-up, something director Roger Zemeckis captures nicely in his depiction of a sad but still charming black-and-white Betty reduced, in *Who Framed Roger Rabbit* (1985), to waiting on tables because she can't star in colour pictures. The Disney Studio would never have considered making a film like

Fleischer's "Minnie the Moocher" (1932), where the artists first rotoscoped then animated Cab Calloway's famous Cotton Club performance of a song about a woman in love with a cocaine addict. The film's beginning is a live-action piece showing Calloway and his band engaging in call and response with the white audience. Calloway's figure soon becomes a ghost (that is, white) that performs in a cave against a black ground. As problematic as that (and other) representation was, it seemed enlightened compared to the African Americans appearing in *Dumbo* (1941) as crows, the literal embodiment of the Jim Crow laws maintaining apartheid in the South. The crows were the new, happy not-slaves there to perform the role of magical African American for the two encoded white characters (Timothy Mouse and Dumbo). The main African-American crow (the character's name is in fact "Jim Crow"—the other crows don't have names at all) has the idea that Dumbo can fly if he believes in himself and holds a single magical black crow feather. It was hardly anything for an African American to rejoice about.

While the New York films dealt with race, they enthusiastically showed heterosexual male fantasies. Betty Boop's dress got shorter as the years went by, and she often managed to dance in front of a flame or bright light so the animators could silhouette her nearly naked figure, until finally the Hays Office abolished such scenes, as well as her garter. Disney shifted the action to a mythic, often Edenic, garden, encoding the liminal characters bordering on transgressive as "bad." Tinkerbell and Snow White's evil queen are depicted in openly erotic ways, particularly when compared to Tiger Lily, Snow White, or Wendy, all of whom are prissy young women or girls so mature beyond their years that they assume maternal roles. These virgins are asexual matrons. It isn't as though the Disney animators, many of whom were recent imports from New York, had lost their interest in sex. Shamus Culhane tells about working around the clock to finish *Snow*

White when, in the inordinately tense final days, "there was a spontaneous avalanche of pornographic drawings from all over the studio. Drawings of Snow White being gang raped by the dwarfs, mass orgies among the dwarfs themselves. Even the old witch was involved." Culhane notes dryly that Krafft-Ebbing would have been surprised by some of the permutations.[23] But those drawings stayed a Studio secret, and the films they might have produced wouldn't show up in the mainstream until Ralph Bakshi's animated *Fritz the Cat* (1971) and *Heavy Traffic* (1973) over thirty years later.

Disney's infantilization and sanitization of animation in the west was so successful that it spread to the rest of animation in America, the worlds of comic strips and comic books, all of which were determined to be children's fare. The view that childhood is a time of purity and innocence created a narrow definition of what one could or should show children. Even the thoroughly recognizable adult world populated by Chuck Jones and his colleagues working at Warner Bros., John and Faith Hubley working on their own creations, and the rare, astonishing, if short, life of the UPA studio (responsible for the short "Gerald McBoing Boing" [1951], a brilliant piece of high modern design) would fail to divert the Disney juggernaut's cultural direction. Post-war animation, as with other graphic media, soon became a sentimental prison into which children were locked. Where America's animation, comic books, and comic strips settled into talking about and to a white, protected middle class and purged resistant voices, European and Asian comics and animated film suffered many fewer limitations. Media that were crippled in America by moral police (the Hays code, the Comics Code Authority) elsewhere went on growing in breadth, depth, and complexity, far transcending saccharine children's fare, comic strips about white heterosexual middle-class suburbia, or teen male power fantasies.

The limiting effects the Studio had didn't mean, however, that the Studio was artistically bankrupt or cut off from the world around it. Just as Walt Disney was signing on to sound cartoons, making a vastly expensive three-year deal with Technicolor, investing in the continued development of the multiplane camera, so he was also sending his animators to class, hiring the influential art instructor Don Graham from Chouinard's Art Institute to teach them to see more complexly. Disney also kept "the animation staff in contact with trends in the contemporary art world ... [reinforcing] its engagement with modernism."[24] Visible in the background art of the later films was the influence of modern regionalists like Grant Wood and Thomas Hart Benton, although the palettes were usually tinted into hues of pastel cotton-candy brightness. Disney brought in all manner of creators, including Frank Lloyd Wright, to talk to the animators.[25] One modernist Disney wholly embraced was critically acclaimed American fine artist Eyvind Earle, who created the visual look for the whole of Disney's *Sleeping Beauty* (1960) before returning to his studio. Earle's impact on the animation world can be tracked by his ghostly presence in the backgrounds of many Warner Bros.' cartoon pastoral scenes, even to the 3D computer graphic environments used by Sony Pictures Animation for its 2006 hit *Open Season*.

Disney seemed divided between the worlds of the new and the sentimental, the modernist and the Victorian. While he supported Earle, he equally favoured Kay Nielsen's Victorian dream landscapes and nightmares. Nielsen's genius drove the black strength of *Fantasia's* "Night on Bald Mountain" sequence. The inky darkness of Arthur Rackham and Carlo Collodi's Victorian mysteries alternated with the clean lines of American woodcut modernism. While Disney's penchant for pastoral scenes suggests he rejected a kind of tougher audience-provoking modernism, in some art forms he was more adventurous. Music, about which Disney originally knew little, fascinated him. With Leopold Stokowski an eager Disney undertook a swift course in music history and modernism. His dream of making feature-length animated films that portrayed a wide range of emotions became a broader wish to create populist art that would educate his audiences. By the late 1930s, as the Studio geared up to make *Fantasia* (released in 1941), Disney brought into the animators' world not only Stokowski, but modernist music by Stravinsky and Prokofiev.[26] All along Disney was pulled in contrary directions: intrigued by modernism he "began experimenting with its forms and techniques. His artistic heart, however, continued to beat to the rhythm of nineteenth-century sentimental realism. This Victorian sensibility continually grappled with an audacious modernism, but neither impulse completely triumphed. The result was an aesthetic and cultural hybrid."[27]

Disney's synthesis also had to be successful enough for the Studio to pay for its next experiments. Both Winsor McCay and Disney were businessmen, but their worldviews were considerably different. McCay had a powerful sense of social outrage that he expressed at length, seeing a world replete with poverty, cruelty, loneliness, and danger. In McCay's animations and comic strips like *The Dreams of a Rarebit Fiend*, *Hungry Henrietta*, *Little Sammy Sneeze*, and *Little Nemo in Slumberland*, pain, shock, eternally disrupted landscapes, loss and the threat of it, homelessness, and missing parents are the norm. There are few of the reassuring endings that Hollywood, Disney particularly, learned to produce for its audiences. If Disney's Mickey found his living parallel in Charlie Chaplin's Little Tramp, McCay's Nemo was much closer to the stone-faced stoicism of Buster Keaton's perpetual survivor who surprised himself as much as his audiences with razor-thin escapes from catastrophe. When Disney dealt with poverty and class he navigated by Dickens, finding in each grim situation an angel (or fairy) who could magic up a solution and convert a beggar into a prince, or at least a middle-class working stiff (as happens in *The Lady and the Tramp* [1955]).

Disney wasn't interested in pulling animation apart as much as making it run more smoothly; he drove viewers toward his vision, not incoherence or fragmentation. He was determined to educate, as the Studio's award-winning modernist short "Toot, Whistle, Plunk and Boom" (1953) designed by Eyvind Earle, displayed. The didactic film proposed to tell the history of music from the dawn of the human race to the present in ten minutes. Igor Stravinsky, who sold the rights to a number of pieces of his music to the Disney Studio, remembered Disney telling him, "Think of the numbers of people who will now be able to hear your music," an appeal to a mass audience that put Stravinsky in an ill mood, causing him to huff, "The mass ads nothing to art."[28] Other modern composers were not only happy to have their work adapted by Disney, they had him in mind while they composed. Sergei Prokofiev approached Disney with the unfinished score for "Peter and the Wolf," telling him "I've composed this with the hope that someday you'll make a cartoon using my music."[29] While radio stations in the heartland might not be inclined to play *Le Sacre du Printemps*, it was sure that Disney's films would get there and return there, initially on film and then by television and user-controlled formats (from Betamax to digital streams).

Disney worked with modernism up to a point. John Hubley, initially a Disney animator who, with his artist-animator wife Faith Elliot Hubley, established the influential Storyboard Studios, obtained a copy of famous Russian animator Ivan Ivanov-Vano's 1934 film *The Tale of the Czar Durandai*, which was set to Dmitri Shostakovich's music.[30] Disney wasn't interested, although other animators were. By the 1950s, modernism, particularly a number of its tropes, had become an accepted cultural style and "the industry also opened its doors to outside talents ... and

Modernists of the time from diverse disciplines were called upon to contribute to animated films."[31]

Searching for modernism in Disney's pre-war films usually leads to a discussion of the intriguing and beautifully made "Pink Elephants on Parade" sequence from *Dumbo*.[32] It is one of the very few times when alcohol is shown as a moderately benign force. Dumbo and Timothy Mouse accidentally drink from (or in Timothy's case, fall into) a bucket into which a champagne bottle has been thrown. As they innocently get drunk, Dumbo begins to blow ever more complex bubbles ("balloonies," as Timothy calls them), until they come to surreal, sometimes nightmarish, sometimes charming, but always visually striking life. Dumbo and Timothy somehow share the same delirium tremens (Why not? After all, it's a film about a talking mouse and a flying elephant) of electric-pink elephants who change shape, scale, mass, and number, fully control their environment, and break through the fourth wall. The animators exploited the chance to work on a dark background and create shifting perspectives, pulling tricks with lines and vanishing points that wouldn't be seen again until the much more fluid, colloquial second music film compilation *Make Mine Music* (1946). It is in this dream that Dumbo first flies. Apart from the obvious cautions about alcohol, the vivid shared images suggest a wonderful, at times frightening, mindscape that even the most innocent possess. Dumbo and Timothy exist in the shadow of an uncaring, exploitative world: as the clowns plan the ways in which Dumbo will make them wealthy, they get soused and are shown in silhouette against their circus tent, greedy, conniving drunkards who Langer typifies as belonging to the "underclass" replete with "vulgarity, cruelty."[33]

While the pink elephants sequence in *Dumbo* deserves the attention it gets, it's surprising that other equally modernist, arguably more striking passages don't come in for similar discussion. What connects all of these works of art, those that are sentimental as well as others that are much less so (the narrative accompanying Stravinsky's *Le Sacre du Printemps*, depicted by the Studio as the development of life on the planet, is largely devoid of empathy; the audience is not asked to identify with any of the creatures), is the oscillating modernism that informs it all—complex, at times foraging, at others almost nonexistent. Cultural scholar T. J. Jackson Lears notes that this was common to modernism in many guises: "All the idioms of modernism contained contradictory elements of protest and affirmation, longings for transcendence as well as desires to merge with the commonplace."[34]

What was commonplace about the interwar years was the worker's (or unemployed person's) plight, rarely better captured than by Chaplin in *Modern Times* (1936). A piece of gristle jammed in the machine's teeth, the Little Tramp monomaniacally goes on tightening two bolts until he's taken away to an asylum. Disney's Mickey, Donald, and Goofy often work together at exciting jobs, and *Snow White's* dwarfs have their hymn to labour. What's interesting about the dwarfs is that they are differentiated from each other. Disney's interpretation of the fable was the first to give each dwarf his own distinctive character that then dictated his behaviour. In this Disney not only pushed character in animation well beyond anything that had come before, but also indicated that, while all the men worked and were workers, all men were not also the same worker. Comparing Disney's treatment of the seven miners with the undifferentiated massed workers in Friz Lang and Thea von Harbou's *Metropolis* (1927) clarifies that the first shows triumphal individualism where the second refuses to see the workers as anything but brutalized exchangeable pieces.

Disney artists were understandably sympathetic to the worker. The Depression-era animators were grateful to have work when so many in America didn't. At the same time, Walt Disney had promised that everyone would benefit from the Studio's profits. Disney also kept asking the workers to wait, that he needed to fund his next groundbreaking idea. As the Depression came to a close and the Studio prospered, the animators' patience gave out: in the middle of 1941 they went on strike. The strike was bad for everyone—it was at this point that many talented animators left the studio they had been instrumental in building. The focus on stories about kingdoms and royalty take on additional irony in light of the strike. The workers, who didn't then and don't now own either their labour or intellectual property, operate in the context of films like *Beauty and the Beast* (1991, rebooted in 2017), where the servants-become-objects are unhappy if they cannot engage in the menial labour that gives them purpose, as the candlestick-footman Lumiere sings to Belle, "Life is so unnerving/For a servant who's not serving."

The magical objects that populate the Beast's castle are servants twice over: they are in service to the castle's lord, and are then once more reduced to household items. Belle dreams of more, of reading books and getting away from her provincial existence, but Lumiere, Cogsworth, and Mrs. Potts just want to return to being unpaid help living below stairs. Dreams are not for their class. Animation scholar Steven Watts notes that, "while the industrial revolution had made machinery the great enemy of art, this cartoonist had begun to reconcile the two with his production techniques and narrative themes."[35] Nowhere was the marriage of production, high technology, special effects, and content clearer than in the *Sorcerer's Apprentice* section of *Fantasia*.

Set to French composer Paul Dukas's late-nineteenth-century music, the story shows the magician, a thinly disguised Disney (the animators unofficially named the sorcerer's "Yen Sid," and his typical single raised eyebrow was a perfect caricature of a cogitating Disney) complete with wizard hat, performing knowledge work. As he stands at his table, imposing and in charge of nature, he conjures a resplendent luminous butterfly that blinks a few times before it is destroyed by its dissatisfied creator. Mickey, the physically labouring Apprentice who literally wipes the sweat from his brow, humbly fills the well with two buckets and looks on admiringly as the Sorcerer works. Once the Sorcerer leaves, the Apprentice rushes to put on the hat, pushes up his sleeves and takes command. Rather than go on slaving away at what appears to be a pointless, certainly thankless, and ignoble job, the Apprentice commands a broom to life, causes it to sprout two woody arms that pick up buckets and start filling the well.

Of course the worker doesn't have management's imagination or experience to foresee what will happen if things are not properly planned; Mickey just wants to be free of his job. Having settled the broom to working autonomously, he falls asleep and dreams of running the universe. Awoken to find the cellar flooded with water, Mickey tries to countermand the broom, finally assassinating it with an axe. The broom's death (shown as shadows on the wall) is beautifully emphasized by the transition from increasingly strong tomato reds and electric blues—the colours' complements make the image that much more vivid—to an almost completely achromatic scene when the broom seems to have been subdued. For a heartbeat there's no colour, no music, no life. The broom is in splinters and the music seems to be over until a solitary bassoon's note warns the audience and Mickey that the broom isn't finished. It's an autonomous, Taylorized system. Each splinter now rises up with two bucket-wielding arms, marches over the prone Mickey to overfill the well, the cellar, and the wizard's castle.

What comes to life is something the worker cannot control—the very assembly line required to produce new animations like *The Sorcerer's Apprentice*. The Studio rationalized and divided into its main components the job of creating an animated film. The managers plan what films will or will not be made; the idea is handed to the story department that writes a script; the script is passed to the layout, character, special effects, and background departments; the animators draw the characters' key poses; other animators (called "in-betweeners") draw the frames between each key frame; the drawings are handed to the ink and paint department (for a long time work done by women, who were rarely allowed to animate) where the cels are made; the cels go to the camera operators, who assemble and shoot them; music and sound work parallel this whole process. The complex, expensive multiplane camera is a metaphor for the whole operation: each frame is divided between multiple levels, all requiring planning and execution. Disney's process streamlined a handcrafted, irregular, wildly variable product, converting it into a recognizable brand. With an ugly strike about to break at the Studio, it's hard not to reconsider Mickey's displeasure at carrying water for his master. In Mickey the animators drew themselves, all capable of dreaming creative dreams, all an indispensable part of the whole machine. But Yen Sid, the Sorcerer, has the final say when he descends the stairs, parts and banishes the chaotic waters, and spanks Mickey for his temerity. Here was modernism in action: a discussion of labour in and by the very medium it documented, commentary on worker aspirations and maltreatment, the division of labour between the head and the hand.

Ideas of creation suffuse *Fantasia*, from the abstract images that assemble into the music of Bach's Toccata and Fugue in D Minor; the advent, destruction, and renewed beginnings of life in Stravinsky's *Le Sacre du Printemps*; the fight between gods of creation and celebration in Beethoven's sixth symphony; repeated metatheatrical references in Ponchielli's *Dance of the Hours*; the demon Chernabog, gorgeously animated by Vladimir "Bill" Tytla, summons muses from hellfire in Mussorgsky's *Night on Bald Mountain*; and the stabilizing idea of Christianity in the near-abstract pilgrimage accompanying Schubert's *Ave Maria*. Disney created one the earliest, most powerful innovative sound systems with "Fantasound," designed to reproduce what a symphony hall audience would hear. No theatre had ever played sound the way Disney set up his theatres.[36]

Nothing like *Fantasia* had existed before: it was truly the new. It was a unique length (the film's first iteration ran over two hours long), and married the highest of high culture (the music of Bach, Beethoven, Schubert, Stravinsky, Tchaikovsky; ballet as an art form) with Mickey, the exemplar of popular culture, the dancing flora from the Tchaikovsky ballet, and the various fauna in tutus or capes in the Ponchielli, images taken directly from the surreal pen of modernist German illustrator Heinrich Kley.

For one particular reviewer, however, the attempt to impress the audience was entirely too much, too manipulative, and too dangerous. Dorothy Thompson, who had witnessed Hitler's rise to power and was expelled from Germany for her reporting of it, saw *Fantasia* in New York and wrote in her *New York Herald-Tribune* review that, as she "staggered out" of the theatre all she could think "was 'Nazi.' The word did not arise out of an obsession, Nazism is the abuse of power, the perverted betrayal of the best instincts, the genius of a race turned into black magical destruction, and so is the [sic] 'Fantasia.'" Thompson saw in *Fantasia* not just an overwhelming spectacle, but a piece of what would cause the collapse "of the civilized world." Thompson's case is intriguing. She was a powerful journalist with millions of readers. Her identification of what she perceived to be fascist rhetoric in the film's politics and design cannot be written off as the ravings of an unhappy viewer or esthete. She was knowledgeable about Hitler's Germany and had interviewed Hitler during his rise to power. As a side note, she wrote the *Fantasia* review while married to novelist Sinclair Lewis, who had just written *It Can't Happen Here* (1935), in which America becomes a fascist state. The idea that Disney's ability to tap into a strong populist current and produce overwhelmingly powerful texts that work to their own, often invisible, ends is not new in the present. But what Thompson identified was a worrisome similarity in the image handling between America's Disney and Nazi Germany.

It is only recently that animation scholars have learned the extent to which one modernist, Spanish surrealist Salvador Dalí, found a home at the Studio. Disney's invitation to Dalí produced, some sixty years after the collaboration between the two men, the curious anachronism *Destino*. While designed and laid out by Dalí from 1944–1945 when he was in Hollywood working for Hitchcock, the film was not animated until 2002 when Roy Disney dedicated resources to resurrecting the work, of which only eighteen seconds had been filmed. The result is historically interesting, very much a product of its artistic time, with aesthetic sensibilities that are inane in a twenty-first-century setting. Still, for animation historian John Canemaker the film is important because, among other things, it "underlines how comparatively timid today's mainstream producers are, and how animation's unlimited potential remains restricted to child's fare."[37] If *Destino* is now an oddity, a strange piece of art that travelled in time (as befits a work featuring Dalí's soft clocks), the film is, as Pallant says, "a testament to the Studio's continued highbrow aspirations."[38] It was part of a larger project Disney spoke about in 1946, declaring his intention "to give more big artists such opportunities. We need them. We have to keep breaking new trails."[39]

Unexpectedly for just about everyone, Disney and Dalí got along very well. Their warm relationship, and Disney's reported openness to Dalí's nonlinear story telling, was an indicator of the complexity of Disney's understanding of the media around him. As scholar Susan Hegeman argues, "not only was there a great deal of interborrowing between 'high' and 'low' forms in the modernist moment, but the audiences for these forms were more versatile than [cultural historian Lawrence] Levine grants. In this regard we might point to the fact that broadcasts of classical music were some of the earliest and most popular programs on commercial radio."[40] Drawing lines through the culture in order to divide groups based on their perceptions of what is and is not art is unhelpful. We can instead expect to find large blurred areas where people regularly cross back and forth, transiting between different cultural forms. How many people came to understand and seek out high culture because of Disney's pastel faux Greco-Roman version of it in Beethoven's *Pastoral*? How many went away with their beliefs confirmed that elite culture was not for them? How many were, like paleontologist and evolutionary biologist Stephen Jay Gould, inspired to a life of study by seeing the dinosaurs "of Disney's *Fantasia* panting to their deaths across a desiccating landscape to the tune of Stravinsky's *Rite of Spring*"?[41] The fact that the Studio released a second *Fantasia* in 2000 suggests that, even with Walt Disney gone, the Studio, now part of one of the most powerful global brands, saw value in the ongoing popularization of high culture (the second film took its greatest risk by including a piece by Shostakovich).

The interwar Disney Studio had not yet found a comfortable distance with modernism (the idea of attaining a happy relationship with modernism contradicts the concept of something that is perpetually shocking—but then few things remain constantly disruptive). Disney was personally finding his way, pulling his studio along with him. The result, for Watts, was that "Disney's aesthetic paradigm thus offered a series of cultural compromises. The filmmaker and his artists tried to pursue artistic innovation without leaving their popular audience lost, confused, groping for meaning. Sentimental modernism, like much else with this Hollywood innovator, served as a mediating impulse—between modernism and realism, art and commerce, aesthetics and entertainment, elitism and populism."[42] Continuing oscillation between the accessible sentimental and the taxing avant-garde became the pattern for design in that pre-war cultural moment. Twenty to thirty years later much of the design uncertainty would be resolved.

By 1941 Mickey Mouse had accrued the kind of cultural power that was proleptic of the brand today. Even in Hitler's Germany Mickey was enormously popular. Films that struck America's interwar audience as morale boosters (particularly the first of the *Three Little Pigs* [1933] films, which made the song "Who's Afraid of the Big Bad Wolf" into a national anthem about resisting despair) connected equally strongly in Germany, although the wolf, appearing at one point with a long fake nose, was framed as a predatory Jew. The relationship between the design worlds is evident in Goebbels's 1937 Christmas gift to Hitler of eighteen Mickey films (evidently Hitler was also a fan of *Snow White*).[43] In 1943, with America neck deep in the war and after the remarkable artistic chances Disney had taken with *Pinocchio* (1940), *Dumbo* (1940), and *Fantasia* (1941) behind him, over 90 per cent of the Studio's work consisted of government contracts for the military.[44] Where the Disney brothers had largely been the masters of their own ship, the war aligned the Studio's work more closely with public relations, propaganda, and advertising. Instead of pleasing a mass audience, the Studio now had to please the military and its wartime government, both of which required more support and money from Americans than ever. Disney would be crucial to selling America to Americans, especially during the seven increasingly desperate major bond drives that funded the war.[45] It was a task that called for the right mixture of signs and myths in order to produce an identifiable, desirable vision of America. The war became, as told by public relations' writers, "a struggle for the American way of life ... that to them made America great."[46] That meant appealing to large discrete groups, disconnected masses of people who would need to share their cultural imaginings if the war was to be supported emotionally.

Asked to create a film instructing citizens about paying income tax, a new thing for millions of Americans (the income tax structure initiated during the war was responsible for paying for the majority of it), the Studio produced *The New Spirit* (1942).[47] The first of the overt Disney propaganda films, *The New Spirit* showed the audience, through a baffled and typically distraught Donald Duck, how to pay the tax. Seeing a corporation about to make a war profit, congressional representative John Taber questioned the film's $80,000 cost, asking the House why so much money that could "go to [building] a bomber" should instead "be spent for a moving picture to entertain people?"[48] Facing a congressional veto against paying the Studio, Disney duly forfeited all costs, understanding how bad the Studio would look in a fight for money (it was eventually paid by the Treasury Department). The Studio thereafter made all of its government films at cost.[49] It is hard to imagine Ford or GM, crucial to war manufacturing, being asked to do the same thing. Congressional blocks on appropriations for image production reinforces how much Americans underestimated the propaganda machine that had already steamrollered them.

The Studio wasn't just making films for the war effort: it was also increasingly busy producing special designs for what would eventually be over 1,200 individual unit insignia. Disney handed over the job of the unit designs to Henry "Hank" Porter, telling him: "Mister, you have yourself a job .... Just settle down to it."[50] Working at the head of a team of six artists, Porter was responsible for about 80 per cent of the designs, representing the staggering output of roughly one new design each day.[51] Offering the Studio's work gratis to the military, Disney requested only that no civilian contractor be allowed to profit from reproducing his characters. Asked later about this remarkable generosity while the Studio was in debt, then toughing out the damaging strike, Disney answered, "Those kids [soldiers] grew up on Mickey Mouse. I owed it to them."[52] Disney's generosity to the soldiers, but not the animators responsible for making his groundbreaking films possible, is yet another of the contradictions in his character and an illustration of the different value put on building bombers as opposed to doing artistic work.

American heraldry now entered a unique phase. Talented, experienced artists trained in design, colour, character, and composition, and with no ties to heraldic patterns or traditions, took on the branding of a huge swath of the military. The Disney patches represented not only a significant piece of design work for the Studio, but the expression of a newly minted vernacular, a form of sentimental modernism that would make the insignia desirable to Mickey's fans now old enough to be carry weapons. The patches broke with all previous understandings of what constituted heraldic codes, even in a country whose heraldry was already a free-for-all. As Hank Porter began creating unit insignia based on requests from commanders as well as individual soldiers, pilots, and sailors, a few basic rules came into practice. There was a general reticence about using the most famous Disney characters in the service of killing, partly because the Studio feared the public would think it was profiting from public service, partly because the Studio was protecting its brand. The most obvious shelter was extended to Mickey. Understood to be a nice guy and "not warlike by nature," he was exempt from carrying weapons, dropping bombs, and generally looking belligerent. Mickey's limited appearances were kept to representations "on behalf of a signal corps or a chaplains' unit," a fascinating commentary on the perception that Mickey needed to remain innocent to be effective.[53] The children who had grown up on Mickey garnered no such protection.

Lining up with his history as a perpetually youthful grown-up, an innocent adult engaged in but largely untouched by the world, Mickey's position as a citizen was, in Rawls's view, "quite satisfactory for peacetime America, but with the country at war this small-town boy simply could not be visualized in warlike poses."[54] Because Mickey generally refused to see evil, there was no real evil in his world. But if Mickey was the everyman he appeared to be, then his job was to get into uniform and soldier on, toughening up as required by the exigencies of facing Hitler. Like another famous American, Marion Morrison, who was too valuable to be allowed to fight, Mickey was indispensable. Mickey's battlefield shyness pushed the irascible, largely incoherent Donald Duck to the fore. Donald would fight Hitler; Donald would, if briefly, be a Nazi (*Der Fuhrer's Face* [1943]); Donald would be the new taxpayer (*The New Spirit* [1942]); Donald would become a willing soldier and enraged citizen. Over sixty years later brand specialists Riesenbeck and Perrey approve of taking Mickey off the battle roster: "When using celebrities as part of the marketing campaign, it is important that the media image of the chosen celebrity should not be too discordant with the brand's current image position. Otherwise, it will be difficult to make the communication believable. Even if the individual selected represents the ideal *target* positioning of the brand, it is probably better in the case of a large gap to work with several celebrities with less pronounced traits."[55] While Mickey might seem to be the best choice in order to reach the demographic (the "kids" he raised), still it didn't seem right to have the same mouse send them to war. That job was left to the lesser stars in the Disney firmament, producing some eyepopping contrasts, as in the case of a chortling Thumper riding a bomb on its way to destruction (the 799th Bombardment Squadron and Marine Base Defense Aircraft Group 41), or Timothy Mouse complete in circus hat gleefully uncorking a couple of bombs from a B-24 Liberator on behalf of the 831st Bomb Squadron. This was the Disney brand—happy, cute—at war.

There were other characters who could not serve or survive at the tip of the spear. Dumbo was one. If one could imagine Bambi throwing bombs or wading into the surf of an amphibious landing, one could also presumably see Dumbo in a steel helmet: neither character had it in them to fight this way. Instead Dumbo supported a barrage balloon unit (303rd Coastal Artillery). The much bloodier and probably fatal business of handling machine guns was given to the more ambiguous Gremlins (a patch for the Royal Netherland Military Flying School), based on characters created by British novelist Roald Dahl. The surprise of seeing Thumper joyfully riding bombs the way Stanley Kubrick's Major Kong was to do in *Dr. Strangelove* suggests that the minor characters were dispensable. Where Mickey, Bambi, and Dumbo's legacies required protection, others designed to be equally charming (Pegasus's children from *Fantasia*, Flower the skunk from *Bambi*, Huey, Dewey, and Louie, the Country Mouse) might well find themselves brandishing weapons, flying with or carrying large pieces of military equipment like tanks and aircraft. Bambi does make an appearance on behalf of the 421st Coast Artillery Battalion, but it is as an adult character, perhaps even his father, sporting a full rack of antlers.

I've discussed the United States military's habit of using generic images of Native Americans, the first of which we saw in the Lafayette Escadrille flying in First World War France. Disney revived and pushed that image much farther. Disney produced two particularly infamous images of Native Americans. The first came in the 1937 Silly Symphony *Little Hiawatha*, which was a mock-heroic spoof of Longfellow's popular poem. The film converted the young man Hiawatha into a six- or seven-year-old child whose greatest struggle is keeping his pants on and up. Even the woodland chorus laughs at Hiawatha in his quest to save Nokomis's daughter Minnehaha: only when threatened by a bear does nature assist Hiawatha. If Longfellow's 1855 "Song of Hiawatha" was already problematic in its depiction of Native Americans as a backward people awaiting the advent of Christianity (which is where the poem concludes), Disney's Silly Symphony more cruelly mocked the Native culture at the centre of the narrative. Disney's Hiawatha is just a child playing with bows and arrows, and is the subject of paternalistic concern for both audiences (the woodland animals, and Disney's viewers).

Things were arguably worse when the Studio produced the 1953 adaptation of J. M. Barrie's *Peter Pan*, where the unhappy "What Makes the Red Man Red?" song did further stereotypical racial damage to Native Americans' collective communities. In 1942 Hiawatha was part of an acceptable, sweet Disneyfication of a high-culture hero, a child who can't bear to kill a rabbit that makes soulful eyes at him. Because the character is young and appealing, he generally escaped use for infantry unit designs, and was instead recruited for signals or reconnaissance. That exemption didn't extend to tank and bomber units, though. A tertiary character who didn't reappear in the films (although he proved to be popular over the longer term), Hiawatha was one of the disposables, what Riesenbeck and Perrey would call a celebrity "with less pronounced traits" than Mickey. In most cases Hiawatha sports an ill-fitting headband with a lone feather at the back intended to denote him as a brave. On occasion he wears the familiar stereotyped headdress of a Plains Native American. The juxtaposition of the innocent child barely capable of surviving in the wild, wearing oversized pants that appear to be more like diapers, holding bombs and planes or pulling bows with bombs for arrows, is painfully ironic. Here is a representative of a population cruelly persecuted, recruited to fight for the oppressor and in the process infantilized and belittled. The occasional adult Native American who appears is outfitted with a breechclout, a disproportionately long nose (the same racist stereotype appears in *Peter Pan*), and a generally sly look.[56]

The African-American population fared no better at the hands of the Disney insignia artists, who used the same designs the Studio had developed for *Dumbo*. On the African-American side of town the two encoded white characters (how Timothy and Dumbo, a brown mouse and a grey elephant, are signified white has in large part to do with the way Timothy speaks and acts, and the understanding that the hero is a little white boy) find themselves being teased by the "brother" crows, a band of recognizable wise-guy (the word "uppity" hangs in the air) African-American stereotypes with suspenders, bowler hats, and in Jim Crow's case, a dickey, spats (but no shoes), and striped shirtfront with pearl stickpin. These racist representations lasted well into the 1970s when Ralph Bakshi's *Coonskin* (1975—rereleased as *Streetfight*) finally gutted the image. Jim Crow regularly appears riding on or carrying bombs to their destinations for bombardment squadrons. That the biggest, cleverest of the crows appeared on the insignia, as well as often on airplane nose art (itself another form of heraldry), when African Americans themselves were refused the right to integrate or serve in "white" units, let alone fly heavy bombers, hammers home the stark cultural divide between using morale-boosting African American images but denying the people themselves full citizenship.[57] Although the Tuskegee airmen were finally permitted to form their own fighter-bomber squadron, the fully trained African-American crews were never integrated or allowed to fly heavy bomber missions. The patches, however, flew.

It was less ironic when Donald, the usually flightless duck, appeared on many air service patches. Rawls notes that "Donald Duck was by far the most frequent Disney draftee for military service insignia. He made at least 216 appearances, several times the next runner-up: Pluto, who turns up some forty-five times. Surprisingly, Goofy came in third, with assignments too varied to mention."[58] Rawls's note about Goofy is astute: Goofy suited combat as little as, possibly less than, Mickey. The characters possess a certain flexibility, but there are limits: the result of pushing those limits may be overall damage to the brand. Because Donald spends roughly half of his screen time baffled by or apoplectic about the world around him, his quick rages and oscillating moods suited the badges as diverse as a Carrier Division (the

24th), or Signal Service 969th Engineer Construction Battalion (a particularly bellicose patch that showed the camera-toting duck facing uphill into a torrent of bullets). While there were patches showing Donald and his nephews smiling or laughing (the Carrier Division or the 51st Services Squadron, 310 Service Group), there was no shortage of a bomb-wielding, rifle-carrying, aircraft-flying angry duck.

The Studio's main characters saw a large amount of service, but it was the generic Disney figures (octopi, fish, seahorses, a variety of bugs, spiders, mosquitoes, bees, and grasshoppers) that did most of the work. The one exception to the horde of unnamed insects was Jiminy Cricket, usually looking shocked or surprised. *Pinocchio* viewers would immediately identify and sympathize with the character. For the Gardena Auxiliary Police, Jiminy looks like he's about to be run over, caught in the headlights of an approaching vehicle. It's a clever adaptation of the character because his shadow, Jiminy's own conscience, takes the shape of a human police officer complete with star where Jiminy's gold medal would normally go. He's equally unhappy with events in the 2nd Weather Squadron, Jefferson Proving Ground, where the frowning Cricket uses his miniscule umbrella to protect his weather records from a gale. Jiminy was another a one-time player who immediately became part of the Disney canon. It was impossible to see a character like him (or any of the major actors like Donald or Goofy) and not connect the war with Disney. The brand was fighting the war, and that meant that the line between America, its military, and Disney, a private company, was erased. Disney and America had become the same forces.

A host of much meaner, visibly enraged bugs posed on behalf of the 307th Pursuit Squadron, 31st Pursuit Group; pugilistic mosquitoes with fearsomely long rapier noses led the Motor Torpedo Boat Squadron 36; bees carrying Thompson submachine guns or lightning bolts accompanied signal corps and infantry. Some insects, like wasps, fit naturally into the war environment (particularly for the USS *Wasp*). These creatures were rarely cuddly (perhaps Jiminy Cricket was the exception—helped along by his frock coat, spats, umbrella, and top hat) or were the stuff of phobias, images that register in propaganda's psychology as understood by Sam Keen's *Faces of the Enemy*.

Propaganda, argues Keen, first constructs a binary that separates the in-group and its home place of safety and beauty from the out-group's strangeness, ugliness, and life-threatening qualities. Signs instruct us about who is to be excluded and included: in Hitler's Germany, the yellow Star of David meant exclusion and death, the swastika meant inclusion and life. The propaganda power of these signs is evident from their naturalization. What is always present cannot go on drawing the same kind of attention it once did. Ubiquity will rationalize even the most irrational of signs. But there are other signs one can use to provoke arousal, to elicit reflex responses: in general it takes longer for these to be exhausted because they're wired into the human animal as well as the culture. From late-nineteenth- through early-twenty-first-century propaganda, the enemy is often represented as some slimy, loathsome creature. Keen gives much visual evidence to support his argument that "we regularly use a whole repertoire of animal, reptile, and insect images to dehumanize our enemies," a fact that further "shows us the extent to which modern technological societies are rooted in a metaphysic of war against nature."[59] Equating the enemy with pestilence, whether it is bugs, a disease, or non-mammalian creatures we find disgusting, either because they have no arms and legs (snakes, worms, maggots) or entirely too many (spiders, millipedes, octopi, squid), or because even thinking about them causes us to have bodily reactions, to itch, to feel ill (mosquitoes, fleas, lice), means that we are closer to being able to eradicate such an enemy with fewer moral qualms. Adapting a pesticide for use in their gas chambers made the Nazis' operation of the death camps self-exculpatory: the victims weren't human because humans don't die this way.

The Disney Studio's use of these same phobia-inducing creatures to fight on behalf of the homeland is intriguing. The octopus or mosquito could be called on to fight for the homeland, but it had to point outward. Only the enemy should face these images, particularly the fearsome, fired up, TNT- and bomb-tossing octopus wearing the US Navy's small white "dixie-cup" hat (NCDU-ATB Underwater Demolition Team 20). The malignant, unpleasant parts of nature weren't for the folks at home, but for Hitler-as-rat or fascists depicted as drooling subhumans (the famous American propaganda posters "This is the Enemy" and "The New Order" showed leering enemies, and in the latter, a German officer in a phallic, bullet-headed, thick-necked, slavering profile). The apparently bad parts of nature would fight for the Allies: even a pestilence has its good side if it's wiping out your enemies.[60] On the Disney patches, "if one were to add the 'bee/hornet/wasp' category, winged creatures would overwhelmingly outnumber any other grouping."[61] We are now very far from early worries about brand protection and are entirely at war.

A timeline showing character changes can be instructive when we search for what makes something appealing. The tendency for popular, long-lived cartoons is to become rounder, sweeter, and younger over time. Mickey Mouse (originally quite rat-like), Felix the Cat (with a long, squared-off head, initially), Bugs Bunny, and Daffy Duck (both were originally long and angular), Walt Kelly's Pogo (thin and unkempt at the beginning, short, fluffy and dapper by the late 1960s), Charles Schulz's Snoopy (his nose and stomach rounded and shortened considerably), Berke Breathed's penguin Opus from *Bloom County* (his nose became boxier and bigger as he became plumper and more like the stuffed dolls made, ironically, to look like him), even Bill Watterson's Calvin, all underwent significant shortening, rounding, and redesign. The struggle to make the unpalatable acceptable is beautifully explained by two of Disney's most famous animators Frank Thomas and Ollie Johnston.

Confronted with bringing the python Kaa, a somewhat foolish, if deadly, villain, to life in the 1967 *The Jungle Book*, Thomas and Johnston catalogue all the problems they had with making the character work on screen. As they note, "Bill Peet, one of our better storymen, had tried to sell Walt on a story with a snake as a main character for a propaganda film during the war, but even Walt shied away from that idea."[62] Just hearing there might be a snake character was enough for people to declare they wouldn't see the film. The animators set out to discover what precisely made the snake so intolerable. It came down to some key physical characteristics—the lack of distinction between head and the rest of the body; the unblinking reptilian eyes; the slithering; the tongue. As the animators addressed each of these they progressively rendered Kaa less upsetting, and finally, even funny. They learned to turn the snake's head so that he appeared to have shoulders, gave him "silly Ping-Pong ball eyes," added eyelids, and finally gave him a big nose, noting "for some reason, people and cartoon characters are never considered to be mean or really sinister if they have big noses."[63] The character was such a success that the Studio wrote a snake into *Robin Hood* (1973), where King John's sidekick Sir Hiss plays the comic relief (the problem of shoulders was resolved by having Sir Hiss wear a small cape where the character's neck would be). To make characters repellent one needed to reverse the Kaa process: elongate the body, make the limbs angular and hairy, point the nose like a needle, add more than two arms and legs, add another torso. Thinning, sharpening, elongating, and multiplying became codes for attack. It was in this vein that the Studio put Ben Ali, the predatory alligator from Ponchielli's *Dance of the Hours* sequence in *Fantasia*, to work as a sly and thorough killer for various amphibious assault and air attack squadrons.[64] On every patch the leering, squinting Ben Ali shows a mouth cracked open in the reptile's natural grin, a jaw full of teeth, coiling his long tail for effect. The roaring dinosaurs from *Fantasia*'s *Le Sacre du Printemps* came predesigned for aggressive patches.

Here there were no static designs, no frozen images or stationary shields: all the characters were alive and in the midst of action. Even the most sedately posed characters followed every rule the Disney animators had learned about providing what Thomas and Johnston call "the illusion of life." One of the early challenges animators posed themselves was having an object with no recognizable features, like a pillow, come to life. In the hands of these now expert artists, a pillow could display an enormous variety of emotions (the same kinds of attitudes allow a rug in *Aladdin* [1992] to become a strong character, even though it has no features and can't speak). Giving life to inanimate objects, like Mickey's broom in *The Sorcerer's Apprentice*, is part of Disney's modernism. The world was awake and thinking: things had their own teleologies. Those attributes could be harnessed on patches for heavy bomber units flying the biggest, most dangerous (both to crew and their targets) weapon systems in the air. While bombardment patches often showed a Disney character preparing to throw a missile (or in the case of the 452nd Bombardment Squadron, 3rd Air Force, a cruelly grinning Lampwick cueing up to pocket a smoking cannonball), many of the patches showed the bombs themselves now alive and on the go.

These agents of war are not our familiar woodland friends, but machinery with arms and legs come to life, poised or jumping off diving boards, as pugilists, beating the enemy (in the case of the "KAYO to Tokyo Club," a red-white-and-blue striped bomb pounds a red Japanese octopus with buck teeth and slanted eyes— the very reversal of the octopi that fight on behalf of the Allies), or are adult bombs instructing young ones at school (56th Flight School Squadron, AAF Advanced Flying School). The machine has been recruited for the natural world and is shown in boy-time pursuits—swimming, diving, boxing, going to school, and even engaged in family life composed of adult and child bombs. Some images seem to be a fusion of futurism and surrealism: a grimacing bomb with a cannonball head and missile body riding a bomb horse, posed like some mechanistic headless horseman. Everything is bombs or missiles: feet, heads, tails, even what can be mistaken for testicles (452nd Bombardment Squadron, 3rd Air Force). Sentimental modernism has given way to a world of living destruction where nothing human remains. The strength of these machines is that they are autonomous, purpose-driven to explode. Everything has become a bomb, and the only humans that exist are out of sight on the ground. Everything in the path of these living weapons will perish. No sorcerer Yen Sid will descend into the dungeon, part the waters, and kill the brooms. The brooms are the world.

In the wartime articles from the June 1943 *National Geographic* issue illustrating the then current state of US military heraldry, Gilbert Grosvenor reproduced over 300 Air Force insignia, including some from the Disney Studio. The collection shows that what the Disney artists under Hank Porter produced was in keeping with the repeated themes used by the various insignia and design sections of the military. Heroic animals (eagles, charging bison and rams, Pegasus, bears, broncos, lions, tigers, griffins, and dragons) kept company with generic racist images of Native Americans, spears, stars, and above all, bombs flying at or about to be dropped on the ground. The Disney insignia are superior. They have a unified style, are equally well designed and executed.

Disney as a design house was now synonymous with America: Mickey was as much a citizen as Chaplin's Little Tramp, all standing for the game worker-become-soldier. There was no way the disorganized United States heraldic effort could compare to Disney's machine. The Disney patches came not only from a design house with a unified style, but one that was informed by a singular worldview in which images of home and family were paramount, the hero was good natured and law-abiding, the heroine gracious and committed to middle-class values of child-rearing and consensus. A whole ethos complete with understandings of fairness, justice, mercy, and punishment informed the ideas that became the patches.

The dangerous rebels and outcasts, true threats to the system, like *Dumbo*'s drunken clowns, Stromboli, the Little Coachman, the Fox and the Kitty from *Pinocchio*, the black force of Chernobog and the heedless dinosaurs from *Fantasia*, all of whom inhabited a world of terrors, would gradually be bleached out of the narrative until they were only silhouettes of powers that had once been. *Snow White*'s queen and Maleficent would be replaced by the dangerous but foolish Cruella De Vil and Captain Hook. Even Tick-Tock the crocodile would become more cause for humour than fear. Villains became increasingly unbalanced and laughable, successful only temporarily or by accident more than due to their dark natures. Even when sure killers like *The Jungle Book*'s tiger Shere Khan were around, Baloo the Bear, played by Phil Harris intertextually channelling John Wayne, would make sure Mowgli never came to harm. Just knowing a version of John Wayne was in the film guaranteed that all would be well. Pinocchio's greatest miracle is that he continues to survive in a world of con artists and slavers, unlike the dogs and cats of *The Lady and the Tramp* (1955) and *The Aristocats* (1970), whose safety was never in any doubt. The idea of nature gone terribly wrong, embodied by the insanely raging Monstro, would never reappear, not in *Fantasia 2000*'s depiction of the Firebird from Stravinsky's eponymous ballet.[65] Even *The Lion King*'s (1994) fratricidal Scar, who kills Mufasa, the kind of parental death (no trauma is worse in Disney's narrative) rarely seen in Disney, can be written off as a fading drag queen missing his salad days.

Disney's insignia took all the force of sentimental modernism and balanced it with the military's needs for attractive, remarkable (in the original sense of that word), but altogether new kinds of signifying. About the Air Force insignia, the *Geographic* writer Gerard Hubbard says, "In the quick tempo and brilliant colors of paintings upon the sides of aircraft the young American seems to say: 'Me? Not a care in the world! It's all fun!'"[66] After such an overt propaganda statement it's worth considering how the young men, the "boys" as Paul Fussell rightly calls them, "those kids," in Disney's words, who were initially so eager to have Disney-designed patches, felt about those same insignia after flying combat missions.[67] After seeing their fellow air crews shot down, burned alive, or dismembered by flak, how did it feel to wear a badge displaying Thumper or Dumbo? Those of Mickey Mouse's kids who went to war, saw action, and survived certainly didn't return as children.[68]

The idea "It's all fun!" suggests that Americans were as good at war as Disney was at making cartoons. If the world wanted to know what to expect of American forces in battle, they should look at the new irritable star on the bulk of the insignia—Donald Duck. The Duck might be mostly incoherent, but his actions were incontrovertible. As enraged and frustrated as he got, he always won in the end: his good nature, a key American quality, was always restored when he had vanquished his foe. If Donald was painted on the side of a heavy bomber, then winning meant unloading hundreds, thousands, of bombs, all part of the colloquial, devil-may-care mission Hubbard describes. The laughing, sentimental, and often bloodthirsty images (Thumper on the side of a long-range plane dropping "block busters" in a saturation bombing campaign) made war new again. This was an industrial war served up with a deadly sweetness. It's one thing to have a city flattened by carpet-bombing, another to have the bombers decorated with laughing cherubic cartoon characters.

Against the variety of different kinds of design I've chosen to consider here, from the official pieces of heraldry that followed the First World War to the carefully done work by the Disney Studio, there was in Germany a much more focused kind of signifying practice. Where America pursued a haphazard policy that was rarely unified, later brought together under the auspices of The Institute of Heraldry, it was and to a great extent remains a design Wild West. As one retired Army lieutenant who attacks the vast array of mistakes committed by TIOH says about it: "TIOH fails at properly teaching US Army officers about heraldry by not making the information readily accessible," concluding disgustedly that what TIOH produces is just "crap."[69] If the American approach to design was scattershot, vernacular, often sentimental or arbitrary, the Nazi approach could not have been more calculated, controlled, or rigidly policed by the remarkable *Organisationsbuch* of design rules. Where America sprayed designs across its various military arms and their materiel, the Nazis cleaved without fail to a limited signifying system. Around that one idea all designs—architectural, industrial, graphic, sartorial, vexillogical—orbited. At the same time, with all of its contradictions, the tension between the modern and sentimental, the corporate and the heraldic, the Disney war utterance was the most coherent, unified, popular, and powerful: the American answer to the whole of the swastika project.

EXIT

BUYER'S REMORSE

WHAT IS IT TO WIN A WAR? FOR THE GREATEST GENERATION and its successors, the end of the Second World War became the signature happy ending against which all others would be measured: the homeland (apart from Pearl Harbor) remained unscathed, the enemy had been decimated, the countryside, cities, and industries ruined, the revelation to the public about the staggering atrocities in the concentration camps proving the victory was both moral and justified, a feeling that was reinforced by the official war crimes trials in Nuremburg. Despite fears of a post-war depression, the American economy was restored, with the country becoming the leader of the Allied nations. It was an ending fit for Hollywood. No other American war since has come close to such success, not even the first Gulf War, which, according to then-president George H. W. Bush, proved that America had "kicked the Vietnam syndrome once and for all."[1] There the "bad guy" wasn't really punished, and the proof of misdeeds was countered by questions about the United States' long support of Saddam Hussein's regime. If anything, the war did more to raise the issue of the so-called "friendly dictators" that the United States had aided and financed over the decades. In pursuit of the fleeing Iraqi army United States forces created the infamous "highway of death," kilometers of road crammed with over a thousand military and civilian vehicles both that were boxed in and bombed, over the course of ten hours, to smoking ruins. The number of human casualties varies depending on the source, but that it was a massacre, or what a previous Attorney General Ramsey Clark called a "turkey shoot," is certain.[2] The terrible ordeals in southeast Asia, in Korea and Vietnam, could in no way be made to conform to the Second World War narrative, and left behind serious questions about how and why the wars had been fought, as well as the United States' role as a global superpower. The public discussion about the 1968 My Lai massacre caused the nation to reconsider the idea that American soldiers necessarily behave well in wartime, leading to the Winter Soldier Investigation and Fulbright hearings. The dual wars of occupation in Iraq and Afghanistan, now entering years fourteen and sixteen respectively, have no planned ends in sight; assume at least another fifteen years for Afghanistan, about which retired Lieutenant Colonel John Nagl (author of a famous book on counterinsurgency warfare) says "it's going to take a long time—we're halfway there." The situation is so complex that even framing the definition of "win" is next to impossible, or as Nagl says lamely, "it's not a very satisfying end state."[3] When I give public talks about propaganda, it's the Second World War people are anxious to talk about. I end my discussions with examples from Iraq and Afghanistan, but people my age and older don't want to talk about those wars and their moral implications. The Second World War is familiar, friendly, as Studs Terkel called it, initially sarcastically, the "'Good War.'" When I insist on talking about Afghanistan and Iraq, people get upset and leave. They're anxious, but not for conversation.

War is offered as a way to ensure the right kind of peace; as a route to human development; a way to create and perform gender identities; a way to establish individuality through heroism in, paradoxically, a common cause; as a spur to economic, scientific, and technological progress. Each of these propositions contains an implicit or explicit exchange that benefits the survivors (and, depending on your point of view, the dead: many consider a life swapped for honourable death to be a reasonable deal), assuming they're not too wracked by various forms of suffering, anxiety, illness, and pain. Even if the individual dies, there is the promise that the struggle itself was worthwhile, that sacrifices will not have been made in vain. At the very least the survivors can hold defiantly to the notion that the deaths were meaningful and served some greater purpose.

Now in the rust belt's dim light, the roaring post-war factories that appeared to drive America's economy through the late 1960s seem like a mirage. Americans across the depressed heartland might look with some bitterness on Germany and Japan's thriving economies when they compare them to Detroit, once modernity's show piece, now a nearly abandoned husk containing, ironically, some of modernism's most astonishing successes in the Detroit Institute of Arts. Modernism has survived even modernity. When it comes to memory and memorialization, the gap between the original and the representational artifact has, for many, been filled by mass culture. A great deal of winning a war is recounting stories that not only make sense to survivors and their children, but that people take deep and lasting pleasure in hearing. They are stories that people want retold; they become classics because there is a sense of rightness, if not accuracy, to them—this is the way it felt and should have been. It can be a short step to replace the reality with the desire: "it should have been" becomes "it was." Texts like *American Sniper* don't have to explain themselves if they feel right—they're more powerful when they don't. *American Sniper's* popularity mirrored the success that followed Audie Murphy's re-enacted biographical film *To Hell and Back* (1955) that was Universal's top earner until it was pushed out twenty years later by *Jaws* (1975), directed by the new master of the fabular epic, Steven Spielberg, who would extend American mythology with his war texts for large and small screens (*Saving Private Ryan* [1998], *Band of Brothers* [2001], *The Pacific* [2010]).

Roger Griffin points out that scholars like art historian Peter Adam who "dismiss Nazi classicism, along with all other products of Nazi culture, as 'the expression of a barbaric ideology' would also do well to consider Brandon Taylor's observation that the symmetrical use of massive blocks of polished stone under Nazism evoked not an 'Aryan' past, but the supposedly 'eternal' qualities of smoothness, geometry, and proportion, central features of international modernism."[4] It may have been a useful myth in the first few post-war decades to declare that modernism was a canary in the coal mine of freedom, tolerated by democracies but not by authoritarian states. But if modernism could be used, even embraced and exploited by authoritarian politics, then its existence didn't provide the reassuring cultural bulwark against fascism it once had. If fascists could also be modernists, then perhaps fascism and democracies could co-exist. In everything, complexity must be the answer to reassuring myths we treasure. Complexity is hard. It requires deep reserves of patience, a sense that things are moving, but at times geologically slowly. It is certainty that gives great pleasure—the sure hero (*The Hurt Locker's* Sergeant James, *American Sniper's* Chris Kyle, *Lone Survivor's* Marcus Luttrell) who, despite being an outcast, a maverick at once the curse and pride of the military, knows what to do and does it, is our favourite. Mired in the fragmented difficulty of daily life, the hero's certainty is enormously appealing. Why can't we be so single-minded in our actions and beliefs, at peace with our decisions? Maybe the better way to live is to simplify the world, come to answers, stand by them and brook no discussion.

We live in a world that has experienced convergence, not just of the *Titanic* and the iceberg, to go back to Thomas Hardy's prescient view of the twentieth century in his poem "The Convergence of the Twain," where the machine's creation simultaneously produces the accident that will demolish not only it but all the human lives caught in its mechanism, but also of media and genres, our individual positions in the marketplace and in terms of the planet. The many-screens-become-one where we live, work, play, prepare to procreate, is also the place where we frequently exchange positions between performing as consumers and producers. When fans can drive, alter, or commission (using various crowd-funding platforms) the narrative arcs of mass-market products, have they also become major stakeholders, people with power, or are they just the best focus group of which a company like McKinsey could possible dream? As digital consumers become content creators, to what extent are we aware that what we fashion will be governed by the programs we use, the way they're shaped and in turn organize information? How aware are we that we are being mediated, let alone propagandized? How offended are we if someone suggests we've fallen prey to propaganda? If we're invested in knowing and governing our own minds, one would think we'd be diligent about scrutinizing ourselves for propaganda's diagnostic signs: that we're certain we haven't been propagandized; that we believe we each think differently and value each others' differences; that only the most grotesque behaviour brings us to eject our fellow citizens from the group. It comes down to how at ease we feel: the more at ease, the more at risk.

As long as the narratives we subscribe to are rooted in myth and advertising, it's likely we're not going to want to truly examine how much our ideas could be the result of propaganda. Advertising, the feeding ground for propaganda, as Sam Keen suggests, "encourages us to turn the natural world into things, and propaganda, which invites us to turn our neighbors into things, are both instruments of a metaphysic of total warfare, a paranoid vision in which we are surrounded by an alien world."[5] A world without products to comfort us may seem unbearable, impossible to imagine. In the twenty-first century corporate brands may form the most tenuous of bridges connecting people. A new product from Apple, which has its own religious aura, Starbucks' coffee, or food from any one of dozens of fast food outlets specializing in highly fatty salty and sweet material, may represent more comfort to us than even the shallowest political beliefs.

Where we turn for our statements about truth are increasingly fluid, subject to little confirmation more than our own sense that these are the facts because they align with our beliefs. As brand expert Simon Anholt concludes, "the walls between marketing, entertainment, politics and the military, always somewhat permeable in the American culture, had truly been dismantled by this stage."[6] True convergence is not just the arrival on one screen of previous device-dependent stand-alone media like television or radio, but of information made liquid, a liquid that may be tainted or have no particular hygiene practice involved in its creation and maintenance. Information may want to be free, as citizens working on the Net often said, but what kind of information, how trustworthy and reliable it is, takes work and money to determine. Information is the only thing in our heads. If we don't want to pay for clean information, then what's in our heads will reflect that.

Had the outcome of the Second World War been as the Hollywood story suggested it was, there might not be a problem. But the happy Hollywood reality of war stories where democracy flourishes isn't what I found when I began digging, nor is it what's on exhibit here. It is unutterably more complex, hard to learn about, harder to keep up with. The war winners were the corporate entities now moving with vast dexterity across the planet; the force of advertising, design, and marketing; the shift from product to experiential sales, to lifestyles, and to the brand as the highest expression of these united forms. This is the convergence resulting from the Second World War. The agrarian metaphor of a "natural" cycle of life, death, decay, and renewed life doesn't, for Riesenbeck and Perrey, hold any water when it comes to brands: "Strong brands are like living organisms. The lifecycle theory, which predicts that brands generally die off after passing through phases of boom and then saturation, has been shown to be wrong."[7]

Brands suggest that democracy and the free market, such as they exist at the current moment, are yet more pieces of the crustal plate on the move, always being pulled under to make way for new mountains to build. Although propaganda generally cannot overcome the worst realities, there are times, as with the wave of suicides accompanying the Reich's collapse, when people become true believers in a system, no matter how bent on death it is—this is the road of total war that answers for the dread of being alive, afraid, and human.

NOTES

ENTRANCE: GORGEOUS WARNING

1   Tim O'Brien, *The Things They Carried* (New York: Broadway Books, 1998), 81.

2   Michael Herr, *Dispatches* (New York: Vintage, 1991), 248–9.

CHAPTER 1: SAME OLD NEW

1   Karl Marx and Friedrich Engels, *The Communist Manifesto*, trans. Samuel H. Beer (Arlington Heights: Harlan Davidson, 1955), 28.

2   Zygmunt Bauman. *Liquid Modernity* (Cambridge: Polity Press, 2000), 6.

3   Gilles Deleuze and Félix Guattari, *Anti-Oedipus: Capitalism and Schizophrenia*, trans. Robert Hurley, Mark Seem, Helen R. Lane (Minneapolis: University of Minnesota Press, 1983), 258.

4   Frederick Jackson Turner, *The Frontier in American History* (Tucson: University of Arizona Press, 1986), 30.

5   Daniel Joseph Singal, "Towards a Definition of American Modernism," *American Quarterly* 39, no. 1 (Spring 1987): 7.

6   Modris Eksteins, *Rites of Spring: The Great War and the Birth of the Modern Age* (London: Bantam, 1989), 67, 70.

7   Jonathan Vance, *Death So Noble* (Vancouver: UBC Press, 1999).

8   Michael Levenson, "Introduction," in *The Cambridge Companion to Modernism, Second Edition*, ed. Michael Levenson (Cambridge: Cambridge University Press, 2011), 3.

9   Mark Seltzer, *Bodies and Machines*, (London: Routledge, 1992), 157.

10   Roger Griffin, *Modernism and Fascism: The Sense of a Beginning under Mussolini and Hitler* (Basingstoke: Palgrave Macmillan, 2007), 116.

11   David Harvey, *The Condition of Postmodernity: An Enquiry into the Origins of Cultural Change*, (Oxford: Blackwell Publishers, 1990), 35.

12   Michael Kammen, *Mystic Chords of Memory: The Transformation of Tradition in American Culture* (New York: Vintage, 1993), 443.

13   Henry Adams. *Henry Adams: Novels, Mont Saint Michel and Chartres, The Education of Henry Adams*, (New York: Library of America, 1983), 1067; Thomas Hardy, *Tess of the D'Urbervilles* (London: Penguin Books, 1979), 436.

14   Terry Smith. *Making the Modern: Industry, Art, and Design in America* (Chicago: University of Chicago Press, 1994), 8.

15   Marshall Berman, *All That Is Solid Melts into Air* (New York: Penguin, 1988), 15.

16   Lewis Mumford, "American Condescension and European Superiority," *Scribner's*, May 1930, 525.

17   Peter Gay, *Modernism: The Lure of Heresy* (New York: W. W. Norton & Company, 2010), 18.

18   T. Smith, *Making the Modern*, 200.

19   Leo Marx *The Machine in the Garden: Technology and the Pastoral Ideal in America*. 35th anniversary ed. (New York: Oxford University Press, 1999), 356.

20   T. J. Jackson Lears. *Fables Of Abundance: A Cultural History Of Advertising In America* (New York: Basic Books, 1995), 346.

21   Raymond Chandler, *The Long Goodbye* (New York: Vintage, 1988), 86.

22   Chandler, *The Long Goodbye*, 90.

23   Warren I. Susman, *Culture As History: The Transformation of American Society in the Twentieth Century* (New York: Pantheon, 1984), 192.

24 Kathleen Morner and Ralph Rausch, *NTC's Dictionary of Literary Terms* (Lincolnwood: McGraw-Hill Education, 1991), 138; Karl Beckson and Arthur Ganz, *Literary Terms: A Dictionary*, 3rd ed (New York: Farrar, Straus and Giroux, 1989), 165; Joseph Childers and Gary Hentzi, eds., *The Columbia Dictionary of Modern Literary and Cultural Criticism* (New York: Columbia University Press, 1995), 192; David Macey, *The Penguin Dictionary of Critical Theory* (Penguin Books, 2000), 258.

25 Gay, *Modernism*, 1.

26 Singal, "Towards a Definition of American Modernism," 7.

27 Susan Hegeman, *Patterns for America: Modernism and the Concept of Culture* (Princeton, NJ: Princeton University Press, 1999), 22.

28 Patrick McDonnell, Karen O'Connell, and Georgia Riley de Havenon, *Krazy Kat: The Comic Art of George Herriman* (New York: Harry N. Abrams, 2004), 80, 218.

29 Laurence Cutler and Judy Goffman Cutler, *J. C. Leyendecker: American Imagist* (New York: Harry N. Abrams, 2008), 37, 74.

30 Ludwig Hohlwein, *Ludwig Hohlwein, 1874–1949: Kunstgewerbe und Reklamekunst* (Munich: Klinkhardt & Biermann, 1996), 168, 170.

31 Carole Turbin, "Fashioning the American Man: The Arrow Collar Man, 1907–1931," *Gender & History* 14, no. 3 (2003): 488.

32 Kammen, *Mystic Chords of Memory*, 300.

33 Kammen, *Mystic Chords of Memory*, 355, 316.

34 "Welcome-Guide-2017-Feb-April.Pdf," accessed May 10, 2017, https://www.thehenryford.org/documents/default-source/default-document-library/welcome-guide-2017-feb-april.pdf?sfvrsn=0.

35 T. Smith, *Making the Modern*, 150.

36   Raymond Chandler, *The Simple Art of Murder* (New York: Ballantine Books, 1977), 20.

37   Gay, *Modernism*, 89.

38   Michele Helene Bogart, *Artists, Advertising, and the Borders of Art* (Chicago: University of Chicago Press, 1995), 141.

39   Robert Hughes, *American Visions: The Epic History of Art in America* (London: Harvill Press, 1997), 259.

40   Alice Carter, *The Red Rose Girls: An Uncommon Story of Art and Love* (New York: Harry N. Abrams, 2000), 16–17.

41   Gay, *Modernism*, 87.

42   Bogart, *Artists, Advertising, and the Borders of Art*, 140.

43   Bogart, *Artists, Advertising, and the Borders of Art*, 142.

44   Lears, *Fables of Abundance*, 302.

45   Stuart Ewen, *All Consuming Images: The Politics of Style in Contemporary Culture*, rev. ed. (New York: Basic Books, 1990), 145.

46   Miles Orvell, *The Real Thing: Imitation and Authenticity in American Culture, 1880–1940* (Chapel Hill: The University of North Carolina Press, 1989), 182.

47   T. Smith, *Making the Modern*, 359.

CHAPTER 2: MACHT FREI

1   Peter Adam, *Art of the Third Reich* (New York: Harry N. Abrams, 1992), 124–5.

2   Gay, *Modernism*, 18.

3   Griffin, *Modernism and Fascism*, 26.

4   Jeffrey Herf, *Reactionary Modernism: Technology, Culture, and Politics in Weimar and the Third Reich* (Cambridge: Cambridge University Press, 1986), 234–5.

5   Adolf Hitler. *Mein Kampf*, trans. Michael Ford (Camarillo: Elite Minds, 2009), 226.

6   Steven Heller, *Iron Fists: Branding the 20th-Century Totalitarian State* (London: Phaidon Press, 2008), 49.

7   *Max*, directed by Menno Meyjes, Lions Gate (2002).

8   Herf, *Reactionary Modernism*, 232–3.

9   Steinweis draws on the internal reports written by the SS known as the *Meldungen aus dem Reich* published between 1939 and 1944. Intended to sample the Reich's emotional temperature, these were collated surveys taken for the SS and other high-ranking party members. Alan E. Steinweis, *Art, Ideology, and Economics in Nazi Germany: The Reich Chambers of Music, Theater, and the Visual Arts* (Chapel Hill: University of North Carolina Press, 1993), 151.

10   Adolf Ziegler, the most famous of the Nazi painters, said in his opening comments at the *Entartete Kunst* exhibit that he "would need several freight trains to clear our galleries of this rubbish," a chilling forecast of what was to befall millions of humans, let alone works of art (qtd. in Adam, *Art of the Third Reich*, 123).

11   Adam, *Art of the Third Reich*, 122.

12   Jeff Clark, *Uniforms of the NSDAP: Uniforms—Headgear—Insignia of the Nazi Party* (Atglen, PA: Schiffer Publishing, 2007), 62.

13   Lears, *Fables of Abundance*, 343.

14   Brandon Taylor. "Post-Modernism in the Third Reich," in *Nazification of Art: Art, Design, Architecture Music and Film in Third Reich*, ed. Brandon Taylor and Wilfried van der Will, Winchester Studies in Art and Criticism (Winchester: Winchester School of Art Press, 1990), 143.

15   Griffin, *Modernism and Fascism*, 68.

16   Peter Fritzsche, "Nazi Modern," *Modernism/Modernity* 3, no. 1 (1996): 6.

17   David Welch. *The Third Reich: Politics and Propaganda*, 2nd ed. (New York: Routledge, 2002), 51.

18   Brandon Taylor and Wilfried van der Will, "Aesthetics and National Socialism," in *The Nazification of Art: Art, Design, Music, Architecture and Film in the Third Reich*, ed. Brandon Taylor and Wilfried van der Will, Winchester Studies in Art and Criticism (Winchester: Winchester School of Art Press, 1990), 6.

19   Jan Nelis, "Modernist Neo-classicism and Antiquity in the Political Religion of Nazism: Adolf Hitler as Poietes of the Third Reich," *Totalitarian Movements and Political Religions* 9, no. 4 (2008): 475.

20   Nelis, "Modernist Neo-classicism," 481.

21   Herf, *Reactionary Modernism*, 224.

22   Taylor and van der Will, "Aesthetics and National Socialism," 4.

23   Griffin, *Modernism and Fascism*, 260.

24   Natalie Jarvey, "'The Man in the High Castle' Is Amazon's Most-Watched Original," *The Hollywood Reporter*, December 21, 2015, http://www.hollywoodreporter.com/live-feed/man-high-castle-is-amazons-850422.

25   Walter A. Strauss, "Gottfried Benn: A Double Life in Uninhabitable Regions," in *Fascism, Aesthetics, and Culture*, ed. Richard J. Golsan (London: University Press of New England, 1992), 69. Apart from the discussion of Nazi kitsch, which has its own studies (cf. Rolf Steinberg), there is also Gillo Dorflés' (q.v.) wonderfully droll study of kitsch across wartime and beyond.

26   Natalia Skradol, "Fascism and Kitsch: The Nazi Campaign against Kitsch," *German Studies Review* 34, no. 3 (2011): 597, 599.

27   S. Heller, *Iron Fists*, 50.

28   S. Heller, *Iron Fists*, 55.

29   Jonathan Petropoulos, *Art as Politics in the Third Reich*, rev. ed. (Chapel Hill: University of North Carolina Press, 1999), 47.

30   Petropoulos, *Art as Politics*, 23.

31   Selle qtd. in Jeremy Aynsley, *Graphic Design in Germany: 1890–1945* (Berkeley: University of California Press, 2000), 180.

32   Taylor, "Post-Modernism," 142.

33   Andrew Hewitt, "Fascist Modernism, Futurism, and Post-modernity," in *Fascism, Aesthetics, and Culture*, ed. Richard J. Golsan (Hanover, NH: University Press of New England, 1992), 43.

34   S. Heller, *Iron Fists*, 56.

35   S. Heller, *Iron Fists*, 56.

36   S. Heller, *Iron Fists*, 61.

37   Peter Schjeldahl, "Hitler as Artist," *The New Yorker*, August 19, 2002, http://www.newyorker.com/magazine/2002/08/19/hitler-as-artist.

38   Kate Connolly, "Gypsies' Fate Haunts Film Muse of Hitler," *The Guardian*, August 18, 2002, https://www.theguardian.com/world/2002/aug/18/artsandhumanities.germany.

39   Gregory Maertz, "'The Invisible Museum': Unearthing the Lost Modernist Art of the Third Reich," *Modernism/Modernity* 15, no. 1 (2008): 65.

40   Maertz, "'The Invisible Museum'," 65. Maertz's research and his ability to persuade a number of government and military bureaucracies to open their vaults has been a fascinating development in the field. Until now the existence of such an art cache has been speculated on by other scholars. We now await Maertz's forthcoming book.

41   Maertz, "'The Invisible Museum'," 80.

42   Maertz, "'The Invisible Museum'," 78.

43   Griffin, *Modernism and Fascism*, 253.

44   Petropoulos, *Art as Politics*, 24–5; Griffin, *Modernism and Fascism*, 28.

45   Maertz, "'The Invisible Museum'," 65.

46   Maertz, "'The Invisible Museum'," 78–9.

47 Fritzsche, "Nazi Modern," 6.

48 Gay, *Modernism*, 421.

49 John Heskett, "Modernism and Archaism in Design in the Third Reich," in *The Nazification of Art: Art, Design, Music, Architecture and Film in the Third Reich*, ed. Brandon Taylor and Wilfried van der Will, Winchester Studies in Art and Criticism (Winchester: Winchester School of Art Press, 1990), 118.

50 Gay, *Modernism*, 332.

51 Petropoulos, *Art as Politics*, 26.

52 Heskett, "Modernism and Archaism," 118.

53 S. Heller, *Iron Fists*, 49.

CHAPTER 3: TRUE COLOURS

1 J. A. Reynolds, *Heraldry and You: Modern Heraldic Usage in America*, (Edinburgh: Nelson, 1961), 18.

2 Reynolds, *Heraldry and You*, 77.

3 Reynolds, *Heraldry and You*, 59.

4 David Boven, "The United States Army Institute of Heraldry, Its Background, and Its Predecessors," *Alta Studia Heraldic* 3 (2010): 148.

5 Robert E. Wyllie, *Orders, Decorations and Insignia, Military and Civil; with the History and Romance of Their Origin and a Full Description of Each* (New York: G. P. Putnam's sons, 1921), 211.

6 Guido Rosignoli, *The Illustrated Encyclopedia of Military Insignia of the 20th Century: A Comprehensive A - Z Guide to the Badges, Patches and Embellishments of the World's Armed Forces* (Seacaucus: Chartwell Books, 1986), 11.

7 Eugene Zieber, *Heraldry in America* (Philadelphia: Dept. of Heraldry of the Bailey, Banks & Biddle Co., 1895), 77.

8 Arthur Charles Fox-Davies, *A Complete Guide to Heraldry*, (London: T.C. & E.C. Jack, 1909), 5.

9   "National Arms of Canada: Coat of Arms of National Arms of Canada (Crest, Armoiries)," Heraldry of the World, accessed May 22, 2017, http://www.ngw.nl/heraldrywiki/index.php?title=National_Arms_of_Canada.

10   Zieber, *Heraldry in America*, 33.

11   Zieber, *Heraldry in America*, 33.

12   Qtd. in Kammen, *Mystic Chords of Memory*, 421.

13   Reynolds, *Heraldry and You*, 13.

14   Boven, "United States Army Institute of Heraldry," 135.

15   Arthur E. DuBois, "The Traditions and Glamour of Insignia," *National Geographic Magazine*, June 1943: 652.

16   United States, *The Quartermaster Corps. [Prepared under the Direction of Thomas M. Pitkin, Chief, Historical Section, Office of the Quartermaster General]*, ed. Erna Risch and Chester L. Kieffer, United States Army in World War II: The Technical Services (Washington: Office of the Chief of Military History, Dept. of the Army, 1953), 75.

17   Rosignoli, *Illustrated Encyclopedia of Military Insignia*, 41.

18   Barry Jason Stein. *U.S. Army Patches, Flashes and Ovals: An Illustrated Encyclopedia of Cloth Unit Insignia* (Greenwich, CT: Insignia Ventures, 2007), xv.

19   Cussans qtd. in Zieber, *Heraldry in America*, 76.

20   Danny Hakim, "The Coat of Arms Said 'Integrity.' Now It Says 'Trump'," *New York Times*, May 28, 2017, https://www.nytimes.com/2017/05/28/business/trump-coat-of-arms.html?_r=1.

21   Boven, "United States Army Institute of Heraldry," 137.

22   Stein, *U.S. Army Patches, Flashes and Ovals*, xiii.

23   Wyllie, *Orders, Decorations and Insignia*, 241–2.

24   Zieber, *Heraldry in America*, 3.

25   Reynolds, *Heraldry and You*, 118.

26 Stansbury F. Haydon and Frederic P. Todd, "Notes on the Insignia of the Twenty-Fourth Corps," *Military Affairs*, January 1, 1947, 182.

27 Wyllie, *Orders, Decorations and Insignia*, 211.

28 Wyllie, *Orders, Decorations and Insignia*, 238.

29 Paul Fussell, *Uniforms: Why We Are What We Wear* (New York: Houghton, 2002), 199.

30 William Fowler, *American Military Insignia* (New York: Bdd Promotional Book Co., 1990), 43.

31 Wyllie, *Orders, Decorations and Insignia*, 214.

32 James L. Abrahamson, "Army, U.S.: 1900–41," in *The Oxford Companion to American Military History*, ed. John Whiteclay Chambers (New York: Oxford University Press, 1999), 53; Graham A. Cosmas, "Army, U.S.: Since 1941," in *The Oxford Companion to American Military History*, ed. John Whiteclay Chambers (New York: Oxford University Press, 1999), 54.

33 Boven, "United States Army Institute of Heraldry," 140.

34 Alex Abella, *Soldiers of Reason: The RAND Corporation and the Rise of the American Empire* (Orlando: Houghton Mifflin Harcourt, 2008), 17; Randall Thomas Wakelam, *The Science of Bombing: Operational Research in RAF Bomber Command* (Toronto: University of Toronto Press, 2009), 25.

35 Rosignoli, *Illustrated Encyclopedia of Military Insignia*, 8.

36 Paul Fussell. *Wartime: Understanding and Behavior in the Second World War* (New York: Oxford University Press, 1989), 3.

37 Spike Milligan, *Adolf Hitler, My Part in His Downfall* (London: Penguin Books, 1973), 36.

38 Rosignoli, *Illustrated Encyclopedia of Military Insignia*, 148.

39 Fussell, *Wartime*, 70.

40 Rosignoli, *Illustrated Encyclopedia of Military Insignia*, 163.

41 Rosignoli, *Illustrated Encyclopedia of Military Insignia*, 148.

42 DuBois, "Traditions and Glamour," 659.

43   Stein, *U.S. Army Patches, Flashes and Ovals*, xii.

44   Sullivan qtd. in Stein, *U.S. Army Patches, Flashes and Ovals*, ix.

45   Rosignoli, *Illustrated Encyclopedia of Military Insignia*, 12.

46   Fussell, *Uniforms*, 181.

47   Mircea Eliade, *The Myth of the Eternal Return: Or, Cosmos and History*, trans. Willard R. Trask (Princeton, NJ: Princeton University Press, 1971), 5.

48   Alison Smale and Steven Erlanger, "Ukraine Mobilizes Reserve Troops, Threatening War," *New York Times*, March 1, 2014, http://www.nytimes.com/2014/03/02/world/europe/ukraine.html.

49   Hajo Riesenbeck and Jesko Perrey, *Power Brands* (Weinheim: Wiley-VCH, 2007), 13.

50   Reynolds, *Heraldry and You*, 13.

51   George Pasch, "Semiotic Vexillology." *The Flag Bulletin* 22, no. 3–4 (1983): 141.

52   David Arnold, *The Handbook of Brand Management* (Reading, MA: Addison-Wesley, 1992) 2.

53   Ernest Beck and Julie Lasky, "In Iraq, Flag Design, Too, Comes Under Fire," *New York Times*, April 29, 2004, http://www.nytimes.com/2004/04/29/garden/in-iraq-flag-design-too-comes-under-fire.html.

54   Ahmed Al-Mallak, personal communication, March 2019.

55   Qtd. in Vidiot, "Vexillological Vexations," *Metafilter*, April 26, 2004, http://www.metafilter.com/32731/Vexillological-Vexations.

56   Qtd. in Beck and Lasky, "Iraq, Flag Design."

57   Qtd. in Beck and Lasky, "Iraq, Flag Design." That this article from *The New York Times* would take a heraldic query about vexillology to brand specialists and marketers instead of vexillologists is an intriguing direction for the future of armorial studies and confirms that heraldry has shifted from representing tribal and national to corporate power.

58 Artur Beifuss and Francesco Trivini Bellini, *Branding Terror: The Logotypes and Iconography of Insurgent Groups and Terrorist Organizations* (London: Merrell, 2013), 51.

59 Ted Kaye, *Good Flag, Bad Flag* (Trenton, NJ: North American Vexillological Association, 2006).

60 Lt. Col. Oscar H. Stroh, *Heraldry in the U. S. Army* (Self-published booklet), 2.

61 Pasch, "Semiotic Vexillology," 157.

62 George Pasch, "Drapeaux Nationaux," *Semiotica* 15, no. 3 (1975): 289.

63 Pasch, "Semiotic Vexillology," 157.

64 Marc Gobé, *Emotional Branding: The New Paradigm for Connecting Brands to People*, rev. ed. (New York: Allworth Press, 2010), 80.

65 Gobé, *Emotional Branding*, 80.

66 Stroh, *Heraldry in the U.S. Army*, 4.

67 The "We Deliver" motto may come from what is known as a "Friday patch," which is an authorized but not completely official patch typically used on a casual Friday. Trevor Paglen, *I Could Tell You but Then You Would Have to Be Destroyed by Me: Emblems from the Pentagon's Black World* (Brooklyn: Melville House, 2007), 6.

68 Another typical approved contradiction is the vaunted power of the small shareholder who delivers a spirited address at the annual meeting: all sit quietly knowing the shareholder has no power, despite corporate protestations to the contrary. It is a necessary part of the ritual. John Kenneth Galbraith. *The New Industrial State*, 3rd ed. (Boston: Houghton Mifflin, 1978), 117.

CHAPTER 4: INSTANT CLASSIC

1 Malcolm Quinn, *The Swastika* (New York: Routledge, 1994), 132.

2   The concept of the prince of creation from whom all myths flow is one I will revisit in a later section on Walt Disney. I am not drawing any parallel between a sociopathic fascist dictator and an entertainer, but instead indicating that from the public's vantage point Disney was seen to be responsible for everything the studio produced (for instance, that he invented and drew Mickey Mouse, he animated all the films, he made the theme parks), which indicates a similarity between two stories about creators who understood myth and the power of their place in it.

3   Hitler, *Mein Kampf*, 408.

4   Robin Lumsden, *A Collector's Guide to Allgemeine SS* (Hersham: Ian Allan Publishing, 2002), 13–14.

5   Eliade, *Myth of Eternal Reason*, 20.

6   Adam, *Art of the Third Reich*, 66.

7   Griffin, *Modernism and Fascism*, 71; David Littlejohn, *The SA 1921–45: Hitler's Stormtroopers* (London: Osprey Publishing, 1990), 19; L. Milner, *Political Leaders of the NSDAP* (London: Almark Publishing, 1972), 54.

8   Littlejohn, *The SA 1921–45*, 17.

9   Hitler, *Mein Kampf*, 407.

10   Z. A. B. Zeman, *Nazi Propaganda*. 2nd ed. (Oxford: Oxford University Press, 1973), 13.

11   Frederic Spotts, *Hitler and the Power of Aesthetics* (Woodstock: Overlook TP, 2004) 101.

12   Taylor and van der Will, "Aesthetics and National Socialism," 2.

13   Hitler, *Mein Kampf*, 408.

14   Jilek. "Nazi and Communist Flags," 24–5.

15   Gobé, *Emotional Branding*, 80.

16   Gobé, *Emotional Branding*, 83.

17   Jilek, "Nazi and Communist Flags," 24.

18 Tilman Allert, *The Hitler Salute: On the Meaning of a Gesture* (New York: Metropolitan Books, 2008), 55.

19 Gobé, *Emotional Branding*, 190.

20 Gobé, *Emotional Branding*, 190.

21 Qtd. in Welch, *The Third Reich*, 122.

22 Paul Virilio, *War and Cinema: The Logistics of Perception*, trans. Patrick Camiller (London: Verso, 2000), 57.

23 Jo Fox, *Film Propaganda in Britain and Nazi Germany: World War II Cinema* (New York: Bloomsbury Academic, 2007), 265.

24 Steffan Postaer, "The Story of 'Not Your Father's Oldsmobile.' Or How Some Really Bad Advertising Changed the Culture Forever!" Gods of Advertising, October 14, 2008, https:// godsofadvertising.wordpress.com/2008/10/14/this-is-not-your-fathers-oldsmobile-how-a-portfolio-tarnishing-piece-of-creative-changed-our-culture-forever/.

25 Simon Anholt, *Brand America* (London: Marshall Cavendish, 2010), 37.

26 Ian Ryder, "Anthropology and the Brand," in *Beyond Branding: How the New Values of Transparency and Integrity Are Changing the World of Brands*, ed. Nicholas Ind (London: Kogan Page, 2004), 141.

27 Allert, *The Hitler Salute*, 39.

28 Allert, *The Hitler Salute*, 28.

29 Allert, *The Hitler Salute*, 13.

30 Jacques Ellul, *Propaganda: The Formation of Men's Attitudes* (New York: Vintage, 1973), 225.

31 Spotts, *Hitler and the Power of Aesthetics*, 61.

CHAPTER 5: ONE PUNCH MACHINE

1 Steven Heller, "Wilhelm Deffke: Modern Mark Maker," *Design Observer*, January 24, 2008, http://designobserver.com/ feature/wilhelm-deffke-modern-mark-maker/6477.

2   S. Heller, "Wilhelm Deffke."

3   Naomi Klein, *No Logo: Taking Aim at the Brand Bullies* (Toronto: Vintage Canada, 2000), 7.

4   Gobé, *Emotional Branding*, 133.

5   *Roger & Me*, dir. Michael Moore, Warner Bros., 1989.

6   Denzil Meyers, "Whose Brand Is It Anyway?" in *Beyond Branding: How the New Values of Transparency and Integrity Are Changing the World of Brands*, ed. Nicholas Ind, (London: Kogan Page, 2004), 23.

7   Deffke qtd. in S. Heller, "Wilhelm Deffke."

8   S. Heller, "Wilhelm Deffke."

9   Steven Heller, *The Swastika: Symbol Beyond Redemption?* (New York: Allworth Press, 2000), 84.

10   S. Heller, *Swastika*, 3.

11   Spotts, *Hitler and the Power of Aesthetics*, 51.

12   J. Clark, *Uniforms of the NSDAP*, 116.

13   Hitler, *Mein Kampf*, 408.

14   Declan Stone and Garech Stone, *LOGO R.I.P.* (Amsterdam: BIS Publishers, 2003), 124.

15   S. Heller, *Swastika*, 23.

16   Sherwin Simmons, "Hand to the Friend, Fist to the Foe: The Struggle of Signs in the Weimar Republic," *Journal of Design History* 13, no. 4 (2000): 325.

17   Simmons, "Hand to the Friend," 325.

18   Wolfgang G. Jilek, "Nazi and Communist Flags," *Flag Bulletin* 40, no. 1 (2001): 25.

19   Jilek, "Nazi and Communist Flags," 26.

20   Gobé, *Emotional Branding*, 125.

21   Doug Guthrie, "Corporations: Personhood Conferred; Citizenship Earned," *Forbes*, accessed October 29, 2014, http://www.forbes.com/sites/dougguthrie/2012/02/14/corporations-personhood-conferred-citizenship-earned/; Binyamin Appelbaum, "What the Hobby Lobby Ruling

Means for America," *New York Times*, July 22, 2014, http://www.nytimes.com/2014/07/27/magazine/what-the-hobby-lobby-ruling-means-for-america.html.

22 The case has recently been overturned on appeal, making the future of private military operations in foreign countries even more dangerous for their citizens. Matt Apuzzo, "In Blackwater Case, Court Rejects a Murder Conviction and Voids 3 Sentences," *New York Times*, August 4, 2017, https://www.nytimes.com/2017/08/04/world/middleeast/blackwater-contractors-iraq-sentences.html.

23 Paul von Zielbauer, "Blackwater Softens Its Logo from Macho to Corporate," *New York Times*, October 22, 2007, https://www.nytimes.com/2007/10/22/business/media/22logo.html.

24 Gobé, *Emotional Branding*, 125.

25 The one ur-corporation I exclude here is the medieval Catholic church.

26 Riesenbeck and Perrey, *Power Brands*, 95.

27 George Creel, *How We Advertised America; the First Telling of the Amazing Story of the Committee on Public Information That Carried the Gospel of Americanism to Every Corner of the Globe* (New York and London: Harper & Brothers, 1920), 5.

28 Creel, *How We Advertised America*, 3.

29 Max Lenderman, *Experience The Message: How Experiential Marketing Is Changing The Brand World* (Toronto: McClelland & Stewart, 2005), 302.

30 Lenderman, *Experience The Message*, 32.

31 Lenderman, *Experience The Message*, 20.

32 *POM Wonderful Presents: The Greatest Movie Ever Sold*, dir. Morgan Spurlock, Snoot Entertainment, 2011.

33 Riesenbeck and Perrey, *Power Brands*, 2.

34 Gobé, *Emotional Branding*, xxix.

35 Allert, *The Hitler Salute*, 39.

36 Arjun Appadurai, "Disjuncture and Difference in the Global Cultural Economy," *Theory, Culture and Society* 7, no. 2–3 (1990): 307.

37 Lenderman, *Experience The Message*, 302

38 Quinn, *The Swastika*, 109

39 Claude Lanzmann, *Shoah: The Complete Text of the Acclaimed Holocaust Film* (New York: Da Capo Press, 1995), 92–4.

40 Stone and Stone, *LOGO R.I.P.*, 124.

41 Jilek, "Nazi and Communist Flags," 30.

42 Quinn, *The Swastika*, 110.

43 Klein, *No Logo*, 30.

44 S. Heller, *Iron Fists*, 8.

45 Peter Batty, *The House of Krupp: The Steel Dynasty That Armed the Nazis*, updated ed. (New York: Cooper Square Press, 2001), 12.

46 Steven Greenhouse, "3 Walmart Suppliers Made Goods in Bangladesh Factory," *New York Times*, December 5, 2012, http://www.nytimes.com/2012/12/06/world/asia/3-walmart-suppliers-made-goods-in-bangladeshi-factory-where-112-died-in-fire.html.

47 Greenhouse, "3 Walmart Suppliers."

48 "Loblaw & Joe Fresh Will 'Vigorously Defend' against $2B Bangladesh Factory Lawsuit," CBC News, accessed June 14, 2017, http://www.cbc.ca/news/business/loblaw-will-vigorously-defend-lawsuit-over-rana-plaza-factory-collapse-1.3055872.

49 Anholt, *Brand America*, 154.

50 Joseph Heller, *Catch-22* (New York: Everyman's Library, 1995), 317.

51 J. Heller, *Catch-22*, 321.

52 Celia Lury, *Brands: The Logos of the Global Economy* (New York: Routledge, 2004), 10.

53 S. Heller, *Iron Fists*, 8.

CHAPTER 6: LOYALTY PROGRAM

1 Susman, *Culture as History*, 199.

2 Mircea Eliade, *The Forge and the Crucible: The Origins and Structure of Alchemy*, 2nd ed. (Chicago: University of Chicago Press, 1979), 102.

3 Wendy Kaplan, *Designing Modernity: The Arts of Reform and Persuasion 1885-1945* (New York: Thames & Hudson, 1995), 143.

4 Lears, *Fables of Abundance*, 320.

5 Watson qtd. in Lears, *Fables of Abundance*, 301.

6 Frank Thomas and Ollie Johnston, *The Illusion of Life: Disney Animation* (New York: Disney Editions, 1995), 315.

7 Jilek, "Nazi and Communist Flags," 30.

8 S. Heller, *Iron Fists*, 14.

9 Spotts, *Hitler and the Power of Aesthetics*, 106.

10 T. Smith, *Making the Modern*, 448.

11 Gobé, *Emotional Branding*, 125.

12 Mark Pendergrast, *For God, Country, and Coca-Cola: The Definitive History of the Great American Soft Drink and the Company That Makes It*, 3rd ed. (New York: Basic Books, 2013), 225–7.

13 Edwin Black, *IBM and the Holocaust: The Strategic Alliance between Nazi Germany and America's Most Powerful Corporation* (New York: Crown Publishers, 2001), 362, 265.

14 Black makes reference to an IBM supercomputer named "Watson" (after the firm's founder) that competed on the TV show *Jeopardy* in 2011 and beat two previous human champions. Edwin Black, "IBM's Role in the Holocaust: What the New Documents Reveal," *Huffington Post*, February 27, 2012, http://www.huffingtonpost.com/edwin-black/ibm-holocaust_b_1301691.html; Edwin Black, *Nazi Nexus: America's Corporate Connections to Hitler's Holocaust* (Washington, DC: Dialog Press, 2009).

15   Some corporations are judged too poisonous to survive, the most famous of which was I. G. Farben Gesellschaft, one corporation dismantled (or, if the corporation is to be considered a person, dismembered) at the Nuremberg war crimes trials.

16   The decades-long class-action suit against Dow Chemical by thousands of Vietnam War veterans exposed to Agents Blue, White, and Orange is a good example of corporate agility and patience in the face of a nationwide medical and humanitarian catastrophe. The best strategy was summed up accurately by Fred Wilcox in *Waiting for an Army to Die* (Washington, DC: Seven Locks Press, 1989).

17   "America's Army Backgrounder," America's Army, accessed November 5, 2014, www.americasarmy.com/press.

18   Lenderman, *Experience The Message*, 214.

19   Lenderman, *Experience The Message*, 290.

20   Joe Haldeman, *The Forever War*, reprint ed. (New York: St. Martin's Griffin, 2009), 172.

CHAPTER 7: ON YOUR SLEEVE

1   Zieber, *Heraldry in America*, 73.

2   Zieber, *Heraldry in America*, 73.

3   Wyllie, *Orders, Decorations and Insignia*, 238.

4   Reynolds, *Heraldry and You*, 118.

5   Arthur E. DuBois. "Heraldic Branch O.Q.M.G." *US Quartermaster Foundation*, October 1954, http://www.qmfound.com/heraldic_branch_OQMG.htm: 1.

6   Jacqueline M. Hames, "Artwork Made With Honor, Pride," *Soldiers*, November 2010: 33.

7   Stroh, *Heraldry in the U.S. Army*, 2; Hames, "Artwork," 32.

8   Erik Eckholm, "A Federal Office Where Heraldry of Yore Is Only Yesterday," *New York Times*, June 13, 2006, http://

www.nytimes.com/2006/06/13/washington/13heraldry.
html?mcubz=0

9   Boven, "United States Army Institute of Heraldry," 154.

10 DuBois, "Heraldic Branch O.Q.M.G.," 3.

11 Boven, "United States Army Institute of Heraldry," 155.

12 Jacqueline M. Hames. "The Institute of Heraldry Celebrates
    50th Anniversary," U.S. Army, October 27, 2010, https://www.
    army.mil/article/47234/the-in.

13 Jody Rosen. "The Knowledge, London's Legendary Taxi-
    Driver Test, Puts Up a Fight in the Age of GPS," *New
    York Times*, November 10, 2014, https://www.nytimes.
    com/2014/11/10/t-magazine/london-taxi-test-knowledge.html.

14 Boven, "United States Army Institute of Heraldry," 136.

15 Steven Heller, "The Design of American Heraldry: An
    Interview with Charles V. Mugno, " *AIGA, the Professional
    Association for Design*, accessed October 31, 2014, http://www.
    aiga.org/the-design-of-american-heraldry/.

16 Boven, "United States Army Institute of Heraldry," 158.

17 Boven, "United States Army Institute of Heraldry," 156.

18 Reynolds, *Heraldry and You*, 33.

19 Meghan Vittrup, "Institute Creates, Preserves U.S. Military
    Heraldry," *U.S. Department of Defense News*, July 24, 2007,
    http://www.defense.gov/news/newsarticle.aspx?id=46826.

20 A note about terminology: "Native American" is at best an
    awkward collective term in a highly contentious discussion
    about how to refer to so many different peoples grouped
    improperly under one name. The best way to avoid "Native
    American" and the associated problems is to refer to the
    particular tribe involved. However when the cases are,
    as here, stereotypical caricatures, the problem remains
    unresolved and aggravating. American military wartime use
    of "Indian" images are irredeemably racist without exception,
    pictures of half-naked brown men complete with pigtails,

tomahawks, a single- (or multiple-) feather headdress, and fringed buckskin pants. The fraught relationship between North America's hundreds of tribes (Tim Giago suggests that it is impossible to get away from the word "Indian" when referring to the collective population, however it isn't a term a nonNative like me can use appropriately) and the military has been exacerbated by the ongoing naming of helicopters. The most famous helicopter of the Vietnam war, the Bell UH-1E "Huey," was officially named the Bell Iroquois, accompanied by the heavylift Sikorsky Chinook, and was followed by the 1980s' Apache, the Gulf War-era Blackhawk, and most recently, the Comanche. Military appropriation of Native American names and mythology is handled well in Alasdair Spark's "Flight Controls: The Social History of the Helicopter as a Symbol of Vietnam," In *Vietnam Images: War and Representation*, eds. Jeffrey Walsh and James Aulich, 86–111 (London: Macmillan Press, 1989). For more on use of "Indian" see Dennis Gaffney, " 'American Indian' or 'Native American'?" *PBS*, April 24, 2006, http://www.pbs.org/wgbh/roadshow/fts/bismarck_200504A16.html, and Tim Giago, "The Name 'Indian' and Political Correctness," *The Huffington Post*, accessed March 1, 2015, http://www.huffingtonpost.com/tim-giago/the-name-indian-and-polit_1_b_67593.html. For the purpose of this writing I will use "Native American" because the references are almost never to specific tribes but instead to racist caricatures represented most clearly by "Natives" who appear in such texts as Disney's 1937 Silly Symphony "Little Hiawatha" and the studio's 1953 animated feature *Peter Pan*. Walton Rawls, *Disney Dons Dogtags: The Best of Disney Military Insignia from World War II* (New York: Abbeville Press, 1992), 56.

21   Rawls, *Disney Dons Dogtags*, 56.

22   Marie J. Archambeault, "World War I Choctaw Code
     Talkers: 36th Division of the National Guard," *Whispering
     Wind* 37, no. 5 (2008).

23   Simon Anholt and Sicco van Gelder, "Branding for Good?"
     in *Beyond Branding: How the New Values of Transparency and
     Integrity Are Changing the World of Brands*, ed. Nicholas Ind
     (London: Kogan Page, 2004), 42.

24   Reynolds, *Heraldry and You*, 53.

25   Stein, *U.S. Army Patches, Flashes and Ovals*, 35.

26   Virgil J. Vogel, *Indian Names in Michigan* (Ann Arbor:
     University of Michigan Press/Regional, 1986), 71.

27   Stein, *U.S. Army Patches, Flashes and Ovals*, 19.

28   Rosignoli, *Illustrated Encyclopedia of Military Insignia*, 27.

29   Whitney Smith, *Flags through the Ages and across the World*
     (New York: McGraw-Hill, 1975), 268.

30   Yuki Hamasaki, "Saga Prefecture Symbol History (Saga Ken
     No Shinboru Rireki)," personal communication, March 23,
     2015.

31   Joseph Trevithick, "Why Is There a Mosque in U.S. Army
     North's Insignia?" Medium Cool, accessed May 18, 2014,
     https://medium.com/war-is-boring/why-is-there-a-mosque-
     in-u-s-army-norths-insignia-a2c18ea42812.

32   Philip B. Meggs and Alston W. Purvis, *Meggs' History of
     Graphic Design*, 4th ed. (Hoboken: Wiley, 2005), 324–5.

33   Stein, *U.S. Army Patches, Flashes and Ovals*, 12.

34   Stein, *U.S. Army Patches, Flashes and Ovals*, 15.

35   *The Big Red One*, dir. Samuel Fuller, Warner Bros. Home
     Video, 2005.

36   Aynsley, *Graphic Design in Germany*, 51.

37   Meggs and Purvis, *Megg's History of Graphic Design*, 302–3.

38   S. Heller, "The Design of American Heraldry."

39   Steven Heller and Mirko Ilic, *Genius Moves: 100 Icons of
     Graphic Design* (Cincinnati: North Light Books, 2001), 43.

40 Phillips. "Our History, Interactive History 'Why 66?',"
   Phillips 66, accessed May 30, 2015, http://www.phillips66.
   com/EN/about/reports/ViewReports/history.html.

41 Stein, *U.S. Army Patches, Flashes and Ovals*, 40.

42 Capt. James A. Page, "The Story of 'Old Abe,' Famous
   Wisconsin War Eagle on 101st Airborne Division Patch,"
   U.S. Army, accessed April 8, 2015, http://www.army.mil/
   article/91178/.

43 Stein, *U.S. Army Patches, Flashes and Ovals*, 46.

44 Page, "The Story of 'Old Abe'."

45 Damon Runyon, *Runyon from First to Last* (London:
   Macmillan, 1975), 119.

46 DuBois, "Traditions and Glamour," 666.

47 Dwight W. Birdwell and Keith William Nolan, *A Hundred
   Miles of Bad Road: An Armored Cavalryman in Vietnam,
   1967–68* (Novato, CA: Presidio Press, 1997), 4.

48 S. Heller, "The Design of American Heraldry."

49 James Bradley with Ron Powers, *Flags of Our Fathers: Heroes of
   Iwo Jima* (New York: Bantam, 2006), 426.

50 Bradley, *Flags of Our Fathers*, 426.

51 Bradley, *Flags of Our Fathers*, 427.

52 Catherine A. Lutz and Jane L. Collins, *Reading National
   Geographic* (Chicago: University of Chicago Press, 1993), 33.

53 Philip D. Beidler, *The Good War's Greatest Hits: World War
   II and American Remembering* (Athens, GA: University of
   Georgia Press, 1998), 10.

54 Gilbert Grosvenor, "Insignia of the United States Armed
   Forces," *National Geographic Magazine*, June 1943, 651.

55 Grosvenor, "Insignia," 651.

56 "About Us," National Geographic, accessed July 2, 2017,
   http://www.nationalgeographic.org/about-us/.

57 Lutz and Collins, *Reading National Geographic*, 46

58 DuBois, "Traditions and Glamour," 653–5.

59   DuBois, "Traditions and Glamour," 652.

60   Colby Buzzell, *My War* (New York: GP Putnam and Sons, 2005), 234–5.

61   Paglen, *I Could Tell You*, 61.

62   Paglen, *I Could Tell You*, 11.

63   Paglen, *I Could Tell You*, 13.

64   Zieber, *Heraldry in America*, 75.

65   Paglen, *I Could Tell You*, 5.

CHAPTER 8: PLANET SWASTIKA

1   S. Heller, *Swastika*, 135. It is typically the Allies who refer to the swastika (derived from a Sanskrit word)—the Nazis commonly used the more descriptive "hakenkreuz" (hooked cross).

2   S. Heller, *Swastika*, 14–15.

3   Aynsley, *Graphic Design in Germany*, 180.

4   Wallace Terry, *Bloods: Black Veterans of the Vietnam War: An Oral History* (New York: Random House, 1984), 14ff.

5   Piers Platt, *Combat and Other Shenanigans: Tales of the Absurd from a Deployment in Iraq* (NP: CreateSpace Independent Publishing Platform, 2014), 15.

6   Lumsden, *A Collector's Guide*, 49.

7   Lizzie Parry, "Fury at Trendy Fashion Label's Logo That Bears an Astonishing Resemblance to NAZI Eagle," *Mail Online*, May 5, 2014, http://www.dailymail.co.uk/news/ article-2620605/Angry-shoppers-demand-fashion-label-changes-logo-looks-like-NAZI-eagle-symbol.html.

8   Colleen Nika, "Q&A: BOY London on Outfitting the Punk Movement," *Rolling Stone*, accessed July 6, 2017, http://www.rollingstone.com/culture/news/ boy-london-on-outfitting-the-punk-movement-20120920.

9   Gobé, *Emotional Branding*, 133.

10   Quinn, *The Swastika*, 110.

11   S. Heller, *Iron Fists*, 23.

12   Simmons, "Hand to the Friend," 325.

13   S. Heller, *Iron Fists*, 34.

14   Franz J. Huber, "Nazi Propaganda Handbook: Propagandisten-Fibel," German Propaganda Archive, 2005, http://research.calvin.edu/german-propaganda-archive/fibel.htm, 20.

15   S. Heller, "The Master Race's Graphic Masterpiece," *Design Observer*, February 7, 2011, http://designobserver.com/feature/the-master-races-graphic-masterpiece/24358.

16   Dietrich Orlow, *The History of the Nazi Party* (Pittsburgh: University of Pittsburgh Press, 1969), 183.

17   J. Clark, *Uniforms of the NSDAP*, 9.

18   Orlow, *History of the Nazi Party*, 182–3.

19   Robert Ley, *Organisationsbuch der NSDAP*, 2nd ed. (Munich: Zentralverlag der NSDAP, 1940), 576.

20   S. Heller, "The Master Race's Graphic Masterpiece."

21   Riesenbeck and Perrey, *Power Brands*, 216.

22   Riesenbeck and Perrey, *Power Brands*, 216.

23   Milner's book is a much shortened version of the *Organisationsbuch*—it is his translation. The German original is widely available free, in colour, on the web. Milner, *Political Leaders of the NSDAP*, 55.

24   Milner, *Political Leaders of the NSDAP*, 55.

25   Ian Kershaw. *The "Hitler Myth": Image and Reality in the Third Reich*. Reissue ed. (New York: Oxford University Press, 2001), 2–3.

26   Griffin, *Modernism and Fascism*, 315.

27   S. Heller, *Swastika*, 41.

28   Lumsden, *A Collector's Guide*, 10.

29   Gordon Williamson, *Men-at-Arms 401: The Waffen-SS (1) 1. to 5. Divisions* (Oxford: Osprey Publishing, 2003), 7.

30   Rosignoli, *Illustrated Encyclopedia of Military Insignia*, 9.

31   Fussell, *Uniforms*, 19–21.

32   Fussell, *Uniforms*, 19–21.

33   Maximilian Uriarte, *Terminal Lance, Ultimate Omnibus* (New York: Little, Brown and Co., 2018), 12.

34   Alex Preston, "This Man Claims to Have Amassed the World's Largest Collection of Nazi Memorabilia," *Business Insider*, June 24, 2015, http://www.businessinsider.com/this-man-claims-to-have-amassed-the-worlds-largest-collection-of-nazi-memorabilia-2015-6.

35   Preston, "Man Claims."

36   "Flags," Traders of the Lost Surplus, accessed August 19, 2016, http://www.totls.com/index.php?option=com_content& view=article&id=18.

CHAPTER 9: THE UNITED STATES OF ADVERTISING

1   Vatican, "Congregazione per l'Evangelizzazione Dei Popoli: Profilo," The Holy See, accessed July 10, 2017, http://www.vatican.va/roman_curia/congregations/cevang/documents/rc_con_cevang_20100524_profile_en.html.

2   Randal Marlin, *Propaganda and the Ethics of Persuasion*, 2nd ed. (Peterborough, ON: Broadview Press, 2013), 12.

3   *Merriam-Webster*, s.v. "Advertise (2c.)," accessed July 10, 2017, https://www.merriam-webster.com/dictionary/advertise.

4   Anthony R. Pratkanis and Elliot Aronson, *Age of Propaganda: The Everyday Use and Abuse of Persuasion*, rev. ed. (New York: W. H. Freeman, 2001).

5   Neal Stephenson, *Snow Crash*, reprint ed. (New York: Del Rey, 2000), 374.

6   Galbraith, *New Industrial State*, 190–1; Edward S. Herman and Noam Chomsky, *Manufacturing Consent: The Political Economy of the Mass Media* (New York: Pantheon Books, 1988), 14.

7   Kevin Lui, "China Orders Propaganda Videos at Movie Screenings," *Time Magazine*, July 7, 2017, http://time.com/4848569/china-theaters-propaganda-movies-cinema/.

8   Russ Martin, "New Scotiabank Animation Pops Up in Theatres," Marketing, April 18, 2016, http://marketingmag.ca/brands/new-scotiabank-animation-pops-up-in-theatres-172572.

9   "The Pre-Movie Ads Go on, and on ..." *Maclean's*, August 16, 2013, http://www.macleans.ca/politics/the-pre-movie-ads-go-on-and-on/.

10 Patrick Corcoran, "In-Theater Advertising Tops $500 Million," NATO Reel Blog, June 16, 2008, http://www.natoonline.org/blog reel-blog-in-theater-advertising-tops-500-million/.

11 Martin, "New Scotiabank Animation."

12 Ellul, *Propaganda*, xvi.

13 "American Sniper," Box Office Mojo, accessed June 14, 2016, http://www.boxofficemojo.com/movies/?id=americansniper.htm; "American Sniper (2014)," The Numbers, accessed July 12, 2017, http://www.the-numbers.com/movie/American-Sniper.

14 *Redacted*, dir. Brian De Palma, Magnolia, 2007; Sean Alfano, "2 GI's Face Execution For Iraq Rape-Murder," CBS News, October 18, 2006, http://www.cbsnews.com/news/2-gis-face-execution-for-iraq-rape-murder/; *Casualties of War*, dir. Brian De Palma, Sony Pictures, 2006; "Redacted." Box Office Mojo, accessed June 21, 2016, http://www.boxofficemojo.com/movies/?id=redacted.htm.

15 Qtd. in Simon Hattenstone, "No One Wants to Know," *The Guardian*, March 8, 2008, https://www.theguardian.com/film/2008/mar/08/features.iraqandthemedia.

16 See particularly Martin Barker, *A "Toxic Genre,"* (London: Pluto Press, 2011); Patricia Aufderheide, "Your Country, My Country: How Films about the Iraq War Construct Publics," *Framework: The Journal of Cinema and Media* 48, no. 2 (2007);

Tim Blackmore, "Eyeless in America: Hollywood and Indiewood's Iraq War on Film," *Bulletin of Science, Technology & Society* 32, no. 4 (2012); "Lone Survivor," Box Office Mojo, accessed June 14, 2016, http://www.boxofficemojo.com/movies/?id=lonesurvivor.htm.

17 "Whiskey Tango Foxtrot," Box Office Mojo, accessed July 12, 2017, http://www.boxofficemojo.com/movies/?id=untitledtinafeycomedy.htm.

18 Chris Kyle, Scott McEwen, and Jim DeFelice, *American Sniper: The Autobiography of the Most Lethal Sniper in U.S. Military History* (New York: Harper, 2013), 158.

19 Don Van Natta Jr., "Bush Was Set on Path to War, British Memo Says," *New York Times*, March 27, 2006, https://www.nytimes.com/2006/03/27/world/europe/bush-was-set-on-path-towar-british-memo-says.html.

20 The burial practice is important enough that it appears in other recent laudatory films about the SEALs, particularly *Act of Valor* (2012), in which active SEALs play themselves in a semi-fictional rescue thriller (the film was not about Iraq or Afghanistan, and earned back its $12 million production budget six times over).

21 *Taking Chance*, dir. Ross Katz, HBO, 2009.

22 Ellul, *Propaganda*, 52.

23 Ellul, *Propaganda*, 52.

24 Tom Boggioni. "Eastwood Film 'American Sniper' Sets Box Office Record While Setting off Flurry of Racist Tweets," Raw Story, accessed July 2, 2016, http://www.rawstory.com/2015/01/eastwood-film-american-sniper-sets-box-office-record-while-setting-off-flurry-of-racist-tweets/.

25 I'm quoting from some of the better known tweets that appeared at the time, most of which exist on the web as quotations, but in many cases as screen captures. Most of the Twitter authors have since either removed their tweets

or protected their accounts from public view. Michael
Goodier, "American Sniper Box Office Hit Inspires Racist
Tweets," Storify, accessed July 2, 2016, https://storify.com/
michaelgoodier7/american-sniper-box-office-hit-inspires-
racism.

26   Ellul, *Propaganda*, 152.

27   Beidler, *The Good War's Greatest Hits*, 8.

28   Martin Manning and Herbert J. Romerstein, *Historical
Dictionary of American Propaganda* (Westport: Greenwood,
2004), 206.

29   William L. Bird and Harry R. Rubenstein, *Design for
Victory: World War II Posters on the American Home Front*
(New York: Princeton Architectural Press, 1998), 42;
Gordon Calhoun. "Because Somebody Talked!" 1944 Poster.
Hampton Roads Naval Museum, accessed July 2, 2016, http://
hamptonroadsnavalmuseum.blogspot.ca/2012/11/because-
somebody-talked-1944-poster.html.

30   Allan M. Winkler, *The Politics of Propaganda: The Office of War
Information, 1942–1945*, Yale Historical Publications 118 (New
Haven: Yale University Press, 1978), 156.

31   Lears, *Fables of Abundance*, 274.

32   Susman, *Culture as History*, 203.

33   Qtd. in Winkler, *The Politics of Propaganda*, 155.

34   Martin Boisen, Kees Terlouw, and Bouke van Gorp, "The
Selective Nature of Place Branding and the Layering
of Spatial Identities," *Journal of Place Management and
Development* 4, no. 2 (2011): 140.

35   Anholt, *Brand America*, 92.

36   One recent example of persuasion's limits is the 2002 Bolivian
election win by Gonzalo Sanchez de Lozada, engineered
by brand expert and spin wizard James Carville. Lozada's
tenuous victory lasted a few months before collapsing under
its own weight. Carefully watched by Rachel Boynton in

her 2005 documentary *Our Brand Is Crisis,* no amount of Carville's genius could transform Lozada into a better person. Temporarily rebranding and successfully selling him to the Bolivians didn't affect Lozada's disastrous policies. Philip M. Taylor, *Munitions of the Mind: A History of Propaganda,* 3rd ed. (Manchester: Manchester University Press, 2003), 4.

37   Winkler, *The Politics of Propaganda,* 76.

38   Winkler, *The Politics of Propaganda,* 76.

39   Anholt, *Brand America,* 65.

40   George Roeder Jr., *The Censored War: American Visual Experience during World War Two* (New Haven: Yale University Press, 1995), 3.

41   William Manchester, *Goodbye Darkness: A Memoir of the Pacific War,* (New York: Bantam Doubleday Dell Publishing Group, 1987), 23; Roeder, *The Censored War,* 102.

42   Roeder, *The Censored War,* 14.

43   Clayton D. Laurie, *The Propaganda Warriors: America's Crusade Against Nazi Germany* (Lawrence: University Press of Kansas, 1996), 235.

44   Welch, *The Third Reich,* 5.

45   Ellul, *Propaganda,* 104.

46   Stanley Fish, *There's No Such Thing as Free Speech: And It's a Good Thing, Too,* rev. ed. (New York: Oxford University Press, 1994), 104.

47   "Takata Airbag Recall: Everything You Need to Know," Consumer Reports, accessed July 19, 2017, http://www.consumerreports.org/cro/news/2016/05/everything-you-need-to-know-about-the-takata-air-bag-recall/index.htm; Hiroko Tabuchi and Neal E. Boudette, "Automakers Knew of Takata Airbag Hazard for Years, Suit Says," *New York Times,* February 27, 2017, https://www.nytimes.com/2017/02/27/business/takata-airbags-automakers-class-action.html.

48   Anholt, *Brand America,* 62.

CHAPTER 10: PARADED TO DEATH

1   S. Heller, *Swastika*, 69.

2   Welch, *The Third Reich*, 9.

3   Ian Kershaw, "How Effective Was Nazi Propaganda?" in *Nazi Propaganda: The Power and the Limitations*, ed. David Welch (London: Croom Helm; Barnes & Noble, 1983), 182.

4   Robert Edwin Herzstein, *The War That Hitler Won: The Most Infamous Propaganda Campaign in History* (New York: Putnam, 1978), 373.

5   Richard Evans. *The Third Reich at War* (New York: Penguin Press, 2009), 728.

6   Patrick Henry. "Give Me Liberty or Give Me Death." Accessed July 20, 2017. http://www.history.org/almanack/life/politics/giveme.cfm.

7   Griffin, *Modernism and Fascism*, 96.

8   As a child born and raised in North America, I was taught that history here began with successive waves of Spanish, French, and British "explorers" who "discovered" the continent, made peace with friendly natives, established Thanks Giving, and instated parliamentary democracy, starting the country on its course to civilization (I deliberately omit the quotation marks around the final word because there wasn't an ounce of irony in this history as it was delivered to us). There were brief mentions of smallpox-ridden blankets that were handed out by these "explorers," certainly no mention, let alone discussion, of the genocide practiced on aboriginal peoples who once numbered in the tens of millions. Citizens forced to confront the human catastrophe may respond defensively that they didn't have anything to do with these actions, wouldn't have supported them if they'd been alive. At the same time there is plenty of resentment toward aboriginal survivors (Goar). I draw this parallel not to

blame citizens or excuse Magda Goebbels, but to refocus our attention on the ways in which persuasion invisibly naturalizes worldviews, and converts unease into comfortable beliefs that reassert the status quo.

9   Spotts, *Hitler and the Power of Aesthetics*, 54.

10   Taylor and van der Will, "Aesthetics and National Socialism," 1.

11   Jill Stephenson, "Propaganda, Autarky, and the German Housewife." In *Nazi Propaganda*, edited by David Welch (London: Croom Helm, 1983), 118.

12   Herzstein, *The War That Hitler Won*, 257.

13   Littlejohn, *The SA 1921–45*, 8; Lumsden, *A Collector's Guide*, 49.

14   Robin Givhan, "Fashion Firm Discovers Its Holocaust History," *Washington Post*, August 14, 1997, https://www.washingtonpost.com/archive/lifestyle/1997/08/14/fashion-firm-discovers-its-holocaust-history/c3413d98-5e73-4ede-8b9b-4e4cdd57bb4d/.

15   Roger Boyes, "Hugo Boss to Pay Slave Labourers: The Men's Fashion Giant Was Once a Preferred Tailor to the Nazi Party and a Supplier to the German Military," *Vancouver Sun*, April 8, 2000,

16   Melissa Eddy, "Hugo Boss Fashion House Acknowledges It Made Nazi Uniforms," *Associated Press*, August 14, 1997.

17   Roman Köster, "Hugo Boss, 1924-1945. A Clothing Factory during the Weimar Republic and Third Reich," Hugo Boss, September 23, 2014, http://group.hugoboss.com/en/group/about-hugo-boss/history/.

18   Givhan, "Fashion Firm."

19   Walsh.

20   Köster, "Hugo Boss, 1924-1945"; Guy Walters, "Shameful Truth about Hugo Boss's Links to the Nazis Revealed: As Russell Brand Is Thrown out of a Party for Accusing Fashion Designer of Helping Hitler," *Daily Mail*, September 5, 2013, http://www.dailymail.co.uk/news/article-2413371/

Shameful-truth-Hugo-Bosss-links-Nazis-revealed-As-Russell-Brand-thrown-party-accusing-fashion-designer-helping-Hitler.html. Boss paid for the report written by Roman Köster, an economic historian at the Bundeswehr, University of Munich. The company claims not to have influenced the content. Münster ethnologist Elisabeth Timm's earlier work corroborates the report.

21 Paul Fussell, *The Boys' Crusade: The American Infantry in Northwestern Europe, 1944–1945* (New York: Modern Library, 2003), 23.

22 Brian Leigh Davis, *German Army Uniforms and Insignia, 1933–1945*, 2nd rev. ed. (London: Arms and Armour Press, 1973), 9.

23 Rosignoli, *Illustrated Encyclopedia of Military Insignia*, 37–8.

24 Rosignoli, *Illustrated Encyclopedia of Military Insignia*, 12.

25 Milner, *Political Leaders of the NSDAP*, 16.

26 Littlejohn, *The SA 1921–45*, 8.

27 Fussell, *Uniforms*, 23.

28 Fussell, *Uniforms*, 19.

29 Gerard Lefort, "Dans l'album de Famille, Hitler," *Liberation*, November 5, 2009, http://next.liberation.fr/culture/2009/11/05/dans-l-album-de-famillehitler_591913.

30 Riss, *Hitler dans mon salon* (Paris: Editions Les Echappés, 2009).

31 Fussell, *Uniforms*, 22.

32 Susan Sontag, "Fascinating Fascism," in *The Nazification of Art: Art, Design, Music, Architecture and Film in the Third Reich*, edited by Brandon Taylor and Wilfried van der Will (Winchester: Winchester School of Art Press, 1990), 215.

33 Herf, *Reactionary Modernism*, 213, 227.

34 Herf, *Reactionary Modernism*, 206.

35 Fritzsche, "Nazi Modern," 13.

36 Mark Antliff, "Fascism, Modernism, and Modernity," *Art Bulletin* 84, no. 1 (2002): 148.

37 Griffin, *Modernism and Fascism*, 29.

38 Aynsley, *Graphic Design in Germany*, 181.

39 Antliff, "Fascism, Modernism, and Modernity," 148.

40 Nelis, "Modernist Neo-classicism," 476.

41 Griffin, *Modernism and Fascism*, 328.

42 Spotts, *Hitler and the Power of Aesthetics*, 389.

43 Christopher Hurndall, *The Weimar Insanity: Photographs and Propaganda from the Nazi Era* (Lewes: Book Guild, 1996), 128.

44 Robin Fry, *Volkswagen Beetle* (Newton Abbot: David & Charles, 1980), 42.

45 Fry, *Volkswagen Beetle*, 47.

46 Qtd. in Fry, *Volkswagen Beetle*, 79.

47 Qtd. in Gobé, *Emotional Branding*, 109.

48 Blair Dike, "Auto-Emotive Design: Interview with J. Mays, Head of Ford Motor Company Design," Thing.net, accessed November 7, 2016, http://www.thing.net/~lilyvac/pages/writing/writing26.html.

49 Griffin, *Modernism and Fascism*, 314. A contemporary audience might consider how the Reich's imprint on Twitter, Facebook, Instagram, and YouTube would appear.

50 Walter Henry Nelson, *Small Wonder: The Amazing Story of the Volkswagen*, rev. ed. (London: Hutchison, 1967), 65n.

51 Alison Smale and Jack Ewing, "Volkswagen Parts Ways with the Historian Who Chronicled Its Nazi Past," *New York Times*, November 2, 2016, http://www.nytimes.com/2016/11/03/world/europe/volkswagen-vw-emissions-scandal-nazi.html.

52 "VW Asks Historian to Research Role under Brazil Dictatorship," *Canadian Business*, November 3, 2016, http://www.canadianbusiness.com/business-news/vw-asks-historian-to-research-role-under-brazil-dictatorship/.

53 Fritzsche, "Nazi Modern," 13.

54 Spotts, *Hitler and the Power of Aesthetics*, 399.

55   Paul Virilio, *Bunker Archaeology*, trans. George Collins (Paris: Les Editions du Semi-Cercle, 1994), 45.

56   Virilio, *Bunker Archaeology*, 13.

57   Griffin, *Modernism and Fascism*, 31. Unfortunately the word "alternate" and its abbreviation "alt" have been soiled by recent association with neo-Nazis, white supremacists, and racists who prefer coinages like "alternate truths," "alternate facts," "alt right." I still argue Griffin's term is more flexible than Herf's.

CHAPTER 11: KILLER CARTOONS

1   Donald Crafton, *Before Mickey: The Animated Film, 1898–1928* (Cambridge, MA: MIT Press, 1982), 66.

2   John Canemaker, *Winsor McCay: His Life and Art* (New York: Abbeville Press, 1990), 159.

3   Thomas and Johnston, *The Illusion of Life*, 145.

4   Leonard Maltin, *Of Mice and Magic: A History of American Animated Cartoons* (New York: McGraw-Hill, 1980), 51–2.

5   Intriguingly enough *mise-en-abyme*, the expression of or reference to the whole by a part of it, as with Shakespeare's "The Murder of Gonzago" in *Hamlet*, stems from a heraldic term used to describe the placement of a shield on a larger shield. Macey, *Penguin Dictionary of Critical Theory*, 257–9; Childers and Henzi, *Columbia Dictionary of Modern Literary and Cultural Criticism*, 191–3; Andrew Edgar and Sedgwick, *Key Concepts in Cultural Theory* (London: Routledge, 1999), 244–6.

6   Susman, *Culture as History*, 197.

7   Beidler, *The Good War's Greatest Hits*, 15.

8   Jenna Goudreau, "Disney Princess Tops List Of The 20 Best-Selling Entertainment Products," *Forbes*, accessed July 10, 2016, http://www.forbes.com/sites/jennagoudreau/2012/09/17/

disney-princess-tops-list-of-the-20-best-selling-entertainment-products/#2d48c486252d.

9   Shamus Culhane, *Talking Animals and Other People* (New York: St. Martin's Press, 1986), 183.

10 Roeder, *The Censored War*, 102.

11 Fussell, *Wartime*, 268.

12 Office of Marine Corps Communication, "USMC Statement on Iwo Jima Flag Raisers," Official United States Marine Corps Public Website, June 23, 2016, http://www.marines.mil/News/News-Display/Article/810457/usmc-statement-on-iwo-jima-flag-raisers/.

13 "Marines: Man in Iwo Jima Flag Raising Photo Misidentified," Fox News, June 23, 2016, http://www.foxnews.com/us/2016/06/23/marines-man-in-iwo-jima-flag-raising-photo-misidentified.html.

14 Edward T. Linenthal and Tom Engelhardt, eds., *History Wars: The Enola Gay and Other Battles for the American Past* (New York: Holt Paperbacks, 1996).

15 Steven Watts, *The Magic Kingdom: Walt Disney and the American Way of Life* (Boston: Houghton Mifflin, 1997), 104.

16 Watts, *The Magic Kingdom*, 104.

17 Crafton, *Before Mickey*, 13.

18 Mark Langer, "Regionalism in Disney Animation: Pink Elephants and Dumbo," *Film History* 4, no. 4 (1990): 309.

19 John Canemaker, *Walt Disney's Nine Old Men and the Art of Animation*, (New York: Disney Editions, 2001), 24, 224–5.

20 Langer, "Regionalism in Disney Animation," 305.

21 Darlene Geis, *Walt Disney's Treasury of Silly Symphonies* (New York: Harry N. Abrams, 1981), 13–14; John Grant, *Encyclopedia of Walt Disney's Animated Characters* (New York: Harper & Row, 1987), 28.

22   Jack Kinney, *Walt Disney and Assorted Other Characters: An Unauthorized Account of the Early Years at Disney's* (New York: Harmony Books, 1988), 120.

23   S. Culhane, *Talking Animals*, 179–80.

24   Watts, *The Magic Kingdom*, 106.

25   S. Culhane, *Talking Animals*, 158

26   Chris Pallant, *Demystifying Disney: A History of Disney Feature Animation* (New York: Continuum, 2011), 55.

27   Watts, *The Magic Kingdom*, 102–3.

28   John Culhane, *Walt Disney's Fantasia* (New York: Harry N. Abrams, 1983), 117.

29   J. Culhane, *Walt Disney's Fantasia*, 117.

30   Amid Amidi, *Cartoon Modern: Style and Design in 1950s Animation* (San Francisco: Chronicle Books, 2006), 10.

31   Amidi, *Cartoon Modern*, 1.

32   Amidi, *Cartoon Modern*, 13; Langer, "Regionalism in Disney Animation," 317; Maltin, *Of Mice and Magic*, 66; Pallant, *Demystifying Disney*, 47. Robin Allan, *Walt Disney and Europe: European Influences on the Animated Feature Films of Walt Disney* (London: John Libbey, 1999), 178, 186.

33   Langer, "Regionalism in Disney Animation," 317.

34   Lears, *Fables of Abundance*, 300.

35   Watts, *The Magic Kingdom*, 75.

36   Disney's obsession with the audience's experience was foreshadowed by Abel Gance's epic *Napoleon* (1927), which, by using multiple projectors, created an aspect ratio of 4:1 in the theatre as opposed to the standard Academy ratio of 1.33:1. Contemporary theatres are not set up to get an aspect ratio as extreme as Gance's.

37   John Canemaker, "When Dali Met Disney," *Print*, September/October 2005, 76. I think Canemaker refers to the world of American animation, and I agree with his conclusion. When looking more widely, however, animators

and animation directors in other countries have taken wonderful chances with the medium. Anyone who has seen work by Graham Annabale and Anthony Stacchi, Aardman Studios, Michael Arias, Stephane Aubier and Vincet Patar, Satoshi Kon, Jean-François Laguionie, Hayao Miyazaki, Mamoru Oshii, Katsuhiro Otomo, Nick Park, and Isao Takahata would have an idea of just how astonishing animation has come to be.

38   Pallant, *Demystifying Disney*, 54.

39   Ron Barbagallo, "The Destiny of Dali's Destino," Animation Art Conservation, 2003, http://www. animationartconservation.com/the-destiny-of-dali-s-destino. html.

40   Hegeman, *Patterns for America*, 17. Her reference is to Lawrence Levine's *Highbrow/Lowbrow: The Emergence of Cultural Hierarchy in America* (Cambridge, MA: Harvard University Press, 1988).

41   Stephen Jay Gould, *Ever Since Darwin: Reflections in Natural History* (New York: W. W. Norton & Company, 1992), 134.

42   Watts, *The Magic Kingdom*, 105.

43   Richard J. Evans, *Third Reich in Power 1933–1939* (New York: Penguin Press, 2005), 130–1; Martin Goodman, "Dr. Toon: 'Der Führer's' Paintbrush," *Animation World Network*, May 1, 2008, http://www.awn.com/animationworld/ dr-toon-der-f-hrers-paintbrush.

44   Rawls, *Disney Dons Dogtags*, 17.

45   Bradley, *Flags of Our Fathers*, 427.

46   Winkler, *The Politics of Propaganda*, 156–7.

47   W. Elliot Brownlee, "Public Financing and Budgeting for War," in *The Oxford Companion to American Military History*, ed. John Whiteclay Chambers (Oxford: Oxford University Press, 1999), 576–7.

48 David Lesjak, *Service with Character: The Disney Studios and World War II* (NP: Theme Park Press, 2014), 36–7.

49 Rawls, *Disney Dons Dogtags*, 16.

50 Lesjak, *Service with Character*, 113; Charles Zarza, "Reconnaissance Squadron Switches Back to Original Disney Patch," *Citizen Airman* 64, no. 1 (February 2012): 8.

51 Lesjak, *Service with Character*, 113–15.

52 Lesjak, *Service with Character*, 148.

53 Rawls, *Disney Dons Dogtags*, 7.

54 Rawls, *Disney Dons Dogtags*, 38.

55 Riesenbeck and Perrey, *Power Brands*, 153.

56 Rawls, *Disney Dons Dogtags*, 56–9.

57 Jeffrey L. Ethell and Clarence Simonsen, *The History of Aircraft Nose Art: 1916 to Today* (Wisconsin: Motorbooks International, 1991).

58 Rawls, *Disney Dons Dogtags*, 39.

59 Sam Keen, *Faces of the Enemy: Reflections of the Hostile Imagination* (San Francisco: Harper & Row, 1991), 134.

60 Anthony Rhodes and Victor Margolin, *Propaganda: The Art of Persuasion World War II* (Leicester: Motorbooks Intl., 1994), 174.

61 Rawls, *Disney Dons Dogtags*, 40, 63.

62 Thomas and Johnston, *The Illusion of Life*, 421.

63 Thomas and Johnston, *The Illusion of Life*, 421.

64 Rawls, *Disney Dons Dogtags*, 94–5.

65 One recent addition to Disney films that contains a parent's death is 2015's *The Good Dinosaur*, where the child character is left quite bitterly alone for a good deal of the film. The picture earned back nearly triple what it cost to make, but is still a relative underperformer for Disney-Pixar. If you're going to kill a parent in a Disney film, it better pay off heavily when it comes to emotional redemption. At this the *The Good Dinosaur* failed.

66 Gerard Hubbard, "Aircraft Insignia, Spirit of Youth,"
National Geographic Magazine, June 1943: 710.

67 Fussell, *Boys' Crusade*, 7.

68 This is the pivot point for the final scene in Stanley Kubrick's
Full Metal Jacket (1987), when the Marines move forward using
the Mickey Mouse Club song to count cadence.

69 Old-Empresario [pseud], "Why I Dislike the US Army
Institute of Heraldry by Old-Empresario," Old-Empresario.
Hubpages.Com, May 18, 2014, http://old-empresario.
hubpages.com/hub/Why-I-Dislike-The-US-Army-Institute-of-
Heraldry.

EXIT

1 George H. W. Bush, "Remarks to the American Legislative
Exchange Council," March 1, 1991, http://www.presidency.
ucsb.edu/ws/?pid=19351.

2 Ramsey Clark, *The Fire This Time: U.S. War Crimes in the Gulf*
(New York: Thunder's Mouth Press, 1994), 50–4.

3 Julie Hirschfeld Davis and Matthew Rosenberg, "Trump
Seeks a Clear Victory in a Murky War," *New York Times*,
August 22, 2017, https://www.nytimes.com/2017/08/22/world/
asia/trump-afghanistan.html.

4 Griffin, *Modernism and Fascism*, 291–2.

5 Keen, *Faces of the Enemy*, 136.

6 Anholt, *Brand America*, 70.

7 Riesenbeck and Perrey, *Power Brands*, 7.

BIBLIOGRAPHY

Abella, Alex. *Soldiers of Reason: The RAND Corporation and the Rise of the American Empire*. Orlando: Houghton Mifflin Harcourt, 2008.

"About Us." National Geographic. Accessed July 2, 2017. http://www.nationalgeographic.org/about-us/.

Abrahamson, James L. "Army, U.S.: 1900–41." In *The Oxford Companion to American Military History*, edited by John Whiteclay Chambers, 52–3. New York: Oxford University Press, 1999.

Adam, Peter. *Art of the Third Reich*. New York: Harry N. Abrams, 1992.

Adams, Henry. *Henry Adams: Novels, Mont Saint Michel and Chartres, The Education of Henry Adams*. New York: Library of America, 1983.

Alfano, Sean. "2 GI's Face Execution for Iraq Rape-Murder." CBS News, October 18, 2006. http://www.cbsnews.com/news/2-gis-face-execution-for-iraq-rape-murder/.

Allan, Robin. *Walt Disney and Europe: European Influences on the Animated Feature Films of Walt Disney*. London: John Libbey, 1999.

Allert, Tilman. *The Hitler Salute: On the Meaning of a Gesture*. New York: Metropolitan Books, 2008.

American Sniper. Directed by Clint Eastwood. Warner Home Entertainment, 2014.

"American Sniper." Box Office Mojo. Accessed June 14, 2016. http://www.boxofficemojo.com/movies/?id=americansniper.htm.

"American Sniper (2014)." The Numbers. Accessed July 12, 2017. http://www.the-numbers.com/movie/American-Sniper.

"America's Army Backgrounder." America's Army. Accessed November 5, 2014. www.americasarmy.com/press.

Amidi, Amid. *Cartoon Modern: Style and Design in 1950s Animation*. San Francisco: Chronicle Books, 2006.

Anholt, Simon. *Brand America*. London: Marshall Cavendish, 2010.

Anholt, Simon, and Sicco van Gelder. "Branding for Good?" In *Beyond Branding: How the New Values of Transparency and Integrity Are Changing the World of Brands*, edited by Nicholas Ind, 56–68. London: Kogan Page, 2004.

Antliff, Mark. "Fascism, Modernism, and Modernity." *Art Bulletin* 84, no. 1 (2002): 148–69.

Appadurai, Arjun. "Disjuncture and Difference in the Global Cultural Economy." *Theory, Culture and Society* 7, no. 2–3 (1990): 295–310.

Appelbaum, Binyamin. "What the Hobby Lobby Ruling Means for America." *New York Times*, July 22, 2014. http://www.nytimes.com/2014/07/27/magazine/what-the-hobby-lobby-ruling-means-for-america.html.

Apuzzo, Matt. "In Blackwater Case, Court Rejects a Murder Conviction and Voids 3 Sentences." *New York Times*, August 4, 2017. https://www.nytimes.com/2017/08/04/world/middleeast/blackwater-contractors-iraq-sentences.html.

Archambeault, Marie J. "World War I Choctaw Code Talkers: 36th Division of the National Guard." *Whispering Wind* 37, no. 5 (2008): 9–15.

Arnold, David. *The Handbook of Brand Management*. Reading, MA: Addison-Wesley, 1992.

Aufderhelde, Patricia. "Your Country, My Country: How Films about the Iraq War Construct Publics." *Framework: The Journal of Cinema and Media* 48, no. 2 (2007): 56–65.

Aynsley, Jeremy. *Graphic Design in Germany: 1890–1945*. Berkeley: University of California Press, 2000.

Barbagallo, Ron. "The Destiny of Dali's Destino." Animation Art Conservation. Accessed July 15, 2016. http://www.animationartconservation.com/the-destiny-of-dali-s-destino.html.

Barker, Martin. *A "Toxic Genre."* London: Pluto Press, 2011.

Batty, Peter. *The House of Krupp: The Steel Dynasty that Armed the Nazis.* Updated edition. New York: Cooper Square Press, 2001.

Bauman, Zygmunt. *Liquid Modernity.* Cambridge: Polity, 2000.

Beck, Ernest, and Julie Lasky. "In Iraq, Flag Design, Too, Comes Under Fire." *New York Times*, April 29, 2004. http://www.nytimes.com/2004/04/29/garden/in-iraq-flag-design-too-comes-under-fire.html.

Beckson, Karl, and Arthur Ganz. *Literary Terms: A Dictionary.* 3rd edition. New York: Farrar, Straus and Giroux, 1989.

Beidler, Philip D. *The Good War's Greatest Hits: World War II and American Remembering.* Athens, GA: University of Georgia Press, 1998.

Beifuss, Artur, and Francesco Trivini Bellini. *Branding Terror: The Logotypes and Iconography of Insurgent Groups and Terrorist Organizations.* London: Merrell, 2013.

Berman, Marshall. *All That Is Solid Melts into Air.* New York: Penguin, 1988.

The Big Red One. Directed by Samuel Fuller. Warner Bros. Home Video, 2005.

Bird, William L., and Harry R. Rubenstein. *Design for Victory: World War II Posters on the American Home Front.* New York: Princeton Architectural Press, 1998.

Birdwell, Dwight W., and Keith William Nolan. *A Hundred Miles of Bad Road: An Armored Cavalryman in Vietnam, 1967–68.* Novato, CA: Presidio Press, 1997.

Black, Edwin. *IBM and the Holocaust: The Strategic Alliance between Nazi Germany and America's Most Powerful Corporation.* New York: Crown Publishers, 2001.

———. "IBM's Role in the Holocaust: What the New Documents Reveal." *Huffington Post*, February 27, 2012. http://www.huffingtonpost.com/edwin-black/ibm-holocaust_b_1301691.html.

————. *Nazi Nexus: America's Corporate Connections to Hitler's Holocaust*. Washington, DC: Dialog Press, 2009.

Blackmore, Tim. "Eyeless in America: Hollywood and Indiewood's Iraq War on Film." *Bulletin of Science, Technology & Society* 32, no. 4 (2012): 294–316.

————. "McCay's McChanical Muse: Engineering Comic-Strip Dreams." *Journal of Popular Culture* 32, no. 1 (1998): 15–38.

Bogart, Michele Helene. *Artists, Advertising, and the Borders of Art*. Chicago: University of Chicago Press, 1995.

Boggioni, Tom. "Eastwood Film 'American Sniper' Sets Box Office Record While Setting off Flurry of Racist Tweets." Raw Story. Accessed July 2, 2016. http://www.rawstory.com/2015/01/eastwood-film-american-sniper-sets-box-office-record-while-setting-off-flurry-of-racist-tweets/.

Boisen, Martin, Kees Terlouw, and Bouke van Gorp. "The Selective Nature of Place Branding and the Layering of Spatial Identities." *Journal of Place Management and Development* 4, no. 2 (2011): 135–47.

Boven, David. "The United States Army Institute of Heraldry, Its Background, and Its Predecessors." *Alta Studia Heraldic* 3 (2010): 135–58.

Boyes, Roger. "Hugo Boss to Pay Slave Labourers: The Men's Fashion Giant Was Once a Preferred Tailor to the Nazi Party and a Supplier to the German Military." *Vancouver Sun*, April 8, 2000.

Bradley, James, with Ron Powers. *Flags of Our Fathers: Heroes of Iwo Jima*. New York: Bantam, 2006.

Brownlee, W. Elliot. "Public Financing and Budgeting for War." In *The Oxford Companion to American Military History*, edited by John Whiteclay Chambers, 575–8. New York: Oxford University Press, 1999.

Bush, George H. W. "Remarks to the American Legislative Exchange Council," March 1, 1991. http://www.presidency.ucsb.edu/ws/?pid=19351.

Buzzell, Colby. *My War*. New York: GP Putnam and Sons, 2005.

Calhoun, Gordon. "Because Somebody Talked!" 1944 Poster. Hampton Roads Naval Museum. Accessed July 2, 2016. http://hamptonroadsnavalmuseum.blogspot.ca/2012/11/because-somebody-talked-1944-poster.html.

Canemaker, John. *Walt Disney's Nine Old Men and the Art of Animation*. New York: Disney Editions, 2001.

———. "When Dali Met Disney." *Print*, September/October 2005): 76.

———. *Winsor McCay: His Life and Art*. New York: Abbeville Press, 1990.

Carter, Alice. *The Red Rose Girls: An Uncommon Story of Art and Love*. New York: Harry N. Abrams, 2000.

Casualties of War. Directed by Brian De Palma. Sony Pictures, 2006.

Chambers, John Whiteclay, ed. *The Oxford Companion to American Military History*. New York: Oxford University Press, 2000.

Chandler, Raymond. *The Long Goodbye*. New York: Vintage Crime/Black Lizard, 1988.

———. *The Simple Art of Murder*. New York: Ballantine Books, 1977.

Childers, Joseph, and Gary Hentzi, eds. *The Columbia Dictionary of Modern Literary and Cultural Criticism*. New York: Columbia University Press, 1995.

Clark, Jeff. *Uniforms of the NSDAP: Uniforms—Headgear—Insignia of the Nazi Party*. Atglen, PA: Schiffer Publishing, 2007.

Clark, Ramsey. *The Fire This Time: U.S. War Crimes in the Gulf*. New York: Thunder's Mouth Press, 1994.

Clark, Toby. *Art and Propaganda in the Twentieth Century*. New York: Harry N. Abrams, 1997.

Connolly, Kate. "Gypsies' Fate Haunts Film Muse of Hitler." *The Guardian*, August 18, 2002. https://www.theguardian.com/world/2002/aug/18/artsandhumanities.germany.

Corcoran, Patrick. "In-Theater Advertising Tops $500 Million." NATO Reel Blog. June 16, 2008. http://www.natoonline.org/blog/reel-blog/in-theater-advertising-tops-500-million/.

Cosmas, Graham A. "Army, U.S.: Since 1941." In *The Oxford Companion to American Military History*, edited by John Whiteclay Chambers, 53–4. New York: Oxford University Press, 1999.

Crafton, Donald. *Before Mickey: The Animated Film, 1898–1928*. Cambridge, MA: MIT Press, 1982.

Creel, George. *How We Advertised America; the First Telling of the Amazing Story of the Committee on Public Information That Carried the Gospel of Americanism to Every Corner of the Globe*. New York and London: Harper & Brothers, 1920.

Culhane, John. *Walt Disney's Fantasia*. New York: Harry N. Abrams, 1983.

Culhane, Shamus. *Talking Animals and Other People*. New York: St. Martin's Press, 1986.

Cutler, Laurence, and Judy Goffman Cutler. *J. C. Leyendecker: American Imagist*. New York: Harry N. Abrams, 2008.

Davis, Brian Leigh. *German Army Uniforms and Insignia, 1933–1945*. 2nd revised edition. London: Arms and Armour Press, 1973.

Davis, Julie Hirschfeld, and Matthew Rosenberg. "Trump Seeks a Clear Victory in a Murky War." *New York Times*, August 22, 2017. https://www.nytimes.com/2017/08/22/world/asia/trump-afghanistan.html.

Deleuze, Gilles, and Felix Guattari. *Anti-Oedipus: Capitalism and Schizophrenia*. Translated by Robert Hurley, Mark Seem, Helen R. Lane. Minneapolis: University of Minnesota Press, 1983.

Dike, Blair. "Auto-Emotive Design: Interview with J. Mays, Head of Ford Motor Company Design." Thing.net. Accessed November

7, 2016. http://www.thing.net/~lilyvac/pages/writing/writing26.
html.

Doll, William E., and Donna L. Trueit. "Modernism." In
Encyclopedia of Curriculum Studies, edited by Craig Kridel, 3–11.
Thousand Oaks, CA: SAGE Publications: 2010.

Dorfles, Gillo, John McHale, Karl Pawek, Ludwig Giesz, Vittorio
Gregotti, and Aleksa Celebonovic. *Kitsch: The World of Bad Taste*.
New York: Bell Publishing, 1988.

DuBois, Arthur E. "Heraldic Branch O.Q.M.G." *US Quartermaster
Foundation*, October 1954. http://www.qmfound.com/heraldic_
branch_OQMG.htm.

———. "The Traditions and Glamour of Insignia." *National
Geographic Magazine*, June 1943: 652–709.

Eckholm, Erik. "A Federal Office Where Heraldry of Yore Is Only
Yesterday." *New York Times*, June 13, 2006. http://www.nytimes.
com/2006/06/13/washington/13heraldry.html?mcubz=0

Eddy, Melissa. "Hugo Boss Fashion House Acknowledges It Made
Nazi Uniforms." *Associated Press*. August 14, 1997. https://www.
apnews.com/aaef38ab129afea247e74fec6f9674aa.

Edgar, Andrew, and Peter Sedgwick. *Key Concepts in Cultural Theory*.
London: Routledge, 1999.

Eksteins, Modris. *Rites of Spring: The Great War and the Birth of the
Modern Age*. London: Bantam, 1989.

Eliade, Mircea. *The Forge and the Crucible: The Origins and Structure
of Alchemy*. 2nd edition. Chicago: University of Chicago Press,
1979.

———. *The Myth of the Eternal Return: Or, Cosmos and History*.
Translated by Willard R. Trask. Princeton, NJ: Princeton
University Press, 1971.

Ellul, Jacques. *Propaganda: The Formation of Men's Attitudes*. New
York: Vintage, 1973.

Ethell, Jeffrey L., and Clarence Simonsen. *The History of Aircraft Nose
Art: 1916 to Today*. Osceola: WI: Motorbooks International, 1991.

Etlin, Richard A. *Art, Culture, and Media under the Third Reich.* Chicago: University of Chicago Press, 2002.

Evans, Richard J. *The Third Reich at War.* New York: Penguin Press, 2009.

———. *Third Reich in Power 1933–1939.* New York: Penguin Press, 2005.

Ewen, Stuart. *All Consuming Images: The Politics of Style in Contemporary Culture.* Revised edition. New York: Basic Books, 1990.

Fish, Stanley. *There's No Such Thing as Free Speech: And It's a Good Thing, Too.* Revised edition. New York: Oxford University Press, 1994.

"Flags." Traders of the Lost Surplus. Accessed August 19, 2016. http://www.totls.com/index.php?option=com_content&view=article&id=18.

Fowler, William. *American Military Insignia.* New York: Bdd Promotional Book Co., 1990.

Fox, Jo. *Film Propaganda in Britain and Nazi Germany: World War II Cinema.* New York: Bloomsbury Academic, 2007.

Fox-Davies, Arthur Charles. *A Complete Guide to Heraldry.* London: T.C. & E.C. Jack, 1909.

Fritzsche, Peter. "Nazi Modern." *Modernism/Modernity* 3, no. 1 (1996): 1–22.

Fry, Robin. *Volkswagen Beetle.* Newton Abbot: David & Charles, 1980.

Fussell, Paul. *The Boys' Crusade: The American Infantry in Northwestern Europe, 1944–1945.* New York: Modern Library, 2003.

———. *Uniforms: Why We Are What We Wear.* New York: Houghton, 2002.

———. *Wartime: Understanding and Behavior in the Second World War.* New York: Oxford University Press, 1989.

Gaffney, Dennis. " 'American Indian' or 'Native American'?" *PBS*.
April 24, 2006. http://www.pbs.org/wgbh/roadshow/fts/
bismarck_200504A16.html.

Galbraith, John Kenneth. *The New Industrial State*. 3rd Edition.
Boston: Houghton Mifflin, 1978.

Gay, Peter. *Modernism: The Lure of Heresy*. New York: W. W. Norton
& Company, 2010.

Geis, Darlene. *Walt Disney's Treasury of Silly Symphonies*. New York:
Harry N. Abrams, 1981.

Giago, Tim. "The Name 'Indian' and Political Correctness."
Huffington Post. Accessed March 2, 2015. http://www.
huffingtonpost.com/tim-giago/the-name-indian-and-
polit_1_b_67593.html.

Givhan, Robin. "Fashion Firm Discovers Its Holocaust History."
Washington Post, August 14, 1997. https://www.washingtonpost.
com/archive/lifestyle/1997/08/14/fashion-firm-discovers-its-
holocaust-history/c3413d98-5e73-4ede-8b9b-4e4cdd57bb4d/.

Goar, Carol. "Most Canadians Harbour Myths about Aboriginal
People." *Toronto Star*, June 21, 2012. https://www.thestar.com/
opinion/editorialopinion/2012/06/21/most_canadians_harbour_
myths_about_aboriginal_people.html.

Gobé, Marc. *Emotional Branding: The New Paradigm for Connecting
Brands to People*. Revised edition. New York: Allworth Press,
2010.

Golsan, Richard J. *Fascism, Aesthetics, and Culture*. Hanover, NH:
University Press of New England, 1992.

Goodier, Michael. "American Sniper Box Office Hit Inspires Racist
Tweets." Storify. Accessed July 2, 2016. https://storify.com/
michaelgoodier7/american-sniper-box-office-hit-inspires-
racism.

Goodman, Martin. "Dr. Toon: 'Der Führer's' Paintbrush."
Animation World Network, May 1, 2008. http://www.awn.com/
animationworld/dr-toon-der-f-hrers-paintbrush.

Goudreau, Jenna. "Disney Princess Tops List of the 20 Best-Selling Entertainment Products." *Forbes*. Accessed July 10, 2016. http://www.forbes.com/sites/jennagoudreau/2012/09/17/disney-princess-tops-list-of-the-20-best-selling-entertainment-products/#2d48c486252d.

Gould, Stephen Jay. *Ever Since Darwin: Reflections in Natural History*. New York: W. W. Norton, 1992.

Grant, John. *Encyclopedia of Walt Disney's Animated Characters*. New York: Harper & Row, 1987.

Greenhouse, Steven. "3 Walmart Suppliers Made Goods in Bangladesh Factory." *New York Times*, December 5, 2012. http://www.nytimes.com/2012/12/06/world/asia/3-walmart-suppliers-made-goods-in-bangladeshi-factory-where-112-died-in-fire.html.

Griffin, Roger. *Modernism and Fascism: The Sense of a Beginning under Mussolini and Hitler*. Basingstoke: Palgrave Macmillan, 2007.

Grosvenor, Gilbert. "Insignia of the United States Armed Forces." *National Geographic Magazine*, June 1943: 651.

Guthrie, Doug. "Corporations: Personhood Conferred; Citizenship Earned." Forbes. Accessed October 29, 2014. http://www.forbes.com/sites/dougguthrie/2012/02/14/corporations-personhood-conferred-citizenship-earned/.

Hagerman, Edward. *The American Civil War and the Origins of Modern Warfare: Ideas, Organization, and Field Command*. Bloomington, IN: Indiana University Press, 1992.

Hakim, Danny. "The Coat of Arms Said 'Integrity.' Now It Says 'Trump'." *New York Times*, May 28, 2017. https://www.nytimes.com/2017/05/28/business/trump-coat-of-arms.html?_r=1.

Haldeman, Joe. *The Forever War*. Reprint edition. New York: St. Martin's Griffin, 2009.

Hames, Jacqueline M. "Artwork Made with Honor, Pride." *Soldiers*, November 2010: 32–3.

————. "The Institute of Heraldry Celebrates 50th Anniversary."
US Army. October 27, 2010. https://www.army.mil/article/47234/
the-in.

Hardy, Thomas. "The Convergence of the Twain." In *The Norton
Anthology of English Literature, Volume 2*, edited by M. H.
Abrams et al., 4th edition, 2:1779–80. New York: Norton, 1979.

————. *Tess of the D'Urbervilles*. London: Penguin Books, 1979.

Harvey, David. *The Condition of Postmodernity: An Enquiry into the
Origins of Cultural Change*. Oxford: Blackwell Publishers, 1990.

Hattenstone, Simon. "No One Wants to Know." *The Guardian*,
March 8, 2008. https://www.theguardian.com/film/2008/
mar/08/features.iraqandthemedia.

Haydon, Stansbury F., and Frederic P. Todd. "Notes on the Insignia
of the Twenty-Fourth Corps." *Military Affairs*, January 1, 1947:
181–84.

Hegeman, Susan. *Patterns for America: Modernism and the Concept of
Culture*. Princeton, NJ: Princeton University Press, 1999.

Heller, Joseph. *Catch-22*. New York: Everyman's Library, 1995.

Heller, Steven. "The Design of American Heraldry: An Interview
with Charles V. Mugno." *AIGA, the Professional Association
for Design*. Accessed October 31, 2014. http://www.aiga.org/
the-design-of-american-heraldry/.

————. *Design Literacy: Understanding Graphic Design*. 2nd edition.
New York: Allworth Press, 2004.

————. *Iron Fists: Branding the 20th-Century Totalitarian State*.
London: Phaidon Press, 2008.

————. "The Master Race's Graphic Masterpiece." *Design
Observer*, February 7, 2011. http://designobserver.com/feature/
the-master-races-graphic-masterpiece/24358.

————. *The Swastika: Symbol Beyond Redemption?* New York:
Allworth Press, 2000.

———. "Wilhelm Deffke: Modern Mark Maker." *Design Observer*. January 24, 2008. http://designobserver.com/feature/ wilhelm-deffke-modern-mark-maker/6477.

Heller, Steven, and Mirko Ilic. *Genius Moves: 100 Icons of Graphic Design*. Cincinnati: North Light Books, 2001.

Henry, Patrick. "Give Me Liberty or Give Me Death." Colonial Williambsburg. Accessed July 20, 2017. http://www.history.org/ almanack/life/politics/giveme.cfm.

Herr, Michael. *Dispatches*. New York: Vintage, 1991.

Herf, Jeffrey. *Reactionary Modernism: Technology, Culture, and Politics in Weimar and the Third Reich*. Cambridge: Cambridge University Press, 1986.

Herman, Edward S., and Noam Chomsky. *Manufacturing Consent: The Political Economy of the Mass Media*. New York: Pantheon Books, 1988.

Herzstein, Robert Edwin. *The War That Hitler Won: The Most Infamous Propaganda Campaign in History*. New York: Putnam, 1978.

Heskett, John. "Modernism and Archaism in Design in the Third Reich." In *The Nazification of Art: Art, Design, Music, Architecture and Film in the Third Reich*, edited by Brandon Taylor and Wilfried van der Will, 110–27. Winchester Studies in Art and Criticism. Winchester: Winchester School of Art Press, 1990.

Hewitt, Andrew. "Fascist Modernism, Futurism, and Post-Modernity." In *Fascism, Aesthetics, and Culture*, edited by Richard J. Golsan, 38–55. Hanover, NH: University Press of New England, 1992.

Hitler, Adolf. *Mein Kampf.* Translated by Michael Ford. Camarillo: Elite Minds, 2009.

Hohlwein, Ludwig. *Ludwig Hohlwein, 1874–1949: Kunstgewerbe und Reklamekunst*. Munich: Klinkhardt & Biermann, 1996.

Hubbard, Gerard. "Aircraft Insignia, Spirit of Youth." *National Geographic Magazine*, June 1943: 710–22.

Huber, Franz J. "Nazi Propaganda Handbook: Propagandisten-Fibel." German Propaganda Archive, 2005. http://research.calvin.edu/german-propaganda-archive/fibel.htm.

Hughes, Robert. *American Visions: The Epic History of Art in America.* London: Harvill Press, 1997.

Hurndall, Christopher. *The Weimar Insanity: Photographs and Propaganda from the Nazi Era.* Lewes: Book Guild, 1996.

Ind, Nicholas, ed. *Beyond Branding: How the New Values of Transparency and Integrity Are Changing the World of Brands.* London: Kogan Page, 2004.

———. "A Brand of Enlightenment." In *Beyond Branding: How the New Values of Transparency and Integrity Are Changing the World of Brands,* edited by Nicholas Ind, 1–20. London: Kogan Page, 2004.

Jarvey, Natalie. "'The Man in the High Castle' Is Amazon's Most-Watched Original." *Hollywood Reporter,* December 21, 2015. http://www.hollywoodreporter.com/live-feed/man-high-castle-is-amazons-850422.

Jilek, Wolfgang G. "Nazi and Communist Flags." *Flag Bulletin* 40, no. 1 (2001): 2–40.

Kammen, Michael. *Mystic Chords of Memory: The Transformation of Tradition in American Culture.* New York: Vintage, 1993.

Kaplan, Wendy. *Designing Modernity: The Arts of Reform and Persuasion 1885–1945.* New York: Thames & Hudson, 1995.

Kaye, Ted. *Good Flag, Bad Flag.* Trenton, NJ: North American Vexillological Association, 2006.

Keen, Sam. *Faces of the Enemy: Reflections of the Hostile Imagination.* San Francisco: Harper & Row, 1991.

Kershaw, Ian. *The "Hitler Myth": Image and Reality in the Third Reich.* Reissue edition. New York: Oxford University Press, 2001.

———. "How Effective Was Nazi Propaganda?" In *Nazi Propaganda: The Power and the Limitations,* edited by David Welch, 180–205. London: Croom Helm, 1983.

Kinney, Jack. *Walt Disney and Assorted Other Characters: An Unauthorized Account of the Early Years at Disney's*. New York: Harmony Books, 1988.

Klein, Naomi. *No Logo: Taking Aim at the Brand Bullies*. Toronto: Vintage Canada, 2000.

Knight, Damon. "I See You." In *One Side Laughing: Stories Unlike Other Stories*, 55–69. New York: St. Martin's Press, 1991.

Köster, Roman. "Hugo Boss, 1924–1945. A Clothing Factory during the Weimar Republic and Third Reich." Hugo Boss, September 23, 2014. http://group.hugoboss.com/en/group/about-hugo-boss/history/.

Kyle, Chris, Scott McEwen, and Jim DeFelice. *American Sniper: The Autobiography of the Most Lethal Sniper in U.S. Military History*. New York: Harper, 2013.

Langer, Mark. "Regionalism in Disney Animation: Pink Elephants and Dumbo." *Film History* 4, no. 4 (1990): 305–21.

Lanzmann, Claude. *Shoah: The Complete Text of the Acclaimed Holocaust Film*. New York: Da Capo Press, 1995.

Laurie, Clayton D. *The Propaganda Warriors: America's Crusade Against Nazi Germany*. Lawrence: University Press of Kansas, 1996.

Lears, T. J. Jackson. *Fables of Abundance: A Cultural History of Advertising in America*. New York: Basic Books, 1995.

Lefort, Gerard. "Dans l'album de Famille, Hitler." *Liberation*, November 5, 2009. http://next.liberation.fr/culture/2009/11/05/dans-l-album-de-famillehitler_591913.

Lenderman, Max. *Experience The Message: How Experiential Marketing Is Changing the Brand World*. Toronto: McClelland & Stewart, 2005.

Lesjak, David. *Service with Character: The Disney Studios and World War II*. NP: Theme Park Press, 2014.

Levenson, Michael. "Introduction." In *The Cambridge Companion to Modernism*, edited by Michael Levenson, 2nd edition, 1–9. Cambridge: Cambridge University Press, 2011.

Levine, Lawrence. *Highbrow/Lowbrow: The Emergence of Cultural Hierarchy in America*. Cambridge, MA: Harvard University Press, 1988.

Ley, Robert. *Organisationsbuch der NSDAP*, 2nd edition. Munich: Zentralverlag der NSDAP, 1940.

Linenthal, Edward T., and Tom Engelhardt, eds. *History Wars: The Enola Gay and Other Battles for the American Past*. New York: Holt Paperbacks, 1996.

Littlejohn, David. *The SA 1921–45: Hitler's Stormtroopers*. London: Osprey Publishing, 1990.

"Loblaw & Joe Fresh Will 'Vigorously Defend' against $2B Bangladesh Factory Lawsuit." CBC News. Accessed June 14, 2017. http://www.cbc.ca/news/business/loblaw-will-vigorously-defend-lawsuit-over-rana-plaza-factory-collapse-1.3055872.

"Lone Survivor." Box Office Mojo. Accessed June 14, 2016. http://www.boxofficemojo.com/movies/?id=lonesurvivor.htm.

Lui, Kevin. "China Orders Propaganda Videos at Movie Screenings." *Time Magazine*. July 7, 2017. http://time.com/4848569/china-theaters-propaganda-movies-cinema/.

Lumsden, Robin. *A Collector's Guide to Allgemeine SS*. Hersham: Ian Allan Publishing, 2002.

Lury, Celia. *Brands: The Logos of the Global Economy*. London: Routledge, 2004.

Lutz, Catherine A., and Jane L. Collins. *Reading National Geographic*. Chicago: University of Chicago Press, 1993.

Macey, David. *The Penguin Dictionary of Critical Theory*. Penguin Books, 2000.

Maertz, Gregory. "'The Invisible Museum': Unearthing the Lost Modernist Art of the Third Reich." *Modernism/Modernity* 15, no. 1 (2008): 63–85.

Maltin, Leonard. *Of Mice and Magic: A History of American Animated Cartoons*. New York: McGraw-Hill, 1980.

Manchester, William. *Goodbye Darkness: A Memoir of the Pacific War*. New York: Bantam Doubleday Dell Publishing Group, 1987.

Manning, Martin, and Herbert J. Romerstein. *Historical Dictionary of American Propaganda*. Westport: Greenwood, 2004.

"Marines: Man in Iwo Jima Flag Raising Photo Misidentified." Fox News, June 23, 2016. http://www.foxnews.com/us/2016/06/23/marines-man-in-iwo-jima-flag-raising-photo-misidentified.html.

Marlin, Randal. *Propaganda and the Ethics of Persuasion*. 2nd edition. Peterborough, ON: Broadview Press, 2013.

Martin, Russ. "New Scotiabank Animation Pops Up in Theatres." Marketing. April 18, 2016. http://marketingmag.ca/brands/new-scotiabank-animation-pops-up-in-theatres-172572.

Marx, Karl, and Friedrich Engels. *The Communist Manifesto*. Translated by Samuel H. Beer. Arlington Heights: Harlan Davidson, 1955.

Marx, Leo. *The Machine in the Garden: Technology and the Pastoral Ideal in America*. 35th anniversary edition. New York: Oxford University Press, 1999.

Max. Directed by Menno Meyjes. Lions Gate, 2002.

McDonnell, Patrick, Karen O'Connell, and Georgia Riley de Havenon. *Krazy Kat: The Comic Art of George Herriman*. New York: Harry N. Abrams, 2004.

Meggs, Philip B., and Alston W. Purvis. *Meggs' History of Graphic Design*. 4th edition. Hoboken: Wiley, 2005.

Meyers, Denzil. "Whose Brand Is It Anyway?" In *Beyond Branding: How the New Values of Transparency and Integrity Are Changing the World of Brands*, edited by Nicholas Ind, 21–35. London: Kogan Page, 2004.

Milligan, Spike. *Adolf Hitler, My Part in His Downfall*. London: Penguin Books, 1973.

Milner, L. *Political Leaders of the NSDAP*. London: Almark Publishing, 1972.

Morner, Kathleen, and Ralph Rausch. *NTC's Dictionary of Literary Terms*. Lincolnwood: McGraw-Hill Education, 1991.

Mumford, Lewis. "American Condescension and European Superiority." *Scribner's*, May 1930.

My Best Enemy. Directed by Wolfgang Murnberger. Eichholzer Film, 2011.

"National Arms of Canada: Coat of Arms of National Arms of Canada (Crest, Armoiries)." Heraldry of the World. Accessed May 22, 2017. http://www.ngw.nl/heraldrywiki/index. php?title=National_Arms_of_Canada.

Nelis, Jan. "Modernist Neo-classicism and Antiquity in the Political Religion of Nazism: Adolf Hitler as Poietes of the Third Reich." *Totalitarian Movements and Political Religions* 9, no. 4 (2008): 475–90.

Nelson, Walter Henry. *Small Wonder: The Amazing Story of the Volkswagen*. Revised edition. London: Hutchison, 1967.

Nika, Colleen. "Q&A: BOY London on Outfitting the Punk Movement." *Rolling Stone*. Accessed July 6, 2017. http://www.rollingstone.com/culture/news/ boy-london-on-outfitting-the-punk-movement-20120920.

O'Brien, Tim. *The Things They Carried*. New York: Broadway Books, 1998.

Office of Marine Corps Communication. "USMC Statement on Iwo Jima Flag Raisers." Official United States Marine Corps Public Website, June 23, 2016. http://www.marines.mil/News/News-Display/Article/810457/usmc-statement-on-iwo-jima-flag-raisers/.

Old-Empresario [pseud.]. "Why I Dislike the US Army Institute of Heraldry by Old-Empresario." Old-Empresario.Hubpages. Com, May 18, 2014. http://old-empresario.hubpages.com/hub/ Why-I-Dislike-The-US-Army-Institute-of-Heraldry.

Orlow, Dietrich. *The History of the Nazi Party*. Pittsburgh: University of Pittsburgh Press, 1969.

Orvell, Miles. *The Real Thing: Imitation and Authenticity in American Culture, 1880–1940*. Chapel Hill: University of North Carolina Press, 1989.

Our Brand Is Crisis. Directed by Rachel Boynton. eOne Films, 2006.

Page, Capt. James A. "The Story of 'Old Abe,' Famous Wisconsin War Eagle on 101st Airborne Division Patch." US Army. Accessed April 8, 2015. http://www.army.mil/article/91178/.

Paglen, Trevor. *I Could Tell You but Then You Would Have to Be Destroyed by Me: Emblems from the Pentagon's Black World*. Brooklyn: Melville House, 2007.

Pallant, Chris. *Demystifying Disney: A History of Disney Feature Animation*. New York: Continuum, 2011.

Parry, Lizzie. "Fury at Trendy Fashion Label's Logo That Bears an Astonishing Resemblance to NAZI Eagle." *Mail Online*, May 5, 2014. http://www.dailymail.co.uk/news/article-2620605/Angry-shoppers-demand-fashion-label-changes-logo-looks-like-NAZI-eagle-symbol.html.

Pasch, George. "Drapeaux Nationaux" *Semiotica* 15, no. 3 (1975): 285–96.

———. "Semiotic Vexillology." *The Flag Bulletin* 22, no. 3–4 (1983): 141–57.

Pendergrast, Mark. *For God, Country, and Coca-Cola: The Definitive History of the Great American Soft Drink and the Company That Makes It*. 3rd edition. New York: Basic Books, 2013.

Petropoulos, Jonathan. *Art as Politics in the Third Reich*. Revised edition. Chapel Hill: University of North Carolina Press, 1999.

Phillips. "Our History, Interactive History 'Why 66?'" Phillips 66. Accessed May 30, 2015. http://www.phillips66.com/EN/about/reports/ViewReports/history.html.

Platt, Piers. *Combat and Other Shenanigans: Tales of the Absurd from a Deployment in Iraq*. NP: CreateSpace Independent Publishing Platform, 2014.

Postaer, Steffan. "The Story of 'Not Your Father's Oldsmobile.' Or How Some Really Bad Advertising Changed the Culture Forever!" Gods of Advertising. October 14, 2008. https:// godsofadvertising.wordpress.com/2008/10/14/this-is-not-your-fathers-oldsmobile-how-a-portfolio-tarnishing-piece-of-creative-changed-our-culture-forever/.

Pratkanis, Anthony R., and Elliot Aronson. *Age of Propaganda: The Everyday Use and Abuse of Persuasion*. Revised edition. New York: W. H. Freeman, 2001.

"The Pre-Movie Ads Go on, and on ..." *Maclean's*, August 16, 2013. http://www.macleans.ca/politics the-pre-movie-ads-go-on-and-on/.

Preston, Alex. "This Man Claims to Have Amassed the World's Largest Collection of Nazi Memorabilia." *Business Insider*, June 24, 2015. http://www.businessinsider.com/this-man-claims-to-have-amassed-the-worlds-largest-collection-of-nazi-memorabilia-2015-6.

Quinn, Malcolm. *The Swastika*. New York: Routledge, 1994.

Rawls, Walton. *Disney Dons Dogtags: The Best of Disney Military Insignia from World War II*. New York: Abbeville Press, 1992.

Redacted. Directed by Brian De Palma. Magnolia, 2007.

"Redacted." Box Office Mojo. Accessed June 21, 2016. http://www. boxofficemojo.com/movies/?id=redacted.htm.

Reynolds, J. A. *Heraldry and You: Modern Heraldic Usage in America*. Edinburgh Nelson, 1961.

Rhodes, Anthony, and Victor Margolin. *Propaganda: The Art of Persuasion World War II*. Leicester: Motorbooks Intl., 1994.

Riesenbeck, Hajo, and Jesko Perrey. *Power Brands*. Weinheim: Wiley-VCH, 2007.

Riss. *Hitler dans mon salon*. Paris: Editions Les Echappés, 2009.

Roeder Jr., George. *The Censored War: American Visual Experience during World War Two.* New Haven: Yale University Press, 1995.

Roger & Me. Directed by Michael Moore. Warner Bros., 1989.

Rosen, Jody. "The Knowledge, London's Legendary Taxi-Driver Test, Puts Up a Fight in the Age of GPS." *New York Times,* November 10, 2014. https://www.nytimes.com/2014/11/10/t-magazine/london-taxi-test-knowledge.html.

Rosignoli, Guido. *The Illustrated Encyclopedia of Military Insignia of the 20th Century: A Comprehensive A–Z Guide to the Badges, Patches and Embellishments of the World's Armed Forces.* Seacaucus: Chartwell Books, 1986.

Runyon, Damon. *Runyon from First to Last.* London: Macmillan, 1975.

Ryan, Michael, and Douglas Kellner, *Camera Politica: The Politics and Ideology of Contemporary Hollywood Film.* Bloomington: Indiana University Press, 1988.

Ryder, Ian. "Anthropology and the Brand." In *Beyond Branding: How the New Values of Transparency and Integrity Are Changing the World of Brands,* edited by Nicholas Ind, 139–60. London: Kogan Page, 2004.

Schjeldahl, Peter. "Hitler as Artist." *The New Yorker,* August 19, 2002. http://www.newyorker.com/magazine/2002/08/19/hitler-as-artist.

Seltzer, Mark. *Bodies and Machines.* London: Routledge, 1992.

Simmons, Sherwin. "Hand to the Friend, Fist to the Foe: The Struggle of Signs in the Weimar Republic." *Journal of Design History* 13, no. 4 (2000): 319–39.

Singal, Daniel Joseph. "Towards a Definition of American Modernism." *American Quarterly* 39, no. 1 (Spring 1987): 7–26.

Skradol, Natalia. "Fascism and Kitsch: The Nazi Campaign against Kitsch." *German Studies Review* 34, no. 3 (2011): 595–612.

Smale, Alison, and Steven Erlanger. "Ukraine Mobilizes Reserve Troops, Threatening War." *New York Times,* March 1, 2014.

http://www.nytimes.com/2014/03/02/world/europe/ukraine.
html.

Smale, Alison, and Jack Ewing. "Volkswagen Parts Ways with the
Historian Who Chronicled Its Nazi Past." *New York Times*,
November 2, 2016. http://www.nytimes.com/2016/11/03/world/
europe/volkswagen-vw-emissions-scandal-nazi.html.

Smith, Terry. *Making the Modern: Industry, Art, and Design in
America*. Chicago: University of Chicago Press, 1994.

Smith, Whitney. *Flags through the Ages and across the World*. New
York: McGraw-Hill, 1975.

Sontag, Susan. "Fascinating Fascism." In *The Nazification of Art: Art,
Design, Music, Architecture and Film in the Third Reich*, edited by
Brandon Taylor and Wilfried van der Will, 204–18. Winchester:
Winchester School of Art Press, 1990.

Sony Pictures Animation. "'Open Season' Diary: 2D to
3D—Production Design." Animation World Network.
October 4, 2006. http://www.awn.com/animationworld/
open-season-diary-2d-3d-production-design.

Spark, Alisdair. "Flight Controls: The Social History of the
Helicopter as a Symbol of Vietnam." In *Vietnam Images: War
and Representation*, edited by Jeffrey Walsh and James Aulich,
86–111. London: Macmillan Press, 1989.

Spotts, Frederic. *Hitler and the Power of Aesthetics*. Woodstock:
Overlook TP, 2004.

POM Wonderful Presents: The Greatest Movie Ever Sold. Directed by
Morgan Spurlock. Snoot Entertainment, 2011.

Stein, Barry Jason. *U.S. Army Patches, Flashes and Ovals: An Illustrated
Encyclopedia of Cloth Unit Insignia*. Greenwich, CT: Insignia
Ventures, 2007.

Steinberg, Rolf. *Nazi-Kitsch*. Darmstadt: Melzer Verlag, 1975.

Steinweis, Alan E. *Art, Ideology, and Economics in Nazi Germany: The
Reich Chambers of Music, Theater, and the Visual Arts*. Chapel Hill:
University of North Carolina Press, 1993.

Stephenson, Jill. "Propaganda, Autarky, and the German Housewife." In *Nazi Propaganda in Occupied Western Europe*, edited by David Welch, 117–42. London: Croom Helm, 1983.

Stephenson, Neal. *Snow Crash*. Reprint edition. New York: Del Rey, 2000.

Stone, Declan and Garech Stone. *LOGO R.I.P.* Amsterdam: BIS Publishers, 2003.

Strauss, Walter A. "Gottfried Benn: A Double Life in Uninhabitable Regions." In *Fascism, Aesthetics, and Culture*, edited by Richard J. Golsan, 67–80. Hanover, NH: University Press of New England, 1992.

Stroh, Lt. Col. Oscar H. *Heraldry in the U. S. Army*. Self-published booklet.

Susman, Warren I. *Culture as History: The Transformation of American Society in the Twentieth Century*. New York: Pantheon, 1984.

Tabuchi, Hiroko, and Neal E. Boudette. "Automakers Knew of Takata Airbag Hazard for Years, Suit Says." *New York Times*. February 27, 2017. https://www.nytimes.com/2017/02/27/business/takata-airbags-automakers-class-action.html.

"Takata Airbag Recall: Everything You Need to Know." Consumer Reports. Accessed July 19, 2017. http://www.consumerreports.org/cro/news/2016/05/everything-you-need-to-know-about-the-takata-air-bag-recall/index.htm.

Taking Chance. Directed by Ross Katz. HBO, 2009.

Taylor, Brandon. "Post-Modernism in the Third Reich." In *Nazification of Art: Art, Design, Architecture Music and Film in Third Reich*, edited by Brandon Taylor and Wilfried van der Will, 128–43. Winchester Studies in Art and Criticism. Winchester: Winchester School of Art Press, 1990.

Taylor, Brandon, and Wilfried van der Will. "Aesthetics and National Socialism." In *The Nazification of Art: Art, Design, Music, Architecture and Film in the Third Reich*, edited by Brandon Taylor and Wilfried van der Will, 1–13. Winchester Studies in

Art and Criticism. Winchester: Winchester School of Art Press, 1990.

——, eds. *The Nazification of Art: Art, Design, Music, Architecture and Film in the Third Reich.* Winchester Studies in Art and Criticism. Winchester: Winchester School of Art Press, 1990.

Taylor, Philip M. *Munitions of the Mind: A History of Propaganda.* 3rd edition. Manchester: Manchester University Press, 2003.

Terry, Wallace. *Bloods: Black Veterans of the Vietnam War: An Oral History.* New York: Random House, 1984.

Thomas, Frank, and Ollie Johnston. *The Illusion of Life: Disney Animation.* New York: Disney Editions, 1995.

Thompson, Dorothy. "Minority Report." *New York Herald Tribune,* November 25, 1940.

Trevithick, Joseph. "Why Is There a Mosque in U.S. Army North's Insignia?" Medium Cool. Accessed May 18, 2014. https://medium.com/war-is-boring/why-is-there-a-mosque-in-u-s-army-norths-insignia-a2c18ea42812.

Turbin, Carole. "Fashioning the American Man: The Arrow Collar Man, 1907–1931." *Gender & History* 14, no. 3 (2003): 470–91.

Turner, Frederick Jackson. *The Frontier in American History.* Tucson: University of Arizona Press, 1986.

United States. *The Quartermaster Corps. [Prepared under the Direction of Thomas M. Pitkin, Chief, Historical Section, Office of the Quartermaster General].* Edited by Erna Risch and Chester L. Kieffer. United States Army in World War II: The Technical Services. Washington: Office of the Chief of Military History, Dept. of the Army, 1953.

Uriarte, Maximilian. *Terminal Lance Ultimate Omnibus.* New York: Little, Brown and Co., 2018.

Van Natta Jr., Don. "Bush Was Set on Path To War, British Memo Says." *New York Times,* March 27, 2006. https://www.nytimes.com/2006/03/27/world/europe/bush-was-set-on-path-towar-british-memo-says.html.

Vance, Jonathan F. *Death So Noble: Memory, Meaning, and the First World War*. Vancouver: UBC Press, 1999.

Vatican. "Congregazione per l'Evangelizzazione Dei Popoli: Profilo." The Holy See. Accessed July 10, 2017. http://www.vatican.va/roman_curia/congregations/cevang/documents/rc_con_cevang_20100524_profile_en.html.

Vidiot. "Vexillological Vexations." Metafilter, April 26, 2004. http://www.metafilter.com/32731/Vexillological-Vexations.

Virilio, Paul. *Bunker Archaeology*. Translated by George Collins. Paris: Editions du Semi-Cercle, 1994.

———. *The Original Accident*. Translated by Julie Rose. Cambridge: Polity, 2007.

———. *War and Cinema: The Logistics of Perception*. Translated by Patrick Camiller. London: Verso, 2000.

Vittrup, Meghan. "Institute Creates, Preserves U.S. Military Heraldry." *U.S. Department of Defense News*, July 24, 2007. http://www.defense.gov/news/newsarticle.aspx?id=46826.

Vogel, Virgil J. *Indian Names in Michigan*. Ann Arbor: University of Michigan Press/Regional, 1986.

Vonnegut, Kurt. *Slaughterhouse-Five, or The Children's Crusade*. New York: Dell, 1991.

"VW Asks Historian to Research Role under Brazil Dictatorship." *Canadian Business*. November 3, 2016. http://www.canadianbusiness.com/business-news/vw-asks-historian-to-research-role-under-brazil-dictatorship/.

Wakelam, Randall Thomas. *The Science of Bombing: Operational Research in RAF Bomber Command*. Toronto: University of Toronto Press, 2009.

Walsh, Kate. "Boss Man Prays for Bankers to Keep Jobs; In 2008, the Hugo Boss Chief Watched Aghast as His Market Came Apart at the Seams. But the Brand Is Back—and That Awkward Nazi Link Addressed." *Sunday Times*, April 8, 2012.

Walters, Guy. "Shameful Truth about Hugo Boss's Links to the Nazis Revealed: As Russell Brand Is Thrown Out of a Party for Accusing Fashion Designer of Helping Hitler." *Daily Mail*, September 5, 2013. http://www.dailymail.co.uk/news/article-2413371/Shameful-truth-Hugo-Bosss-links-Nazis-revealed-As-Russell-Brand-thrown-party-accusing-fashion-designer-helping-Hitler.html.

Ward, Lynd. *Lynd Ward: Six Novels in Woodcuts*. New York: Library of America, 2010.

Watts, Steven. *The Magic Kingdom: Walt Disney and the American Way of Life*. Boston: Houghton Mifflin, 1997.

Welch, David, ed. *Nazi Propaganda: The Power and the Limitations*. London: Croom Helm, 1983.

———. *The Third Reich: Politics and Propaganda*. 2nd edition. New York: Routledge, 2002.

"Welcome-Guide-2017-Feb-April.Pdf." The Henry Ford Museum. Accessed May 10, 2017. https://www.thehenryford.org/documents/default-source/default-document-library/welcome-guide-2017-feb-april.pdf?sfvrsn=0.

"Whiskey Tango Foxtrot" Box Office Mojo. Accessed July 12, 2017. http://www.boxofficemojo.com/movies/?id=untitledtinafeycomedy.htm.

Wilcox, Fred. *Waiting for an Army to Die*. Washington, DC: Seven Locks Press, 1989.

Williamson, Gordon. *Men-at-Arms 401: The Waffen-SS (1) 1. to 5. Divisions*. Oxford: Osprey Publishing, 2003.

Wilson, Barrie A. *Hermeneutical Studies: Dilthey, Sophocles and Plato*. Lewiston: Edwin Mellen Pr, 1990.

Winkler, Allan M. *The Politics of Propaganda: The Office of War Information, 1942–1945*. Yale Historical Publications 118. New Haven: Yale University Press, 1978.

Wright, Micah Ian, Kurt Vonnegut, and Howard Zinn. *You Back the Attack! We'll Bomb Who We Want!: Remixed War Propaganda*. New York: Seven Stories Press, 2003.

Wyllie, Robert E. *Orders, Decorations and Insignia, Military and Civil; with the History and Romance of Their Origin and a Full Description of Each*. New York: G. P. Putnam's Sons, 1921.

Zarza, Charles. "Reconnaissance Squadron Switches Back to Original Disney Patch." *Citizen Airman* 64, no. 1 (February 2012): 8.

Zeman, Z. A. B. *Nazi Propaganda*. 2nd edition. Oxford: Oxford University Press, 1973.

Zieber, Eugene. *Heraldry in America*. Philadelphia: Dept. of Heraldry of the Bailey, Banks & Biddle Co., 1895.

Zielbauer, Paul von. "Blackwater Softens Its Logo From Macho to Corporate." *New York Times*, October 22, 2007. https://www.nytimes.com/2007/10/22/business/media/22logo.html.

Zito, Joseph. *Missing in Action*. Universal Studios, 2017.

COPYRIGHT ACKNOWLEDGEMENTS

All images in this volume apart from the five noted below and Figure 8.1 are reproduced with the permission of the Army Trademark Licensing Office, United States Army. The appearance of U.S. Department of Defense (DoD) visual information does not imply or constitute DoD endorsement. Figures 3.2 and 3.3 reproduced courtesy Rafat al-Chadirji; Figure 4.1 courtesy International Historic Films, Inc.; Figure 7.1 courtesy Skillman Library, Lafayette College, PA; and Figure 7.4 courtesy Saga Prefecture, Japan.

INDEX

advertising, 36; convergence, 294; corporate authorship 122–23; ethics, 203; importance of anonymity, 123; indirect harm, 204; marketing, 74; modernism in, 37–38, 122; targeted ads, 113; Watson, John, 74

American heraldry, 40; Airborne Divisions, 159, 162–63; appropriation in, 147; arbitrary, 75–76; badly designed, 74, 75; beauty, 78; Big Red One, 149–52; brass, quantity, 77; Civil War, 72, 74; class, 68; colour codes, 133, 156; colour physics in, 145, 153; corporate identity, 159; disorganization, 133; distinctive unit insignia, 5, 71; Eliade, Mircea, 80–81, 157; errors, 136; fake, 68–69; figure–ground relationship, 157; five categories of, 138; gang colours, 173; gentility, 88; illiteracy, 135; insignia as logo, 131; interpretation, 161; Islam, 144; Japanese design, 143–44; Lafayette Escadrille, 139–41; meaning of ranks, 73; modernism, 73; morale, 77–78; myth, 163–64; mythology, 79; and Native American, 139, 142; non-traditional, 69–71; and nuclear war, 89; "Old Abe," 94, 163–64; personal identity, 80; Public Law, 134; racism, 140; reinvention of, 134; Second World War, 69, 72, 133, 138; Shoulder Sleeve Insignia, 71; "Song of Hiawatha," 142; swastika in, 147; tribalism, 79–80; Trump, Donald, 72; and twenty-first-century design, 173; unit pride, 78–79; United States Quartermaster Corps, 71, 76; US Cavalry, 76; US Cavalry guidon, 141; "Wildcats" (US Expeditionary Force 81st Infantry Division), 75. *See also* TIOH

American Sniper, 206–15; and heteronormativity, 211, 224; Hollywood, 206; "Lex Talionis," 210; misogyny in, 211; Old Testament, 213; and propaganda, 213; "savages," 209; SEALs, 212; sheepdog, 212; sniper duels, 209–10; sniper genre, 209; truth claims, 208; Twitter, 214

America's Army video game, 128–30; "advergaming," 129

animation: and corporate authorship, 123; early history, 246; McCay, Winsor, 246–47, 256; New York vs. Los Angeles style, 256–57; UPA (United Productions of America), 260

Bakshi, Ralph, 260, 278

Blackwater USA, 110; rebranded, 110–11

BOY London, 178–81; and brand management, 179–80; Roman Empire, 179